CADKEY Light
A Handbook

CADKEY Light
A Handbook

Clifford E. Horton

University of Colorado, Colorado Springs

MACMILLAN PUBLISHING COMPANY
New York

MAXWELL MACMILLAN CANADA, INC.
Toronto

MAXWELL MACMILLAN INTERNATIONAL
New York Oxford Singapore Sydney

Credits

- Aldus PageMaker is a registered trademark of Aldus Corp.
- CADKEY, CADKEY Light, CADL (CADKEY Advanced Design Language), and CADUTIL are registered trademarks of Cadkey, Inc.
- Halo is a registered trademark of Media Cybernetics, Inc.
- MicroSoft Mouse is a trademark of Microsoft Corp.
- Mouse Systems Mouse is a trademark of Mouse Systems Corp.
- Mecca III is a registered trademark of Amgraf.
- Ventura Publisher is a trademark of Ventura Software, Inc.
- WordPerfect is a registered trademark of WordPerfect Corp.
- All artwork in this handbook was created using CADKEY Light 1.5. Arcdraft America's TRM-MF font was used within CADKEY Light 1.5 for some of the lettering.

Printed in the United States of America

Macmillan Publishing Company
866 Third Avenue, New York, New York 10022

Macmillan Publishing Company is part
of the Maxwell Communication Group of Companies.

Maxwell Macmillan Canada, Inc.
1200 Eglinton Avenue East
Suite 200
Don Mills, Ontario M3C 3N1

ISBN 0-02-357195-0

Printing: 2 3 4 5 6 7 8 Year: 5 6 7 8 9 0 1

Preface

Learning any full-featured computer program means mastering dozens of new techniques, and each trip to the instruction book takes its toll in time and mental energy. My main purpose in writing this handbook is to make these trips as painless as possible.

CADKEY Light 1.5 is the educational version of CADKEY 3.5, and CADKEY Light 4.0 is the educational version of CADKEY 4.0. These educational versions are remarkably complete. They include the most-used features of the parent programs and put no limit on how complex a drawing you can create.

This handbook is for home or office use as well as for use in classes at the college or high-school level. It covers all of CADKEY Light's commands. A series of tutorial exercises gets you started, whether you are in a class or are learning Cadkey on your own.

This book covers only the two CADKEY Light programs, but you can also use it to learn either professional version. Because these versions look and act like CADKEY Light, a good way to get started with them is to concentrate on the commands they have in common with CADKEY Light, adding the more advanced features when you are comfortable with the basics.

Before you use the rest of the book, you need to work through Chapter 1 at the computer. This one session gives you the fundamental skills you need to start working effectively with Cadkey. Rather than cluttering later chapters with repetitions of basic instructions, I assume you have read Chapter 1 and know these details.

In planning Chapter 2, Tutorial, I decided against the usual style of exercises that give you a rigidly defined set of step-by-step instructions. Sometimes it seem that the main purpose of such tutorials is to make programs look easy and trouble-free. Instead, whenever possible, the Chapter 2 exercises give you freedom to experiment with Cadkey. They also lead you into some of the traps that frequently snare beginners, letting you see why things work the way they do and showing you how to recover from problem situations.

This handbook was developed at the University of Colorado at Colorado Springs in an attempt to induce students to read their reference material instead of depending totally on the instructor or neighbors for help. To make it easy to find information, the Reference chapter, which is the one you will use the most, is arranged alphabetically. You can usually avoid the index and go directly to the information you need. The level of detail is deliberately uneven. There is a minimum of explanation where students have shown little difficulty in picking up construction techniques, and more detail where the subject matter is complex.

Sometimes the added detail explains why a command might not always work the way you think it should. For example, you can usually crosshatch two areas in a single operation, but sometimes you cannot, and when you run into a problem like this it helps to know the rules. To spare you technical discussions of problems you may never encounter, explanations of such puzzles are labeled in ways that let you skip those you don't need to read.

I am indebted to many people for the help and encouragement they provided: the people at Cadkey, Inc., particularly Lilian Johnson; Prof. Robert A. Stager at the University of Windsor; John Griffin and Leo Malek at Macmillan Publishing Company; Mike Belding; Dick Theriault; Ruth; and numerous students.

Contents

Chapter 1
Getting Started

One purpose of this chapter is to get you started running CADKEY Light. Another is to cover What Every Reader Needs to Know to read the rest of the book. These two objectives work well together. Most of the things you need to know are the basics of how Cadkey works—the skills that become almost automatic after your first hour or two working with Cadkey. The chapter closes with a short list of items that are not quite so obvious but that you will find useful as you continue to use this handbook.

Because most readers of this book will be learning CADKEY Light or a related version of Cadkey in class, the chances are that your first exposure to Cadkey will be on a computer where it is already installed. But if you need to start from the beginning, refer to Chapter 4 on Installation and Configuration before you try to run Cadkey.

Many schools have batch files that load Cadkey automatically. If you need to load it manually, you must first change to the directory containing the Cadkey program, type the name of the driver for the video card in your computer, and press the Return (or Enter) key. If you have a VGA monitor, the video driver name you enter is probably ibmvga. If you aren't sure what to do, type Cadkey and press Return. Cadkey will try to start; then it will tell you something like **Type ibmvga.exe to load driver before running this application.** This mild scolding tells you what name you need to type to load the video driver. (You don't need to type the .exe part of the file name.) After you type it and press Return, you should see a message saying the driver was loaded. The message also tells you that when you finish with Cadkey you can type ibmvga -r (or something similar) to remove the driver from the computer's memory.

With the driver loaded, type Cadkey and press Return. Cadkey's first request is **Enter part file name ( ):** Pressing Esc (the Escape key) lets you skip this step. If you want to save a drawing for later use, you could enter a file name at this point, but you shouldn't spend your first Cadkey session trying to create something of lasting value.

This chapter, like most of this handbook, is much easier to follow if you are at a computer terminal and running Cadkey. In this chapter to some extent, and in Chapter 3 to a greater extent, part of your understanding of what to do next comes from the computer screen as you watch Cadkey's response to your commands.

The Menu System

The **main menu**, shown in Figure 1-1, appears in the **menu options window**, which is in the upper left corner of the Cadkey display. The numbers 1 through 8 refer to the function keys F1 through F8. Alt-E (press E while holding down the Alt key) lets you end the session by exiting Cadkey. CREATE is the first step in drawing something. If you press F1, the **create menu** (Figure 1-2), appears, letting you choose whether to draw a line, arc, circle, etc. F10 gives you a way to back up one step, and the Esc key lets you back up several steps at a time.

Figure 1-1 Main Menu	Figure 1-2 Create Menu	Figure 1-3 Line Menu	Figure 1-4 Position Menu
1 CREATE	1 LINE	1 ENDPTS	1 CURSOR*
2 EDIT	2 ARC	2 STRING	2 POINT
3 DETAIL	3 CIRCLE	3 PARALEL	3 ENDENT
4 X-FORM	4 POINT	4 TAN/PRP	4 CENTER
5 FILES	5 POLYLIN	5 HRZ/VRT	5 INTRSC
6 DISPLAY	6 FILLET	6 ANGLE	6 ALONGL
7 CONTROL	7 -	7 RECTANG	7 POLAR
8 DELETE	8 POLYGON	8 N-GON	8 DELTA
			9 KEY-IN
	F10 BACK-UP	F10 BACK-UP	F10 BACK-UP
Alt-E EXIT	Esc ESCAPE	Esc ESCAPE	Esc ESCAPE

Figure 1-1 Main Menu

Figure 1-2 Create Menu

Figure 1-3 Line Menu

Figure 1-4 Position Menu

Press F1 again to select LINE. This calls the **line menu** (Figure 1-3), which gives you eight ways to create lines. For example, the first option, ENDPTS, lets you create a line by telling Cadkey where you want its end points.

Press F1 a third time to select ENDPTS. The **position menu** in Figure 1-4 appears. If you press F1 a fourth time, nothing happens. Instead, keys F1 through F6 simply move an asterisk around, showing which of the position menu options is current.

The general nature of the choices offered by the position menu will be noted shortly, but first let's continue to look at ways to move through the menu system. Pressing F7 for POLAR gives a modified position menu, with options 7 and 8 blank. This marks the start of the POLAR routine, a routine that uses a temporary polar coordinate system to specify a position. It is more than we are ready to tackle at the moment. F10, the key for backing up a single step, provides a graceful way out.

Pressing F10 again takes you back one more step to the line menu, Figure 1-3. Pressing it a third time takes you to the create menu, Figure 1-2. Pressing it a fourth time takes you to the main menu, Figure 1-1.

The Escape key has a similar function, but it moves you through the menus in larger steps. It would have taken you out of the POLAR routine and back to the main menu. (When you are in the middle of some routines you may have to press Esc more than once to return all the way to the main menu. If you accidentally press it more times than necessary, you simply remain at the main menu.)

Creating Entities

An entity is anything—a line, circle, dimension, etc.—that Cadkey creates as a part of a drawing. To start with the simplest type, create a few lines.

If the screen does not show the main menu, press Esc. Then press F1 three times. As before, this takes you to the line-drawing routine. The position menu (Figure 1-4) appears, with the asterisk on CURSOR. In this mode, Cadkey locates positions such as endpoints of lines solely by the position of the cursor, the cross in the center of the screen. The other choices in the position menu allow more precise ways to position points, and eventually you will use them most of the time. For now, however, just stick with CURSOR as the easiest way to explore how Cadkey works.

Probably you will move the cursor with a mouse. A more elaborate setup is a digitizer, consisting of a digitizing tablet—a kind of electronic drafting board—and a hand-held tool to indicate positions on that tablet. This positioning device can be a pointed tool called a pen or a stylus, or it can be a tool with cross hairs that lies flat on the tablet, in which case it is called a mouse, cursor, or puck. For convenience, I refer to all of these devices as mice. Cadkey responds the same way to all of them, moving the cursor on the computer screen as the device is moved, and selecting a point on the screen when you press a button on the device.

If you have neither a mouse nor a digitizer, you can move the cursor using the arrow keys. If this is the case, take a minute now to read the ARROW KEYS write-up in Chapter 3.

To draw a line, move the cursor to the desired start point and press the first (left or top) mouse button. A cross appears, marking the point you selected. Then, as you move the cursor again, a "rubber band" appears, connecting the selected point with the present cursor position. Press the button or the space bar again to complete the line construction.

Because Cadkey is programmed to repeat most operations, it now prompts you for the start point of another line. It will continue to draw lines until you use Esc or F10 to exit the line-drawing routine.

A good way to learn more about Cadkey is to see how much you can do without step-by-step instructions. Try STRING in the LINE menu if you want to connect a series of lines end-to-end. Try drawing arcs and circles. If you run into trouble or press the wrong key, use F10 or Esc to back out. You can't hurt anything. I still forget at times and press 1 instead of F1. Cadkey simply ignores this entry and waits for the right one.

The Cadkey Screen Display

As you explore Cadkey, you can get a lot of help from what you see on the computer screen. Figure 1-5 shows the screen as it would look if you were drawing a line and were ready to select its endpoint. A small x marks the start point, and a rubber band connects this point to the **cursor**.

Not labeled in Figure 1-5 is the **viewport**, the drawing area inside the large rectangle. Above the viewport is the **history line**, which shows the steps you took to get to your present place in the menu system. Across the bottom of the screen is the **prompt line**, which tells the next step to take and the way to take it. In this case, the prompt line tells you to indicate the end point of the line you are drawing and to do so by moving the cursor to the desired position and pressing the mouse button.

You already know about the **menu options window**, which lists the choices you can make by pressing one of the function keys. Another feature of this window is that it lets you use the cursor instead of a function key to make your next choice. Try moving the cursor into the menu options window and pressing the mouse button.

Just below the menu options window is the **status window**, which tells you, for example, which view is showing and which level is active. (Chapter 2 will tell you what view and level mean.) The status window shown in Figure 1-5 is what you see if your computer has a VGA monitor. An EGA monitor displays ten status window entries instead of the twelve shown in Figure 1-5. A CGA monitor shows only two. Altogether, there are 23 entries. Using the cursor, select **--more--** to see a second page of entries. Repeatedly selecting --more-- cycles you through the complete list and returns you to the first page.

To see one way to use the status window, look for the entry, S=0.999693 (the number on your screen is probably different). This number says that the scale of your drawing is about one—approximately full size. When you use the cursor to select this entry, the prompt line changes

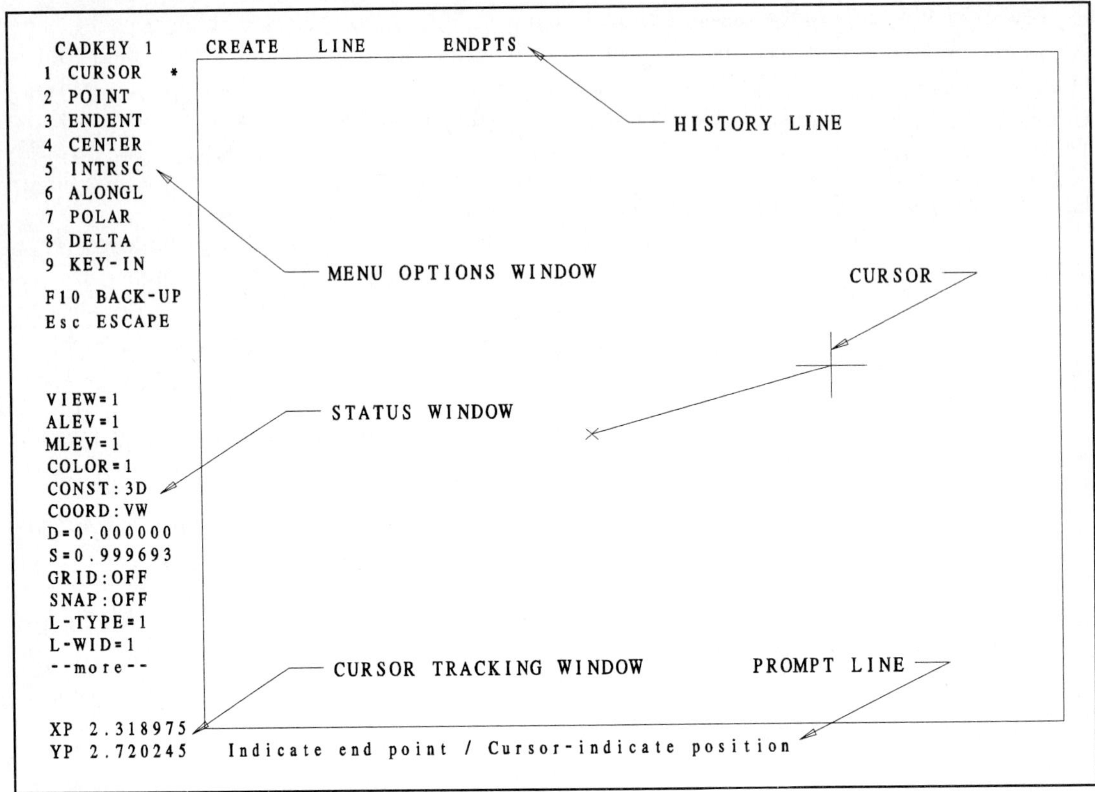

Figure 1-5 Elements of the Cadkey screen display

to **Enter new scale factor (0.999693) = >**. Type .5 and press the Return key (it may be labeled Enter on your keyboard) to specify a half-size drawing. The prompt line now reads **Cursor–indicate new center in viewport**. Whatever point you select with the cursor will be at the center of the screen in the new display. Cadkey clears the screen and redraws it to a scale of 0.5, showing all entities half size.

The **cursor tracking window** usually shows the coordinates of the last point you selected with the cursor. The display changes to MENU AREA when you use the cursor to select something from the menu options window and to STATUS WINDOW when you select an entry there. See CURSOR TRACKING in Chapter 3 if you are curious about this display.

Immediate Mode Commands

You can execute about thirty commands without having to go through the menu structure. Descriptions follow of six of these immediate mode commands. These are commands you will find useful as you continue your initial explorations of how Cadkey works. (See the back cover of this book for a complete list of immediate mode commands.)

Usually you can use these immediate mode commands even when you are in the middle of another operation. Cadkey interrupts that operation to execute the command; then it returns you to the operation at the point where you left off. But watch the history line at the top of the screen. A message in reverse video (dark on a light background) shows when an immediate mode command is active. If the message doesn't appear, the operation cannot be interrupted at that particular point.

To start an immediate mode command, you press a letter key while holding down either the Alt key or the Ctrl key. (These are called the "alternate" and "control" keys.) Alt-A designates an Alt-key combination. ^A, where ^ is shorthand for Ctrl, designates a Ctrl-key combination. The commands are:

^Q gets rid of unwanted entities. Move the cursor to the line, arc, or other entity you want to delete and press the mouse button. Cadkey marks that entity for deletion, either by highlighting it or by placing a small triangle on it. (The marks may be transient or remain on the screen, depending on how Cadkey's CONFIGURATION program is set.) You can mark a series of entities in this way. Press Return when you finish, and the marked entities disappear. If Cadkey marks an entity you intended to keep, press F10 before you mark another entity and Cadkey will cancel the most recent selection. If you think you have selected more than one entity incorrectly, press Esc to cancel all selections and start over.

^U restores (undeletes) the last entity deleted. Try deleting an entity and recalling it with ^U.

^R redraws the screen. When Cadkey deletes entities it sometimes gives the entities that remain a tired look, and ^R refreshes them. Construction and deletion leave small marks on the screen, and ^R removes them. (Don't try to remove them with ^Q. It doesn't work.)

Alt-W creates a WINDOW, a rectangle you construct by using the cursor to select diagonally opposite corners. Cadkey then expands that part of the drawing to fill the screen, letting you see fine detail more clearly.

Alt-A autoscales the drawing; that is, it makes the drawing just large enough to fit comfortably on the screen. This command helps when part of your drawing is hidden because it is off the screen.

^X turns SNAP on. Try hitting this key combination a few times, and watch the results. When you move the mouse with snap off, the cursor moves smoothly across the screen. With snap on, the cursor moves in steps rather than smoothly.

Look in the status window for the entry labeled SNAP, which gives you another way to tell whether snap is on or off. If you move the cursor to this entry, you can use the mouse button instead of ^X to toggle snap on and off.

If you press PgUp (the page-up key), the cursor moves twice as far with each jump. Press PgUp again and the snap distance again doubles. Press the PgDn key to repeatedly cut the snap distance in half.

Snap gives you one way to draw with precision. For example, you can use it to draw lines that are exactly horizontal or to draw a series of rectangles that are exactly the same size.

Exiting Cadkey

Press Esc to get to the main menu, press Alt-E for EXIT, and, unless you want to save your masterpiece, press F1 for NO.

To save your drawing, press F2 for YES. If Cadkey then shows a file name, you can press Return to accept it. If Cadkey does not show a file name or if you want to change the name shown, type a name of eight characters or less and press Return.

The file name you enter can specify a drive and directory. For example, A:\FILENAME names a file FILENAME and directs it to drive A. C:\DRAWINGS\FILENAME puts the file FILENAME in the DRAWINGS directory of disk C:

Things You Need to Know

Press F10 is an instruction you see often in this book. A complete instruction would read, "Either press F10 or move the cursor into the menu options window, select **F10 BACK-UP**, and press the mouse button." Rather than clutter the text with all this detail each time you need to back up a step, I give the detail here, once, in the sentence you just read.

The list that follows tells you a few similar things you need to know.

1. To exit most Cadkey routines, press F10 or Esc. As a rule, whatever Cadkey does, it is ready to do again. After it draws a circle, it is ready to draw another the same size. To go to a different operation, you must back out of the circle routine. F10 backs up just one step, in this example letting you change to a different diameter and draw another circle. Esc (or ESCAPE in the menu options window) also lets you back out of an operation. Esc usually backs up several steps at a time, in this example taking you all the way to the main menu.
2. Some computer keyboards have one key labeled Enter and another labeled Return. Some newer keyboards have both keys labeled Enter. The two keys are equivalent. Only an occasional program distinguishes between them, and Cadkey is not one of them.

   In this book, **Return** refers to either key. Cadkey uses **RETURN** in most of its prompts, but you sometimes see **ENTER**, **RET**, or **CR**. You find all four terms in books about computers.

   Phrases like **enter 2.34** are a brief way of saying that you are to type the number 2.34 and press the Return key. (Unfortunately, this phrase does not always have the same meaning. You see this inconsistency not only in Cadkey, but in other programs as well. When you write or edit a note in Cadkey, the prompt line reads **Enter text:**, even though pressing Return after you type the text can generate a blank line that is sometimes troublesome. But in this handbook, the term **enter** means that you are to type something and then press Return.)
3. Throughout the book there are references to 2D/3D, an article covering the rules for constructing in three dimensions. Look for this topic in Chapter 3 under T, as though its title were spelled TWO D/THREE D.
4. The word **polygon** has two meanings. In lower-case letters, it has the usual meaning of a closed geometrical figure made up of straight lines. But POLYGON, in caps, refers to a special type of entity, one in which an n-sided polygon is a single entity, not a set of n entities. The distinction is important because Cadkey often treats POLYGONS differently than it would treat the individual entities in a polygon. (Don't be disturbed if you don't understand all this yet. Just be aware that a POLYGON is a special kind of entity.)
5. Prompts sometimes remain on the screen after you have responded to them. Meanwhile, the cursor fails to react to your attempts to move it. If Cadkey is telling you to select an entity and you have already done so, be patient. Cadkey is processing the information you have given it and is not ready for more input.
6. Whenever Cadkey asks you to select a position (for example, the start point of a line), the POSITION MENU appears in the menu options window. The directions in Chapter 3 for creating a LINE say nothing to remind you to use the position menu—it's assumed you already know.
7. If computers are really new to you, read the section on DOS in Chapter 3.

Chapter 2

Tutorial

You can learn a lot about CADKEY Light by exploring the menu system, paying attention to what is on the screen, and experimenting with various commands. You can also learn by following step-by-step instructions. The best way is to do some of each, alternating between tutorial sessions and sessions in which you draw whatever strikes your fancy (or whatever strikes your instructor's fancy).

You have two sources of tutorial material. (1) The CADKEY Light package includes a series of tutorial exercises that take you through a wide range of commands. See TUTOR in Chapter 3 for the way to access these exercises. (2) The tutorial exercises in this chapter cover the basics of using Cadkey. They also cover some commands you might not otherwise think to use plus techniques for coping with typical problems.

Even if you strongly prefer to learn just by doing, don't discount the value of these tutorials. It's easy for new users to get in a rut, pushing a limited repertoire of commands to the limit rather than broadening the number of techniques they understand.

The tutorial exercises in this chapter start with fairly complete instructions; nevertheless, you can expect a few problems if you have not worked through Chapter 1 to get at least a superficial familiarity with Cadkey. Many of the points covered in Chapter 1 are repeated, but you will also find, particularly in the later exercises, that explanations become less detailed on the assumption that you have learned something along the way. If you need more information, look for words in upper-case letters that give you the names of topic headings in Chapter 3.

If you get halfway through an exercise, sense that you missed an earlier instruction, and see no way to correct what you have on the screen, just start over. The time spent is not wasted. The exercises go a lot faster the second time through, and the added drill makes it easier to remember how Cadkey works.

The Blank File

Cadkey starts with certain initial settings. The drawing scale is approximately full size, the view number is 1, and so on. Working with Cadkey usually changes these settings. For example, if you use a WINDOW to magnify one part of the drawing, the scale is no longer full size. The tutorial exercises go more smoothly if Cadkey's settings are known rather than random. One way to be sure its initial settings are right would be to have you go down a checklist at the start of each exercise, but it is much easier for you to create a properly configured file named **blank**. Then, to start each exercise, you replace whatever is on the screen with this blank file.

Make the blank file when you have just started Cadkey. If you have been using Cadkey, exit the program and reload it. When Cadkey asks for a file name, enter **blank** (or **a:\blank** if you want to save this file on disk A: and Cadkey is not configured to do so automatically.) The file needs only one set of changes. Set the drawing scale by pressing Alt-S and entering 1. Cadkey asks you to use the cursor to indicate the new center in the viewport. Instead, type 0 (zero). The message **X-CURSOR = 0** appears on the prompt line. Pressing Return expands this to

X-CURSOR = 0 Y-CURSOR =

You can enter 0, or you can simply press Return to accept Cadkey's default value of zero. Either way brings the origin of the coordinate system to the center of the screen.

Press ^F to save the blank file. If Cadkey's prompt is **Enter part file name (blank):** press Return to accept that file name. If there is no file name in the parentheses (this will be the case if you pressed Esc rather than entering a file name at startup), enter **blank** (or **a:\blank**).

To load the blank file later, use FILES—PART—LST/LOAD. Cadkey asks where the file is stored and lists the default path for files of drawings. If that is where you stored the blank file, press Return. Otherwise, enter the path name (probably A:). Use the cursor to select **blank** from the list of part files. Cadkey asks whether to save the drawing that the blank file replaces—the one currently on the screen. (It asks this even if the screen is blank.) Select YES if the drawing on the screen is one you want to keep and you have not yet saved it; otherwise, select NO.

Blank File for Metric Construction

Cadkey comes from the supplier configured to work in inches; consequently these exercises were prepared using inches as the unit of measurement. If the configuration file for your copy of Cadkey is unchanged—if it is still configured for inches—you can skip this section.

If you aren't sure, the STATUS WINDOW can tell you the configuration. Use the cursor to select **--more--** until you see the entries **NH** and **DH**. The numbers show lettering heights for notes and dimensions. If the units are inches, the default heights are 0.300000. If the units are millimeters, the default heights are 8.000000.

If your copy of Cadkey has been configured to work in millimeters, you need to change the blank file. But first, create and save the blank file as just described. You will want it during normal use of Cadkey when you are working in millimeters. Then make the following changes to create a different blank file that you can call **inch**:

> Reset the drawing scale, either by pressing Alt-S or by using the cursor to select S in the STATUS WINDOW. Enter 25. When Cadkey prompts **Cursor-indicate new center in viewport**, type in 0, press Return, and again type in 0 and press Return.
>
> Look for **NH:8.000000** and **DH:8.000000** in the STATUS WINDOW. To see these entries, use the cursor to select **--more--**. Select NH and enter .3; then select DH and enter .3. This reduces the height of letters for notes and the height of numbers for dimensions to a reasonable size for these tutorials.
>
> Finally, assign convenient spacings to the visible and snap grids. With DISPLAY—GRD/SNAP—SNAP INC, set the X and Y snap increments to 0.5. Then press F10 to back up a step and select the GRID=SNP option. This gives the visible grid (an array of dots that you can turn on by pressing ^G) the same spacings as those you just set for the snap grid. Press Esc to return to the main menu.

Use ^F to save the file with these modified parameters. Call the file **inch**, and whenever the tutorial asks you to load the **blank** file, load this file instead.

With these changes, a 3 mm x 4 mm rectangle will be as large on your screen as will a 3" x 4" rectangle on the screen of a computer using Cadkey configured for inches. To convey the illusion of impartiality, the instructions in the tutorials use "units" instead of millimeters or inches to specify dimensional data.

Another way to switch between English and metric units requires a one-time use of the CONFIGURATION program and gives you a more complete change in Cadkey's setups. If you expect to switch often between English and metric units, refer to UNITS in Chapter 3 for descriptions of this alternate procedure and of the results you can expect.

Three-Dimensional Construction

Useful Commands

You need to know seven commands to do this exercise. You have already met the first five in Chapter 1 as IMMEDIATE MODE COMMANDS:

^X toggles SNAP on and off. Use PgUp and PgDn to change the snap distance.

^Q DELETES entities created by mistake or entities such as construction lines you no longer need.

^U restores the entity you deleted most recently.

^R REDRAWS the screen, clearing away marks left by the construction and selection processes.

Alt-A AUTOSCALES the drawing (see ZOOM). Use it if (1) the screen shows only part of your drawing and you want to see it all, (2) the drawing is small and you want to enlarge it to fill the screen, or (3) you see a blank screen when you switch to a new VIEW.

Two new commands that this exercise uses are:

DEPTH sets Cadkey's third dimension, the coordinate perpendicular to the face of the computer screen. Positive values are toward you. You can select this function from the STATUS WINDOW, where it is labeled D, or you can use ^D. Either method invokes the depth menu, letting you choose between VALUE, POSITION, and OFFSET. In this exercise, select VALUE; then enter the depth you want.

CONST in the STATUS WINDOW tells you whether Cadkey is in the **2D** or **3D** construction mode. Selecting CONST or pressing ^W toggles between these two modes.

Despite what you might infer from the names of these two modes, three-dimensional construction often requires both. 2D mode creates a series of flat, two-dimensional drawings on parallel planes, like drawings on parallel sheets of glass. The upper right corner of Figure 2-2 shows an example. To add interconnecting lines, as in the wire-frame drawing in the upper right corner of Figure 2-3, switch to 3D mode.

Construction with 2D and 3D Modes

Cadkey has a display mode that lets you see four views at once. From the main menu (press Esc if the menu options window does not show it) select DISPLAY—VWPORTS—AUTO SET and use the cursor to select the four-viewport option. Move the cursor into the drawing area and select the upper left viewport as the primary one. Press Esc to return to the main menu.

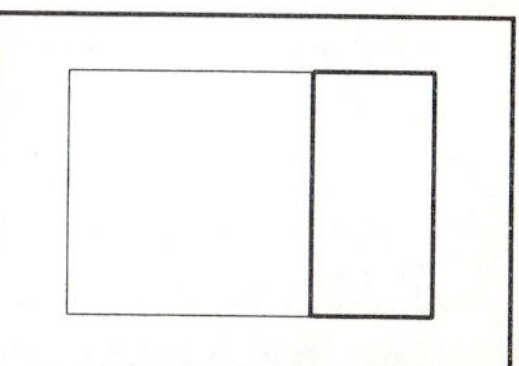

Figure 2-1 Beginning of construction

Turn SNAP on, set CONST to 2D, and set DEPTH to —1.5. In the upper left viewport, construct a large rectangle (Figure 2-1). Use

CREATE—LINE—RECTANG—CORNERS, which lets you draw a rectangle by selecting diagonally opposite corners. Make it about two-thirds the width and two-thirds the height of the viewport.

Set DEPTH to 0 and construct a second rectangle that covers the right end of the first one. The heavy lines in Figure 2-1 show about how big this second rectangle should be. If you need finer control of the cursor position, use PgDn to reduce the snap distance.

Set DEPTH to 1 and draw a third rectangle covering about the left 40% of the first one.

At this point your computer screen should look like Figure 2-2. It shows four views of your drawing in an arrangement that is standard for mechanical drawings: The front view is on the lower left, with the top view above it and the right-side view on its right. The space that remains, on the upper right, shows the isometric.

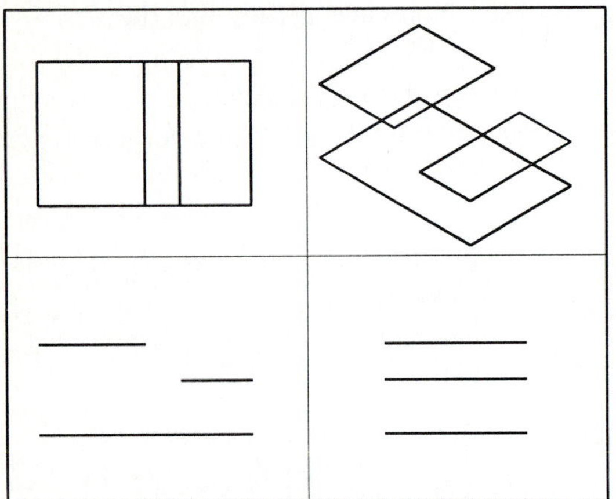

Figure 2-2 Drawing started in 2D mode

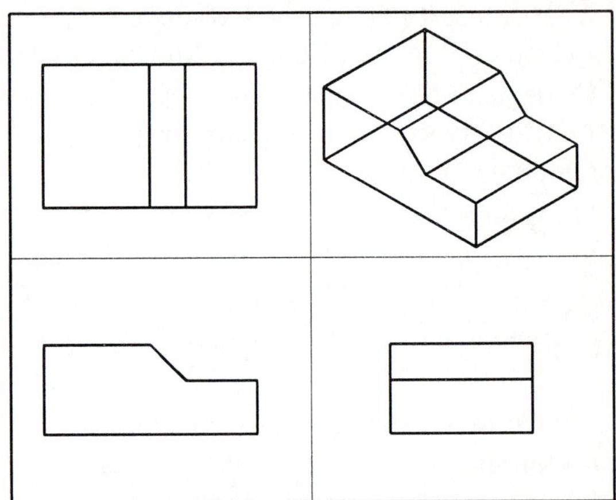

Figure 2-3 3D mode adds interconnecting lines

The next step is to add interconnecting lines and obtain the wire-frame drawing in Figure 2-3. But first let's take a short detour to show what happens when you use the wrong construction mode. Leave Cadkey in 2D construction mode and turn SNAP off.

Use CREATE—LINE—ENDPTS—ENDENT to add the interconnecting lines. (A shortcut way to get there from the RECTANGLE routine is to press F10 twice to get to the LINE menu. Then select ENDPTS and ENDENT.) This command attaches lines to the ends of entities in the partially constructed drawing. In the isometric (upper right) view, draw two or three interconnecting lines. Even if you place the cursor some distance from the points you want to connect, ENDENT starts and ends each line precisely at the endpoints of existing entities.

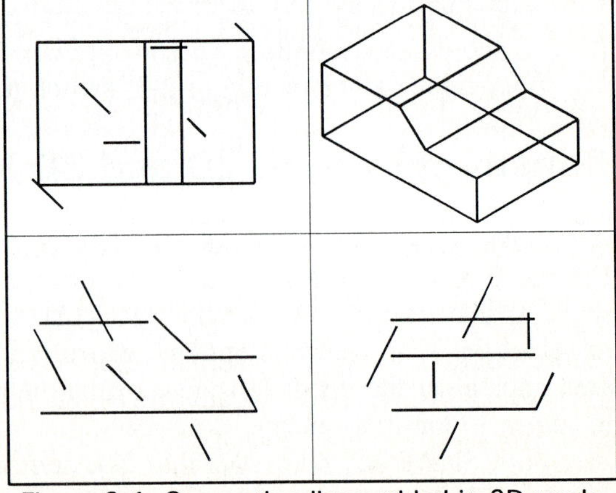

Figure 2-4 Connecting lines added in 2D mode

The isometric is convincingly perfect, but the other views show that something went wrong. The new lines connect in the isometric view but not in space. Your screen won't look exactly like Figure 2-4, but your top, front, and right side views will show that the new lines are detached.

Use ^Q to delete these detached lines, switch CONST to 3D, and again place interconnecting lines in the isometric view. In the 3D construction mode, ENDENT selects points that coincide with the ends of entities not only in the current view, but also in space. Your screen should now look like Figure 2-3.

(A technicality: You could have used 3D mode instead of 2D mode to construct the three rectangles. When you use just the cursor to locate positions, construction is at the current depth, regardless of the mode. But more complex drawings usually involve options such as ENDENT that override the depth setting. In general, when you start a construction by creating a series of flat, parallel drawings, you need 2D mode to be sure that all entities are at the intended depth. See the 2D/3D writeup if you want more detail.)

Constructing with JOIN

The JOIN command provides another way to construct three-dimensional drawings. Although it is limited to producing extruded shapes, it can easily create the drawing in Figure 2-3. The procedure is independent of the construction mode—it can be in either 2D or 3D.

Your screen is probably still in the four-viewport mode, but if it is not, use DISPLAY—VWPORTS—AUTOSET to put it there. Use DELETE—SELECT—ALL DSP to clear the screen of the drawing you just completed. When Cadkey asks you to **Indicate viewport to select all entities in**, you can select any viewport that shows all the entities. Then select ALL from the menu options window. Turn SNAP on. Set DEPTH to —2. (This depth setting makes your drawing more likely to show in all viewports.) Press Esc to return to the main menu.

Working in the front view (the lower left viewport), use CREATE—LINE—STRING to draw an outline shaped something like the one in Figure 2-5. Use F10 to end the string.

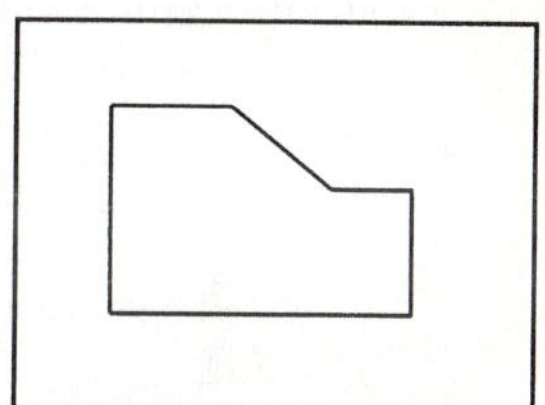

Figure 2-5 Beginning of construction

From the main menu, select X-FORM—TRANS-R—JOIN—WINDOW (CADKEY Light 1.5) or X-FORM—DELTA—JOIN—WINDOW (CADKEY Light 4.0). In any viewport, create a window that completely encloses what you have drawn. (Create it by selecting diagonally opposite corners. If you see that you are not getting the window you want, press F10 and reselect the first point.) Press Return to accept 1 as the number of copies.

Check COORD in the STATUS WINDOW. COORD:VW says you are working in view coordinates; COORD:WLD, world coordinates. Selecting this entry and pressing the mouse button lets you toggle between the two systems. Either can be used for the next step.

If you are in world coordinates, Cadkey's first prompt (dX =) asks for the displacement in the X direction. Press Return to accept the default value, which is zero (or you can do the more obvious thing and enter 0). Enter -3 for DY and zero for dZ. Cadkey copies your drawing, adding lines that join the corners of the copy to the corners of the original. Figure 2-6 shows the result.

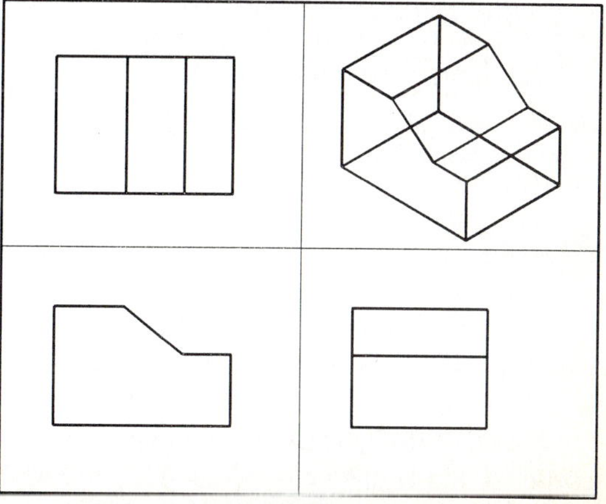

Figure 2-6 Completed construction

If you are in view coordinates, Cadkey asks which viewport to use for the transformation. Pick the front (lower left) view. For the displacement, enter dXV = 0, dYV = 0, and dZV = 3. This transformation also yields the result shown in Figure 2-6.

If you wonder why the displacement was in the negative Y direction in world coordinates but in the positive Z direction in view coordinates, check the inside front cover.

Position Menu

If you are just starting a Cadkey session, enter **blank** as the file name. You may need to include a path name and, for example, enter **a:\blank.** (You did create that blank file, didn't you?) If you have been using Cadkey, or if you just started but pressed Esc when Cadkey asked you for a file name, use FILES—PART—LST/LOAD to clear the screen and load the blank file. Then press Esc to return to the main menu.

1 CURSOR*
2 POINT
3 ENDENT
4 CENTER
5 INTRSC
6 ALONGL
7 POLAR
8 DELTA
9 KEY-IN
F10 BACK-UP
Esc ESCAPE

The POSITION MENU offers several techniques for precise construction. You used ENDENT in the preceding tutorial exercise, but that was just one of seven methods—POINT through DELTA—for selecting points by using specific positions on your drawing. An eighth option, KEY-IN, lets you specify a position by its coordinates in three-dimensional space. This section of the tutorial covers these eight options.

From the main menu, select CREATE–LINE–RECTANG–CORNERS and draw a rectangle like the one shown in Figure 2-5. Its exact size is not important.

Press Esc to exit the RECTANGLE routine and get back to the main menu; then, with CREATE—ARC—THREE-P, create a large arc. Pick a start point, a point near the middle of the arc, and an end point. Put the arc close enough to the rectangle that it would, if extended, intersect the rectangle.

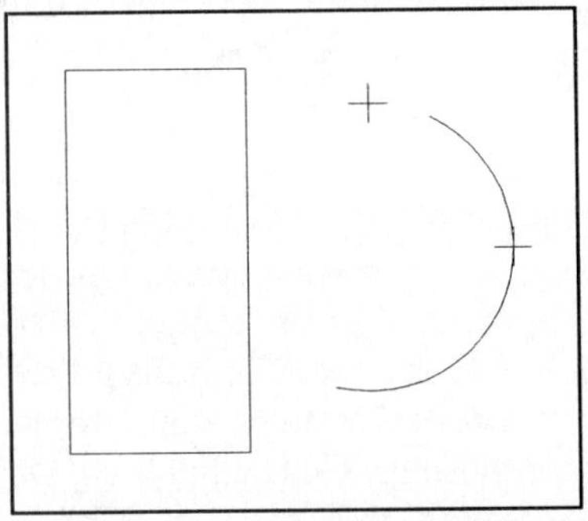

Again press Esc. With CREATE–POINT—ON ARC, put a POINT on the arc. Press Return to accept the default angle of 90 (the 12:00 o'clock position). Because the top of the arc in Figure 2-7 goes only to about 80°, a point at 90° is beyond the end of the arc. Cadkey puts the point on an extension of the arc, then asks for another angle. Enter zero (3:00 o'clock) to place the second point.

Figure 2-7 Starting geometry

POINT

From the main menu, select CREATE—LINE—ENDPTS. The menu options window now shows the position menu, with an asterisk on CURSOR, which, for this exercise, is the least interesting of the nine options listed.

Select **POINT** from the position menu. Try to use this option to select a "point" such as the corner of the rectangle or the bottom end of the arc, Cadkey gives you the error message **Entity not found... press RETURN to continue.**

Now select the two point entities. See how far from each point you can place the cursor and still get Cadkey to find it. If you get the **Entity not found** message, press Return, move the cursor closer, and try again. Cadkey selects the point if the center of the cursor is within about 1/2". Regardless of where you put the cursor to select the points, the line starts and ends precisely at the points (Figure 2-8).

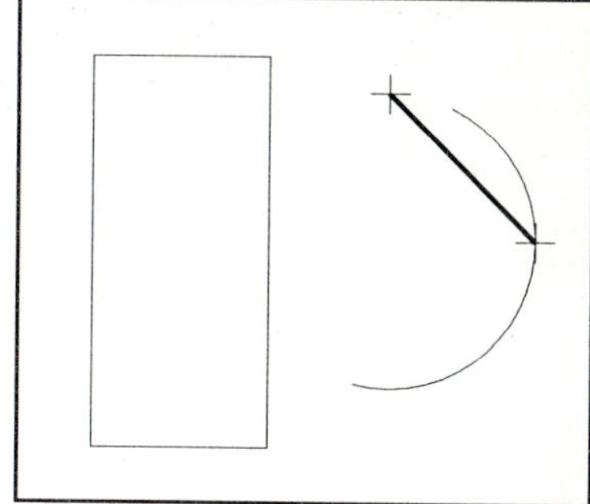

Figure 2-8 POINT example

ENDENT

Select **ENDENT** from the position menu. Experiment with this command by selecting a side of the rectangle, pressing F10 to cancel the selection, and selecting a side again. If you accidentally cause Cadkey to draw a line before you are through experimenting, use ^Q to delete it; then continue the experiment. An X marks each point you select. Note that you get the end of the line as the selection point even though you select the line near its center and almost half an inch away. (To see clearly what is happening, you may need to use ^R to remove the marks made by earlier selections.)

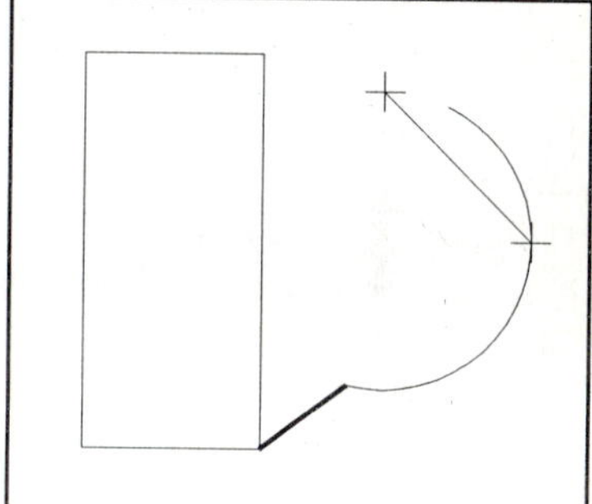

Figure 2-9 ENDENT example

Finally, draw the line shown heavier in Figure 2-9 by starting it at the end of a side of the rectangle and ending it at an end of the arc. When you select the arc, you can be as careless with cursor position as you were when you selected the line. Note, however, that you cannot use F10 to get a second chance here. Cadkey does not mark your selection point with an X, but simply draws the line to it.

CENTER

CENTER gives you the center of an entity. Use this option to select two sides of the rectangle. The result is a line from the center of one side to the center of the other (Figure 2-10). Draw another line from the center of one side to the center of the arc. Figure 2-10 shows this line also. Note that (1) CENTER picks the center of curvature of the arc, not the middle of the curved line, and (2) to select the arc, you select a point on its circumference, not its center of curvature.

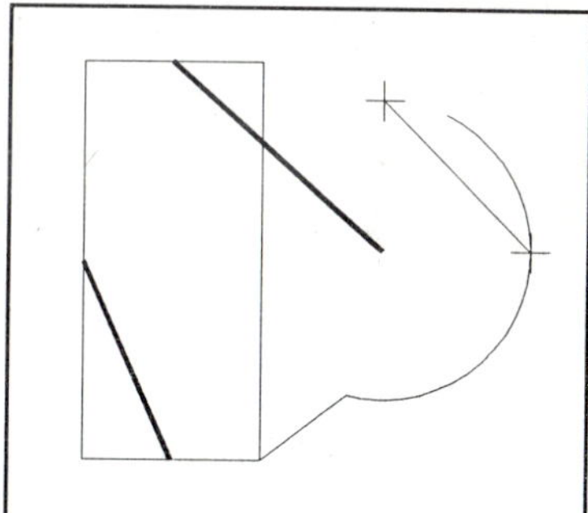

Figure 2-10 CENTER example

INTRSC

INTRSC finds the intersection point of two entities. Select it from the position menu. Choose the arc and the right side of the rectangle as the two intersecting entities. (This works, even though the two don't actually meet. INTRSC can create an imaginary extension of one or both entities to find their virtual intersection.)

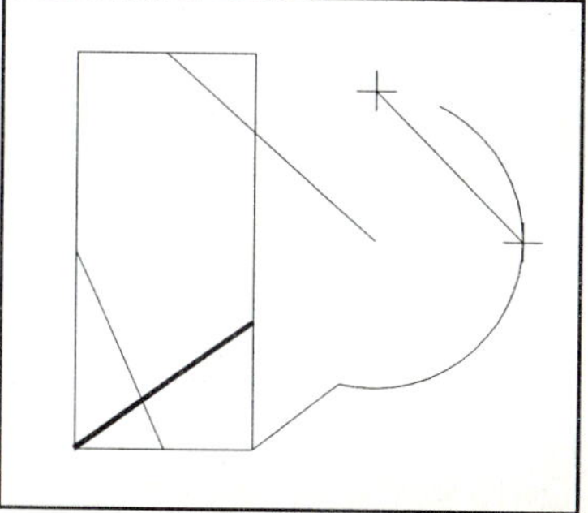

Figure 2-11 INTRSC example

If your drawing is different enough from Figure 2-11 that this intersection won't work—if the arc is so far from the rectangle that extending it would not give an intersection—use another intersection to start the line. Try the top end of the arc and the diagonal between the POINTS.

End the line where two lines intersect at the lower left corner of the rectangle. If Cadkey responds with **Entity not found... press RETURN to continue**, you have fallen into the trap that was set for you. The most likely reason for this message is that you put the cursor squarely on the corner to select the lines. When you do this, Cadkey selects the same line twice. Finding no intersection, it gives you an error message which, in this case, is not up to Cadkey's usual standards of clarity. Reselect the lines, putting the cursor farther from the corner.

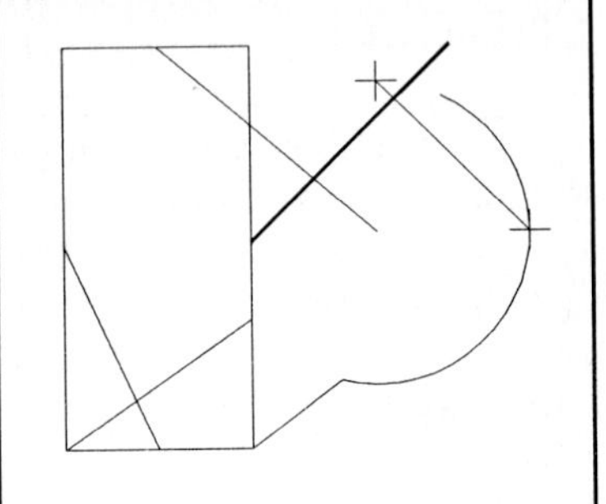

Figure 2-12 ALONGL example

ALONGL

ALONGL gives you a position measured along a line, starting from the end of the line nearest the cursor. Use ALONGL to select the upper portion of the right side of the rectangle. Cadkey responds with something like **Enter distance (2.037193)** =>, where the number in parentheses is the length of the line you selected. Enter 1 and Cadkey will start your new line one unit from the top end of the line. To specify the end point, select the top line of the rectangle near its right end; then enter —1. The negative number tells Cadkey to measure not along the line, but one unit beyond the end of the line, along its extension. The result is a line at a 45° angle (Figure 2-12).

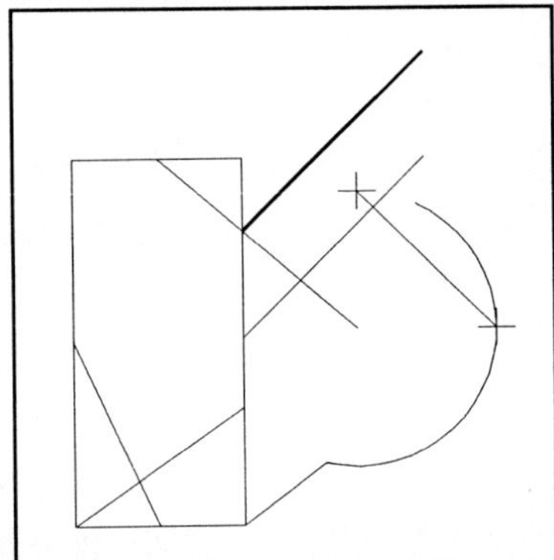

Figure 2-13 POLAR example

POLAR

POLAR and DELTA are commands that involve two steps. First you select a temporary origin; then you specify a position in terms of a displacement from that origin. Because these commands are more complex and ask for more input than the other position menu options, new Cadkey users tend to avoid them. But their unique capabilities can often save you time.

Use **INTRSC** to start the new line shown in Figure 2-13. Select the intersection of the right side of the rectangle with the line that goes to the center of the arc.

Select **POLAR** to position the end of the line. The position menu disappears briefly; then it reappears with the POLAR and DELTA options missing and with the asterisk on CURSOR. Move the asterisk to **INTRSC**, and select, as the **polar origin**, the intersection you used before.

Enter 45 to get an angle of 45°.

When Cadkey asks for a distance, enter **sqrt(2)**. This function and the angle you entered put the start point of the new line 1.414214 units from the temporary origin and in a direction corresponding to a 45° angle. (You may have recog-

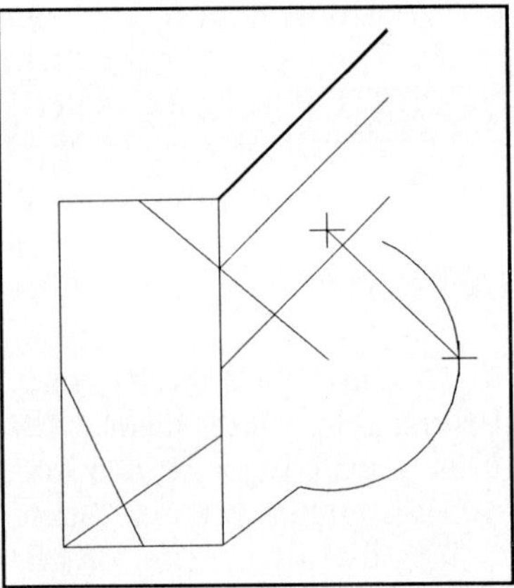

Figure 2-14 DELTA example

nized the function you just used as the square root of 2. See CALCULATOR if you are curious about this and similar functions.) Press F10 to back out of the POLAR menu.

DELTA

To start the line, select **ENDENT** from the position menu and select the upper right corner of the rectangle.

To end the line, select **DELTA** from the position menu; then select **ENDENT** from the abbreviated position menu that appears next. For the **delta reference position**, select the point you selected before—the upper right corner of the rectangle. In response to Cadkey's prompts, set the displacements from this reference position to DXV = 1, DYV = 1, and DZV = 0. This gives you a third 45° line, the same length as the first two (Figure 2-14). Press F10 to exit the DELTA menu.

KEY-IN

KEY-IN lets you specify a position by entering its coordinates. Select KEY-IN from the position menu. Press Return three times to enter zero, the unwritten default value. This sets XV = YV = ZV = 0 and starts the line at the origin of Cadkey's coordinate system, near the center of your screen. KEY-IN the end point of the line as XV = 1, YV = 1, and ZV = 0. The result is a fourth 45° line, located about as shown in Figure 2-15.

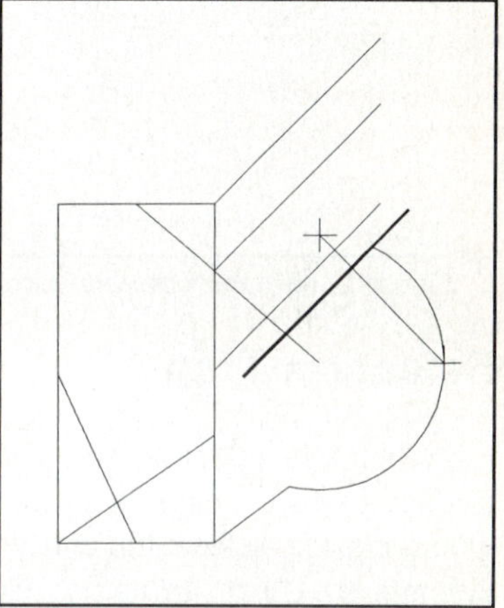

Figure 2-15 KEY-IN example

Selecting Entities

You have selected entities many times. What is new in this exercise is that it covers techniques you need when you have trouble getting Cadkey to select the entity you want.

With FILES—PART—LST/LOAD, load the **blank** file. From the main menu, use CREATE—CIRCLE—CTR+DIA to create a circle. Make it four units in diameter and use KEY-IN to put its center at XV = YV = ZV = 0.

Use X-FORM—SCALE—COPY—ALL DSP—ALL to make 20 copies of the circle. With KEY-IN, put the scaling origin at XV = 0, YV = 0, and ZV = 6. Enter .95 as the scale factor.

With CREATE—LINE—ENDPTS—ENDENT, draw a line between the endpoints of the outer and inner circles. (Cadkey calls the 0° position on a circle the endpoint.) No matter where on the circles you put the cursor, the line should look like the one in Figure 2-16.

But look closely at Figure 2-16 and at your drawing. If you put the cursor squarely on the inner circle when you selected it, Cadkey probably picked the wrong circle—one that is one or two circles away from the inner edge. But if you put the cursor in the open center area and some distance inside the inner circle, Cadkey probably drew the line you expected (Figure 2-17). At work here is Cadkey's **selection trap**, helpful if you understand it, frustrating if you don't.

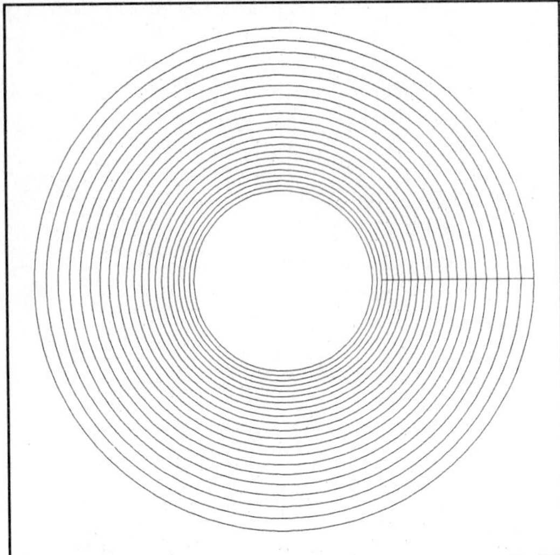
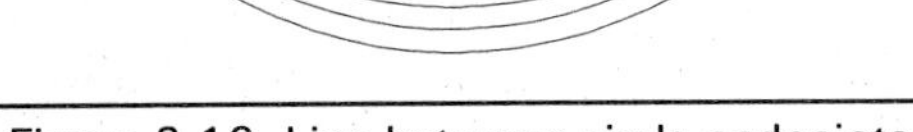

Figure 2-16 Line between circle endpoints

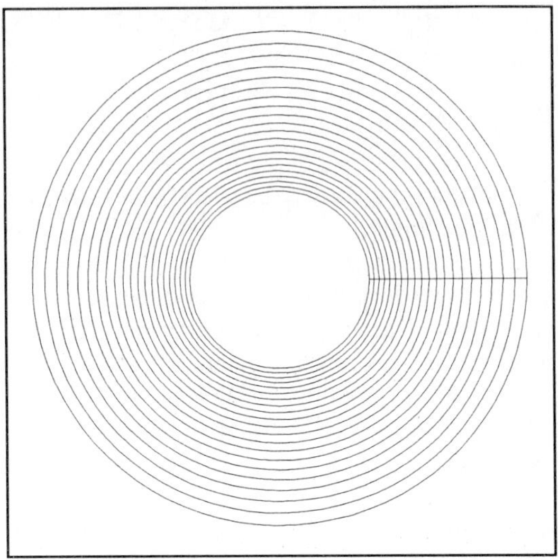

Figure 2-17 Line position corrected

Selection Trap

When you select an entity without putting the cursor particularly close to the one you want, Cadkey looks through its entire database (its record of the entities you have created) and, as you would expect, selects the entity that is nearest the cursor. But when you place the cursor within 2.5 mm (0.1") of an entity, Cadkey's response is different. A circle with a 2.5 mm radius, centered on the cursor, is called the selection trap. As soon as Cadkey finds an entity within this circle, it interrupts its search of the database and selects that entity. If three entities are within 2.5 mm of the cursor, Cadkey doesn't care which of the three is nearest. It picks the first one it finds listed.

In the example in Figure 2-16, putting the cursor squarely on the inner circle puts it within 2.5 mm of the three inner circles. Because the database lists entities in the order in which you create them, and because you created the inner circle last, the circle Cadkey finds first is the third from the center.

Select **--more--** in the STATUS WINDOW and look for the entry DB:FWD. This entry shows that Cadkey is set to read its database FORWARD; in other words, when it looks through the records of your entities it starts with the one you created first. If you move the cursor into the status window and select the DB entry, you can toggle it between DB:BACK and DB:FWD. You can also toggle it between these states by repeatedly pressing Alt-R. Set it to DB:BACK. Now when Cadkey reads the database it starts with the entity you created last. This setting favors selection of the entities created most recently, in this case the inner circle and the line.

Use ^Q to delete the line, placing the cursor within one or two millimeters of it. If the cursor is closer to one of the circles than it is to the line, it shouldn't matter. With Cadkey reading the database backwards, you should have no trouble selecting it instead of one of the circles. Now use CREATE—LINE—ENDPTS—ENDENT to redraw the line. When you select the outer circle, put the cursor a few millimeters outside the circle to avoid selecting the next one in. But when you select the inner circle you can be more daring. Put the cursor on the circle next to the inner one. Cadkey, favoring the circle drawn last, picks the inner circle and draws the line all the way, as in Figure 2-17.

Making a Backup Copy

The next step makes 89 copies of the line. This command could create quite a mess if you pressed a wrong key and the lines fell in the wrong places. To be safe, save a copy of your drawing first. In case of trouble, you can reload the file as it was before the copy operation.

A backup is also a good idea whenever you have a substantial amount if time invested in a drawing. If a thunderstorm interrupts the power to your computer for only a second, your drawing is gone forever unless you have saved it. Disasters are infrequent, but they can take many forms, and the insurance is cheap.

Press ^F to make a backup copy. Enter a file name (eight characters or less) when Cadkey prompts you to do so. After you enter the file name, Cadkey saves your drawing.

In this case, where the drawing is probably nothing you want to keep forever, **back** is a good name for the file. (Although **backup** seems a logical file name, this is Cadkey's default name for its automatic backup feature, and using it could give you trouble.) If you want your backup file on a floppy disk and Cadkey is not configured to put it there automatically, add a disk drive name to the file name. **A:\back** is probably the appropriate file designation.

If the copy operation that follows dumps 89 wrong lines on the screen, use FILES—LST/LOAD to replace what is on the screen with your **back** file. Say NO to the question about saving your current file. Press Return to accept **back** as the name of the file to retrieve. Cadkey deletes what is on the screen and brings back the drawing as it was when you saved it.

Type Masking

Alt-M invokes TYPE MASKING, another way to cope with selection problems. Type masking limits Cadkey's selections to certain types of entities. When you read SELECTING ENTITIES in Chapter 3, you will see that you can impose many restrictions. For example, you can arrange to have Cadkey select only thick, red, dashed lines. Thick, red, dashed circles and solid lines of any color would be immune. In this exercise the masking is simpler, distinguishing only between lines and circles.

From the main menu, select X-FORM—2D ROT—COPY—SINGLE (CADKEY Light 1.5) or X-FORM—ROTATE—COPY—SINGLE (CADKEY Light 4.0). Press Alt-M to invoke type masking and select GEOM, LINE, and DONE. This tells Cadkey to select lines only. When you select the line, try placing the cursor about 10 mm from the line, as though you were trying to select one of the circles instead. If you are too far from the line, Cadkey will say **Entity not found... press RETURN to continue**. Otherwise, it will select the line.

Enter 89 as the number of copies. For the rotation origin, pick CENTER from the position menu and select any of the circles. Enter 4 as the rotation angle. The result should look like Figure 2-18. If it doesn't, retrieve your **back** file and try the copy command again.

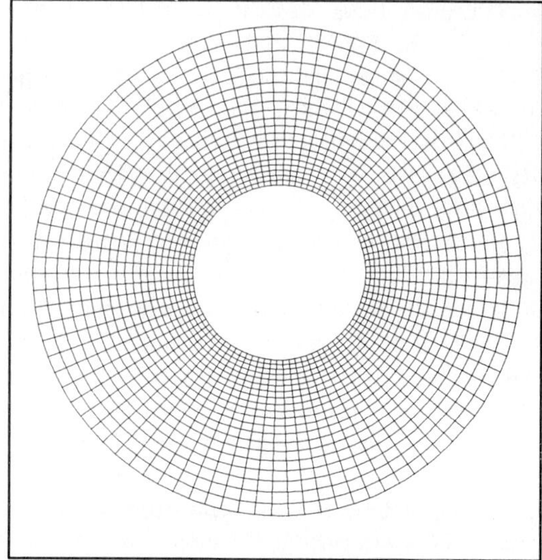

Figure 2-18 Completed mesh

Note that even though you used masking to select only lines, Cadkey let you select a circle to specify the rotation origin. Type masking restrictions are cleared whenever you start a new operation, or, in this case, a new part of an operation.

Just for fun, press Alt-V and enter 7 to see the isometric view. Do you remember making ZV = 6 rather than zero when you specified the scaling origin for copying the circles? This value pulled the drawing into the third dimension, giving the conical shape you now see. To get back to view 1 (the view in Figure 2-18), press Alt-V and enter 1.

Levels and Level Masking

Just before the last COPY operation, you saved your drawing to guard against disaster in case you created multiple wrong copies. There is another way to get similar protection. Cadkey has a feature called LEVELS, which does nothing more than assign each entity a code number from 1 to 256. You can use this code number in many ways. For example, you can delete a particular set of entities, either temporarily or permanently, leaving the rest of the drawing undisturbed.

Don't confuse LEVELS with DEPTH. Levels have nothing to do with Cadkey's third dimension.

To see how levels work, find **ALEV=1** in the status window. (You may have to select **--more--** to make it show.) ALEV=1 says the active level is 1, meaning that as you create new entities, the code number assigned to them is 1. Move the cursor into the status window and select ALEV (or use ^L to do the same thing) and enter 2. Now the level number assigned to new entities will be 2. The conventional way to say this is "new entities are placed on level 2."

It is now safe to bungle a copy operation. Use X-FORM—2D ROT—COPY—SINGLE (CADKEY Light 1.5) or X-FORM—ROTATE—COPY—SINGLE (CADKEY Light 4.0). Select any line. If Cadkey selects a circle instead, press F10 to cancel the selection, use Alt-R to set the database search direction to BACK, and try again. Make 89 copies, use CURSOR to select a rotation origin where you think the center of the circles lies, and enter a rotation angle of 4. Unless you were very lucky (or unless you cheated and had SNAP on), the resulting lines are *almost* right.

There are three ways to get rid of this new array. From the main menu, select DISPLAY—LEVELS—REMOVE and enter 2. Cadkey redraws the display, hiding the entities that are on level 2. To show that the levels are hidden rather than deleted, use DISPLAY—LEVELS—ADD to add level 2. Cadkey adds level 2 to the list of visible levels and the hidden lines reappear.

Now try a more positive way to eliminate these lines. Return to the main menu, select DELETE—LEVEL, and enter 2. This method deletes all entities on level 2, and it does this regardless of whether the level is currently visible or hidden.

But even this operation is not permanent. Use EDIT—RECALL—LEVEL—2 to bring the lines back. When you delete an entity, Cadkey does not remove the record of that entity from its database. Instead, it marks it as deleted and ignores it for all operations except RECALL.

But you don't have to be stuck with those lines forever. When Cadkey saves a file, it does not save records of deleted entities. The following operation removes the lines from the database:

Delete the lines again with DELETE—LEVEL—2. Follow this with FILES—PART—LOAD. Cadkey asks **Save current file first ? (YES).** Press Return to accept the default choice of YES. The prompt line probably reads **Enter part file name (back):** If the default file name is not **back**, it is whatever name you used when you started Cadkey or when you last saved or loaded a file. Press Return if the file name that shows is the one you want to use; otherwise, enter another file name such as **back** or **mesh**.

If you saved a backup file earlier, you can expect the message **File already exists, replace it ? (NO)**, indicating that the disk already contains a file with the name you chose. Probably the file is an earlier version of the current one, in which case it's appropriate to replace the earlier file with the current one. If so, select YES. Otherwise, select NO and pick another name.

Cadkey tells you **Saving part file. . . please wait**, followed by **Enter part file name (back):**, where the name in parentheses is the one you just entered. Press Return to accept this file name. The message **Loading part file... please wait** appears, and your original file reappears, with the database stripped of all records of deleted entities.

The drawing comes back with level 2 still the active one. Reset it to 1. Which level is active makes no difference in what follows, but this step is a reminder of something all too easy to forget: When you finish creating a set of entities on a separate level, switch back to the level that is appropriate for the work you are going to do next.

Window

The most obvious way to make entity selection easier has been saved for last. With Alt-W, draw a window—a small rectangle—over part of the mesh. Make it about 10 mm square. Cadkey expands what this window encloses to make it fill the screen. It is now easy to put the cursor on the entity you want without getting dangerously close to other entities. Alt-B returns you to the view you had previously.

The advantage of WINDOW is its simplicity. A disadvantage is the long time Cadkey takes to redraw the screen when the drawing is complex.

Trimming and Extending

Figures 2-19 and 2-20 illustrate two applications of the TRM/EXT commands. These are not parts you are to draw, but illustrations of what the TRM/EXT commands can do. The drawing in Figure 2-19 started as a rectangle. Then CREATE—LINE—PARALEL—AT DIST added the grid of properly spaced lines. The short diagonal lines connect intersections in this grid. Finally, *trimming* eliminated all but the segments needed in the drawing on the right.

The left side of Figure 2-20 is an isometric view of a wire-frame drawing. The shade lines emphasize the cylindrical contours of this part. ^Q eliminated the hidden lines in this wire-frame drawing, and the TRM/EXT commands trimmed away hidden parts of lines. The result is the pictorial view on the right.

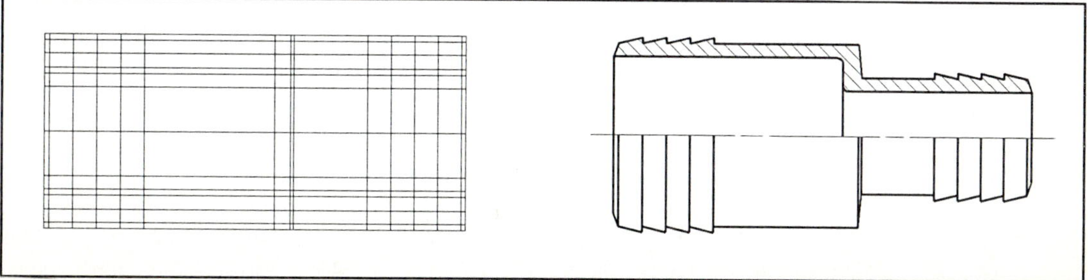

Figure 2-19 Steps in drawing the half section of a PVC coupling

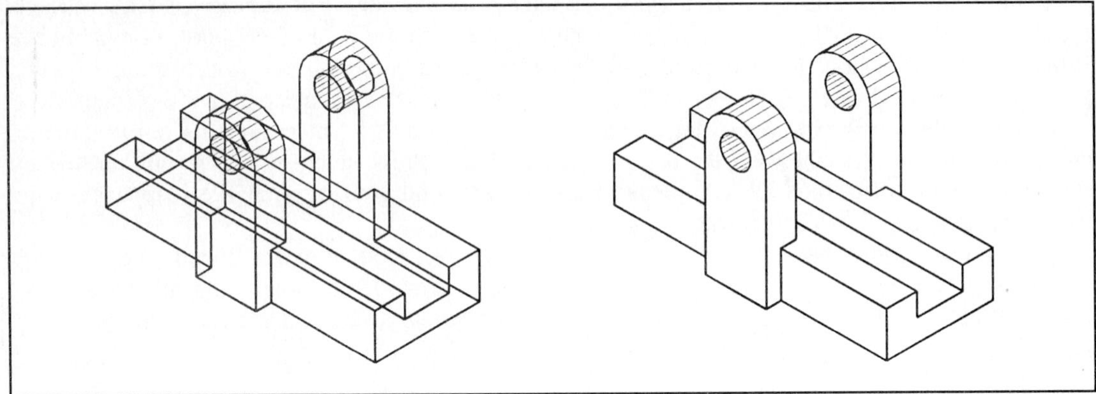

Figure 2-20 Pictorial view created from a wire-frame drawing

To experiment with these trim/extend commands, use CREATE—LINE—RECTANG—CORNERS to create a series of rectangles. Don't copy Figure 2-21, but create your own pattern. Try to be artistic. Eight to ten rectangles is about right. If you get carried away and draw forty, everything will work, but Cadkey may be sluggish in responding to your commands.

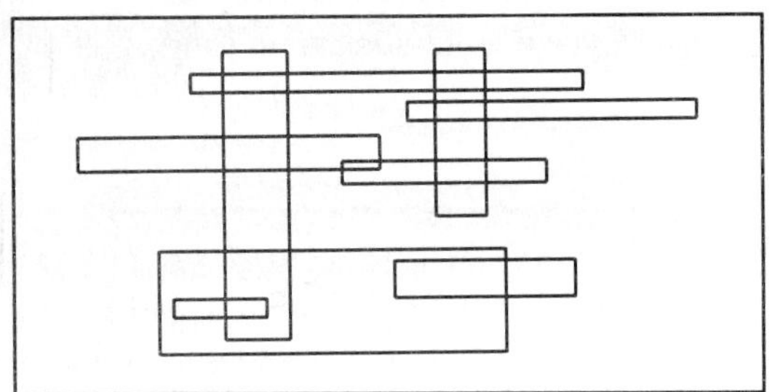

Figure 2-21 Array of rectangles

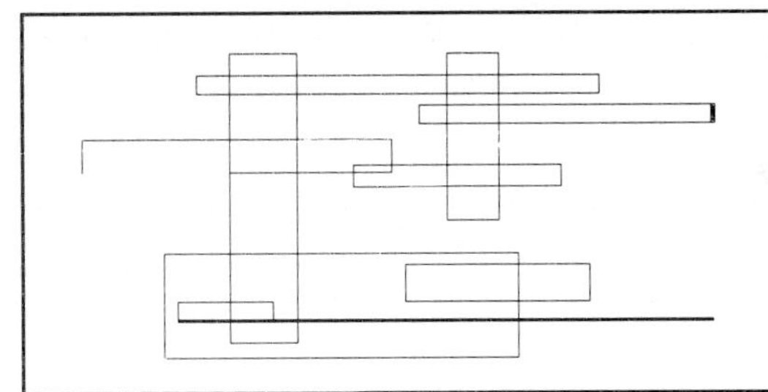

Figure 2-22 Trimming remote lines

With EDIT—TRM/EXT—FIRST, select two lines that cross one another. Cadkey trims the first line you select, and the part of the line that remains is the part you put the cursor on.

Now look at the way TRM/EXT can *extend* a line. Pick two lines that are perpendicular but widely separated. In Figure 2-22, the heavy line near the bottom of the screen was originally just the bottom line of a small rectangle. It was extended by using the short heavy vertical line near the right edge of Figure 2-22 as a trimming entity. Try a few more trimming and extending operations to get the feel of the process.

The next two topics cover problems that you are likely to encounter as you use the TRM/EXT commands and a related command: CREATE—FILLET—ARC—TRIM.

Correcting Errors

If you make a mistake and trim the wrong line or trim the wrong part of a line, the best cure is usually a second trim/extend operation. Figure 2-23 shows how this works. For the line to trim, select one like the line labeled 1 in Figure 2-23a. For the trimming entity, select a line like the one labeled 2. Cadkey trims the first line as in Figure 2-23b. Now assume you didn't really want to trim this line. To restore the line, select 1 again and then select line 3 (Figure 2-23c).

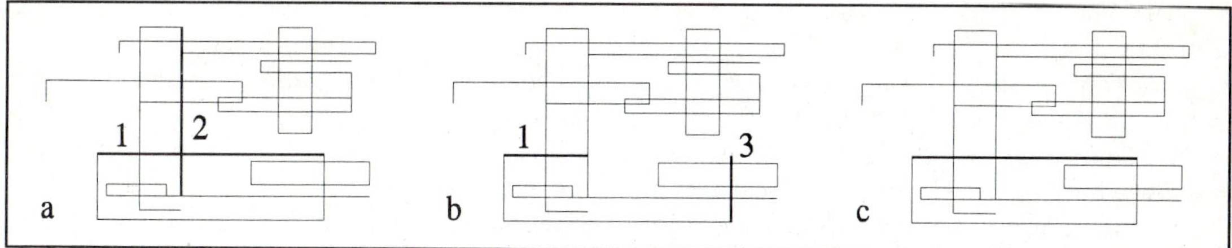

Figure 2-23 Restoration of a trimmed line

You may need to use a similar technique if you use fillets to round corners. Find a fat rectangle or create one well over an inch wide. Select CREATE—FILLET—ARC—TRIM. Enter 0.4 as the radius. Select two adjacent sides, keeping your selection points well away from the corner that joins them. Cadkey trims away the square corner and replaces it with a rounded one. Figure 2-24a shows two corners rounded this way.

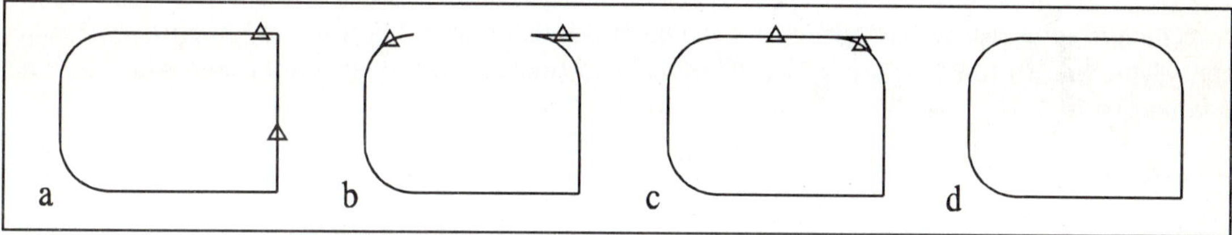

Figure 2-24 A common problem with fillet arcs

Now round another corner, this time putting the cursor close to the corner (closer than 0.4 unit) to select one of the sides. Use selection points like those in Figure 2-24a. Figure 2-24b shows the result. When Cadkey trims the sides of the rectangle, it keeps the parts the cursor was on. In this case, it trims the top side by keeping the short segment between the corner and the end of the arc. When the radius is small, the remaining segment is apt to be so short and inconspicuous that the line seems to disappear altogether. (When this happens, use Alt-W to generate a WINDOW and expand the region to see what is going on.)

The cure for this problem is EDIT—TRM/EXT—FIRST. Select the short line as the entity to trim and the arc on the opposite side of the rectangle as the trimming entity. Figure 2-24b shows the selection points. Cadkey restores the left end of the line (Figure 2-24c). Select the line again and select the arc on the right as the trimming entity. The damage is now corrected (Figure 2-24d).

Lines that Refuse to Disappear

Another problem, one that can be a real mystery if you haven't encountered it before, occurs when two or more lines coincide. Find a fairly long line on your screen. Then, with CREATE—LINE—ENDPTS—ENDENT, draw four more lines that coincide with that line. Trim this composite line, and you will see the trimmed end disappear.

You didn't trim all five lines. When Cadkey erases a line or part of a line, it also temporarily blanks out whatever else was in the same position on the screen. Four lines remain, but they don't show. When you use ^R to redraw the screen, the end that you neatly trimmed away reappears.

This kind of situation is apt to take you by surprise. You think you are rid of the end segment. You forget about it, do some more work on the drawing, and then do something—create a WINDOW or press ^R—that redraws the screen. When the segment suddenly reappears your instinctive reaction is probably to try the trim command again. This time, nothing happens. Of the five lines at the cursor, Cadkey always picks the same one, probably the one you created first. Because you already trimmed this particular line, no change occurs.

To cure the problem, press ^Q to delete the duplicate lines. To avoid deleting the line already trimmed, put the cursor on the end you want trimmed away and more than half an inch from the line you want to keep. Press the mouse button several times. Watch the screen to be sure that Cadkey keeps picking the offending lines. It picks the overlapping lines one after the other until all are selected for deletion. Then, when you pick one line too many, Cadkey either says **Entity not found. . . press RETURN to continue** or it selects another nearby entity. If it does the former, just press Return twice. The first time clears the error message and the second executes the deletion. If it does the latter, press F10 to cancel the most recent selection and press Return to delete the duplicate lines. The entire composite line disappears, but REDRAW restores the one line that was properly trimmed.

There is little risk in this operation. If you accidentally delete the trimmed line or some other entity you wanted to keep, press ^U. This restores (undeletes) the last entity deleted. (Delete a line and try it.)

DIVIDE

As long as you are dealing with lines and arcs but not with circles, there are only two TRM/EXT commands you have to know: FIRST and DIVIDE. The other three commands, BOTH, DOUBLE, and particularly MODAL, can be convenient time savers, but they provide efficiency rather than new capabilities.

EDIT—TRM/EXT—DIVIDE cuts a piece out of the middle of a line or arc, creating two entities where there was only one before. Figure 2-25 shows what DIVIDE might have done to your pattern of rectangles. DIVIDE differs from all the other TRM/EXT commands in that the rules tell you to put the cursor on the part you want to trim away, not on the part you want to keep. (If you violate this rule, Cadkey usually gives you the results you want anyway.)

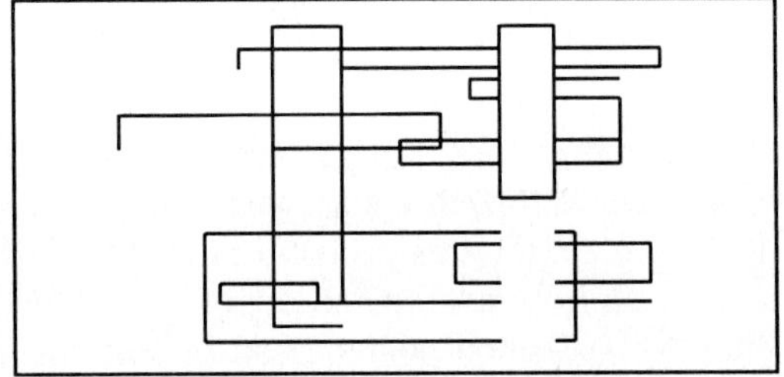

Figure 2-25 Effects of DIVIDE

With DIVIDE, you select the entity to be trimmed; then you select the two trimming entities. Use CREATE—ARC—THREE-P to create a few arcs, and try the command with arcs and lines.

Arcs sometimes behave unexpectedly when you trim them. If you experience any strange results, put your curiosity on hold. You will explore this problem shortly.

MODAL

When you need to trim several entities at a single boundary, MODAL can do it in about half the time that FIRST would take. You need to select the trimming entity only once rather than reselect it for each trim operation. Figure 2-26 shows a number of lines trimmed by using an arc as the trimming entity.

Try one of your lines or arcs as a trimming entity and trim several other lines and arcs. (Use CREATE—ARC—THREE-P to create an arc if you don't already have a suitable one.) To switch to a different trimming entity, press F10.

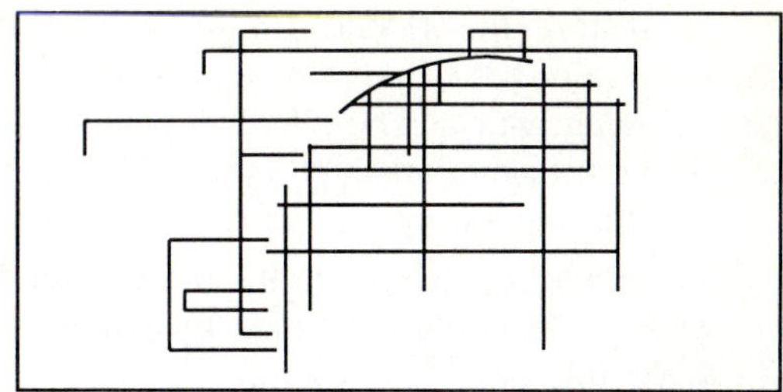

Figure 2-26 Entities trimmed with MODAL

DOUBLE

In its simplest application, DOUBLE trims or extends both ends of a line or arc. Try it. It's equivalent to using FIRST twice—once on one end and once on the other.

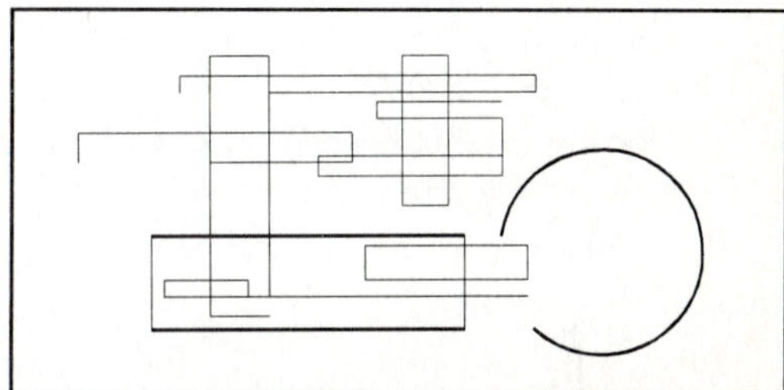

Figure 2-27 Circle trimmed with DOUBLE

DOUBLE comes into its own when you need to take a bite out of a circle (Figure 2-27). None of the other trim/extend commands operate on circles. Use CREATE—CIRCLE—TWO-PTS to add a circle to your drawing (the two points you specify are the endpoints of a diameter), and use EDIT—TRM/EXT—DOUBLE to trim part of it away. Select the circle to trim by putting the cursor on the part you want to keep; then select the two boundaries for trimming. You don't need to remember which command works for circles. If you try to use the wrong one, Cadkey reminds you: **Can only TRIM closed curve with DOUBLE option... press RETURN**.

Problems with Arcs

Use FILES—PART—LOAD to load the **blank** file to clear the screen.

Problems involving arcs often have more than one possible answer, and you need to know how to tell Cadkey which possibility you want. Otherwise, you may see some surprises.

With CREATE—ARC—THREE-P, create an arc like the first arc on the left in Figure 2-28a (the arc marked with the triangle). Make it an inch or two tall, and put it near the left edge of the screen. Use X-FORM—TRANS-R—COPY—SINGLE (CADKEY Light 1.5) or X-FORM—DELTA—COPY—SINGLE (CADKEY Light 4.0) to make 12 copies of the arc, setting dXV = 0.4, dYV = 0, and dZV = 0. Use CREATE—LINE—HRZ/VRT—HORIZTL to add four horizontal lines. Put line 1 below the arcs, but close enough that the arcs, if extended, would intersect it. Put line 2 closer, so it just misses the bottoms of the arcs. Put line 3 just above the bottom ends of the arcs. Finally, use ENDENT to put line 4 through the top endpoints of the arcs.

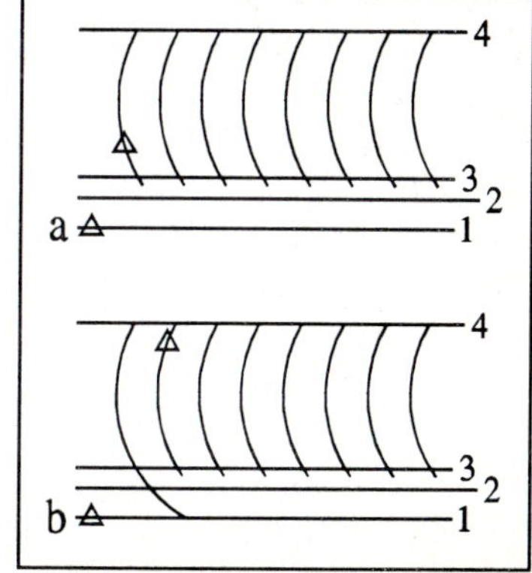

Figure 2-28 Extending and trimming arcs

With EDIT—TRM/EXT—FIRST, extend an arc to the bottom line. When you select the arc, put the cursor near the bottom end, where the triangle is in Figure 2-28a. Figure 2-28b shows the result. Repeat the process for the second arc, this time putting the cursor near the top end of the arc, as indicated by the triangle in Figure 2-28b. Figure 2-29a shows the result, often unexpected, of selecting an arc this way.

To restore the second arc to its original length, select it anywhere along the part you want to keep; then select line 4 as the trimming entity. The selection points shown in Figure 2-29a trim the arc to the length shown in Figure 2-29b.

Use the remaining arcs to answer these questions:

When you select an arc to be extended, you determine which end Cadkey extends by where you put the cursor. What rule does Cadkey follow?

Is the rule different if you extend the arc to line 2, the line closer to the bottom of the arc?

Is the rule different if you trim the arc to line 3, the line that crosses the arc?

Do the results depend on where you put the cursor when you select the trimming entity?

To confirm your answers to these questions, check the last page of this chapter.

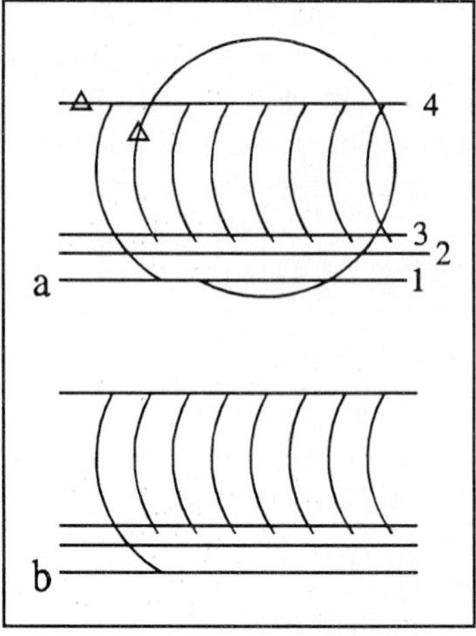

Figure 2-29 More extending and trimming operations

Construction of a Cylindrical Part

The main purpose of the rest of this section is to show how the DOUBLE command trims circles, but another purpose is to alert you to two bugs in CADKEY Light. In this first topic you encounter a minor problem—one you can easily work around but one you are apt to see as you continue to use Cadkey. The next topic involves a more puzzling obstacle but one you are less likely to encounter.

To clear the screen, load the **blank** file. Then use CREATE—CIRCLE—CTR+DIA to draw six circles. KEY-IN the center positions (Cadkey must be in 3D mode for this to work). Recall that you can key in a coordinate of 0 by pressing Return without entering a number.

Diameter	X	Y	Z
1	0	0	0
1	0	0	.5
1.5	0	0	.25
1.5	0	0	.5
2	0	0	0
2	0	0	.25

As soon as you finish constructing a circle, Cadkey is ready to construct another with the same diameter. Simply key in the second set of coordinates. To change to the next diameter, press F10 to back up a step, enter the new diameter, and key in the center coordinates.

Change to view 7; then use Alt-A to AUTOSCALE the drawing and get everything on the screen. You should see the configuration shown in Figure 2-30a.

Press ^W (or select CONST in the status window) to set the construction mode to 2D. With CREATE—LINE—TAN/PRP—TAN TAN, draw lines tangent to the two largest circles. Figure 2-30c shows these as heavy lines. (For now, don't draw in the other tangent lines.) Press F10 between lines; otherwise Cadkey doesn't start fresh, but assumes the first tangency point you picked for the first line is also the first tangency point you want for the second line. Watch the prompt line. If it says **Indicate 2nd tangent entity**, you know the first one is already picked.

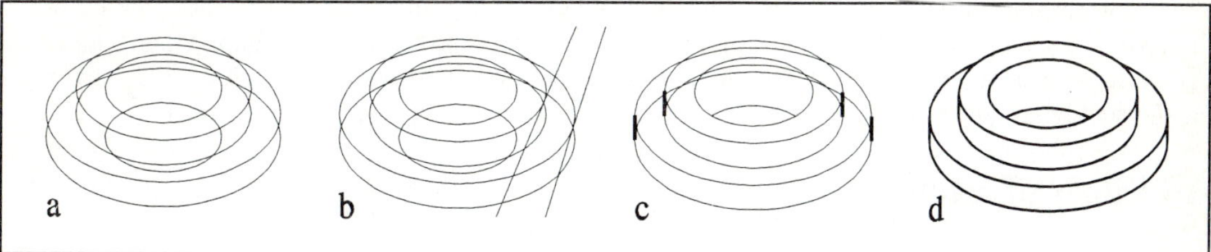

Figure 2-30 Isometric view of cylindrical object

Problems with Tangents to Arcs

Did you have trouble? You may have seen an error message: **Invalid entity combination . . . press RETURN**. If so, Cadkey is in 3D mode (the STATUS WINDOW says CONST:3D) and you need to put it in 2D mode. Or you may have a long line that is tangent to only one of the ellipses, like one of the lines in Figure 2-30b, in which case the explanation is more complicated:

In operations involving tangents, it pays to be careful where you place the cursor when you select the entities to which the new entity will be tangent. Usually this type of problem has more than one solution, and there can be as many as eight. To get the entity you want, you need to put the cursor close to where the points of tangency will be. In the present operation, a bug in CADKEY Light simply requires you to be more careful than usual in placing the cursor. If your selection points are too close to where the ellipses intersect, Cadkey draws a line through that intersection and tangent to only one ellipse.

If you did not get this unwanted line, try creating it deliberately. As you add the rest of the four tangent lines shown in Figure 2-30c, select at least one point close to the intersections of the ellipses to see whether the long diagonal line appears. If it does, use ^Q to delete it. Then reselect the ellipses properly.

Completion of a Cylindrical Part

Use EDIT—TRM/EXT—DOUBLE to trim four circles, putting the cursor on the part of the circle you want to keep. The only trouble that is likely in this operation is that when you try to select the short vertical lines as trimming entities you may get the nearby circles instead. If this happens, press Alt-R to reverse the direction in which Cadkey reads its database. Or place the cursor beside the line rather than on it, thereby getting it farther from the circle you want to avoid. (If you don't remember why this method works, read page 16 again.) Figure 2-30d shows the finished pictorial view.

Technical Notes

When you drew the tangent lines, Cadkey had to be in 2D construction mode. The reason is that you cannot construct a line tangent to two circles in space unless the circles lie in the same plane. In 2D mode, Cadkey can ignore this restriction and draw lines in the plane of the screen to circles projected to the plane of the screen.

Because they were constructed in 2D mode, the vertical lines in Figure 2-30d do not connect in space to the circular arcs. Ordinarily, such lines are perfectly acceptable. Although lines that don't connect in space spoil other views of the object, these other views are usually spoiled anyway by hidden line removal. For example, a correct top view of Figure 2-30d should show three concentric circles, but view 1 shows that hidden line removal has left a gap in the outer one. Figure 2-31f shows this effect. (There are ways around this. For example, before you start work on the pictorial, you can save the complete wire-frame drawing as a separate file.)

Addition of Shade Lines

One reason you might want to connect the vertical lines in Figure 2-30 in space is to create lines that give the drawing a stronger pictorial quality. These notes are more an outline than a detailed set of instructions. See whether you are ready for this. If the instructions seem too brief, go on to other tutorials and come back to this later.

Use TRM/EXT to extend the smallest arc as shown in Figure 2-31a. Use this extension to add one more vertical line to the drawing (Figure 2-31b).

Trim the arcs to make the left end of each arc fall at an endpoint of one of the vertical lines (Figure 2-31c).

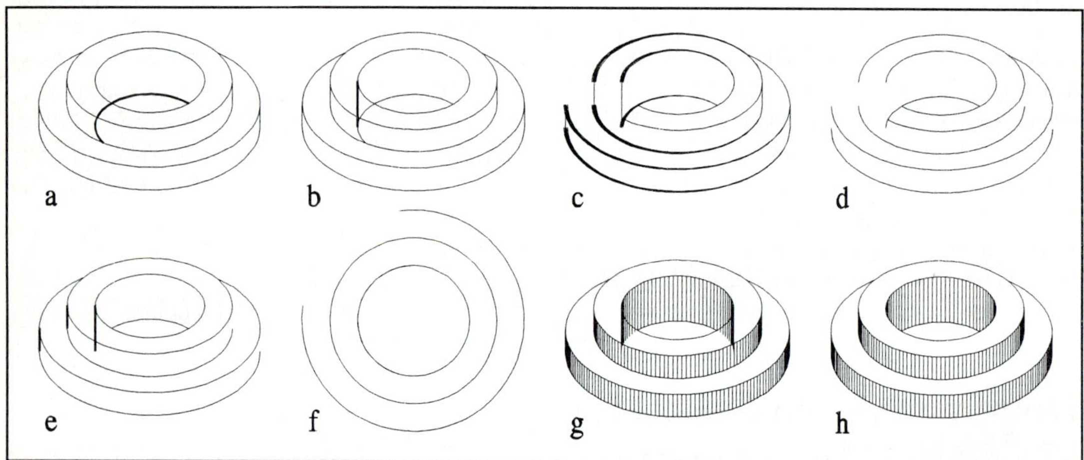

Figure 2-31 Steps needed to add shade lines

Delete all lines (Figure 2-31d). You can do this with DELETE—SELECT—ALL DSP—BY TYPE—GEOM—LINES—DONE, but be careful. If, when you try to select BY TYPE with the cursor, the mouse moves upward slightly as you press the mouse button, you might select ALL instead of BY TYPE. The entire drawing then disappears. To be safe, select BY TYPE by pressing F2 rather than by using the mouse.

The purpose of what you have done is to provide a way to draw vertical lines that connect *in space* to the elliptical arcs. The lines you had before indicated where on the arcs the lines should end. Now you have endpoints of arcs to which you can connect the lines.

Switch the construction mode to 3D.

With CREATE—LINE—ENDPTS—ENDENT, replace the three vertical lines on the left half of the drawing. Use EDIT—TRM/EXT—FIRST to restore the arcs to their original lengths. Figure 2-31e shows these two changes.

Figure 2-31f shows the top view at this point. The vertical lines in Figure 2-31 a, which you have removed, would have shown in this view as disconnected segments. The correct lines that you added do not show because they coincide in this view with the circles.

Use X-FORM—2D ROT—COPY—SINGLE (CADKEY Light 1.5) or X-FORM—ROTATE—COPY—SINGLE (CADKEY Light 4.0) to add shading lines. You have to add these one set at a time; otherwise the lines on the inner surface would be more closely spaced than the lines on the outer one. To be safe, either save your drawing or, with ALEV, make a new LEVEL active.

Select the line at the far left. Ask for 80 copies. To get the correct rotation origin, switch to view 1, select CENTER from the menu options window, and pick one of the circles. Enter 180/80 as the rotation angle. Switch back to view 7 and admire the results.

Press F10 twice to back up two steps. Select SINGLE again to repeat the 2D ROT (or ROTATE) procedure. For the middle line, make 60 copies spaced 180/60 degrees. For the line nearest the center of the object, make 39 copies spaced —180/40 degrees (the minus sign rotates the line clockwise). Figure 2-31g shows what your drawing should look like in view 7.

Use EDIT—TRM/EXT—MODAL to cut these last lines to length and obtain the result shown in Figure 2-31h. Use ^Q to get rid of the line at the left end of this array. (Making only 39 copies eliminated the hidden line that would have been at the right end.)

Had you tried to generate these shade lines using the original lines that did not connect in space, you would have created an interesting pattern of diagonal lines.

Creation of Concentric Ellipses

With FILES—PART—LOAD, load the **blank** file. Use CREATE—CIRCLE—CTR+DIA to create a set of concentric rings. These will become the elliptical rings in Figure 2-32. If you have a color monitor and are tired of the same old colors on the screen, press Alt-X and select a color from the samples you see in the menu options window. The seven rings in Figure 2-32 have diameters of 1, 1.1, 1.14, 1.22, 1.34, 1.42, and 1.46; however, there is nothing sacred about these numbers. You may want to draw more rings or use uniform rather than irregular spacings. Any set of diameters in the 1 to 1.5 range will do. KEY-IN the center of each circle as XV = YV = ZV = 0. To start the next circle, press F10 and enter its diameter. Press Alt-A (AUTOSCALE) to expand the drawing to fill the screen.

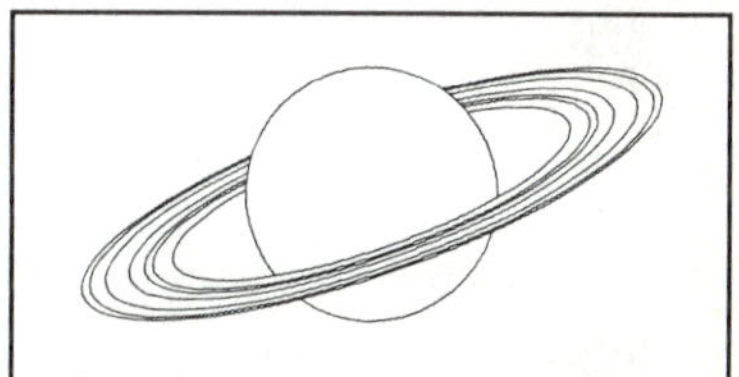

Figure 2-32 Circles trimmed with DOUBLE

Switch to view 5 (press Alt-V and enter 5). You may need to press Alt-A to see the rings. Here they look like a single horizontal line. With X-FORM—2D ROT—MOVE—ALL DSP—ALL (CADKEY Light 1.5) or X-FORM—ROTATE—MOVE—ALL DSP—ALL (CADKEY Light 4.0), rotate the rings. Put the rotation origin at XV = YV = ZV = 0 and use a rotation angle of 75. The horizontal line becomes nearly vertical. When you switch back to view 1, the circular rings show as ellipses.

Trimming a Circle with DOUBLE

With CREATE—CIRCLE—CTR+DIA, create the center circle in Figure 2-33a. Its diameter is 0.6. Specify its center either as XV = YV = ZV = 0 or as the CENTER of any ellipse.

The next step is to create two gaps in the circle where the rings pass in front of it. Figure 2-33b shows these gaps. (To let them show more clearly, five rings were removed.) With EDIT—TRM/EXT—DOUBLE, cut the first gap in the circle. Put the cursor anywhere on the part of the circle you want to keep. Select the inner and outer rings as trimming entities. Because the rings are so closely spaced, you may need to use Alt-W to expand this region of the drawing.

Because the circle has become an arc, it is DIVIDE instead of DOUBLE that cuts the second gap. Press F10 to back up a step; then select DIVIDE. For this command, you select the part of the entity you want to *remove*—the segment between the inner and outer rings. Again, use the inner and outer rings as trimming entities.

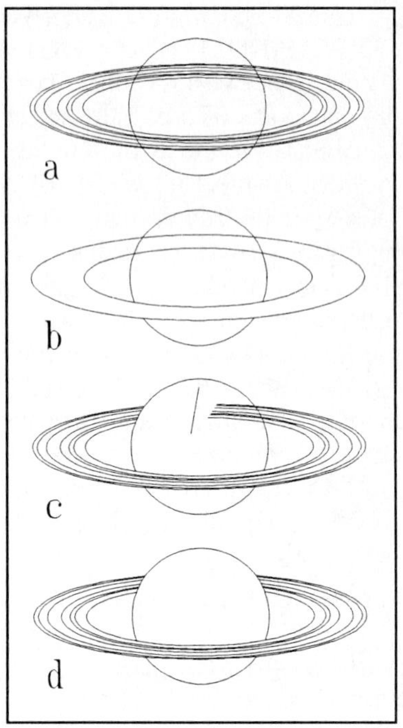

Figure 2-33 Steps in creating the design

Trimming Ellipses with DOUBLE

DOUBLE ought to trim the elliptical rings in the same way that it cut the first gap in the circle, and with CADKEY Light 4.0 it does; but CADKEY Light 1.5 responds with **Intersection not found... press RETURN**. The problem is the second bug you were promised.

If you encounter this bug, use CREATE—LINE—ENDPTS to create a short line like the one in Figure 2-33c. Now use EDIT—TRM/EXT—DOUBLE. Even when DOUBLE cannot cut the rings at both sides of the circle, it cuts them between the line and one side of the circle. With ^Q, delete the line.

Figure 2-33c shows another strange response. Depending on which trimming entity you select first, the arcs may or may not end exactly on the line.

Now that the ellipses have become arcs, you can use MODAL to trim the ends on the right, using the circle as the trimming entity. Trimming proceeds without difficulty to give the configuration in Figure 2-33d.

If you want your picture tilted 20° as in Figure 2-32, use X-FORM—2D ROT—MOVE—ALL DSP—ALL (CADKEY Light 1.5) or X-FORM—ROTATE—MOVE—ALL DSP—ALL (CADKEY Light 4.0). Any rotation origin will do, but if you want to keep the drawing centered on the origin, you can select the CENTER of the circle or any ellipse.

Basic Hole-and-Shaft Dimensioning

A classical engineering graphics problem is dimensioning a hole and shaft to assure a proper fit. If, for example, a shaft is to turn freely in a bearing, the fit must be loose enough to allow for a thin lubricating film but snug enough to prevent chatter and excessive wear.

Setting Up

Load the **blank** file. Press Alt-Y. From the array of lines Cadkey displays, select the next-to-to-the-thinnest (or you can key in a width of 3). This sets the width to be used for this drawing. With CREATE—LINE—RECTANG—WID/HT, create two rectangles. Make the first one 2 units wide by 1 unit high, and KEY-IN its lower left corner as XV = —1, YV = —2, and ZV = 0. Press F10 twice to draw the second rectangle. Make it 1 unit wide by 1.25 units high, with its lower left corner at XV = —0.5, YV = 1, and ZV = 0.

Either press ^X or select SNAP in the status window to turn snap on. With CREATE—LINE—ENDPTS, draw two lines in the lower rectangle as shown in Figure 2-34. Turn snap off for the next step.

The next step is to create the cylindrical break symbol in Figure 2-35d. Use Alt-W to put a window around the top rectangle and enlarge it.

With CREATE—ARC—CTR+RAD, draw the arcs in Figure 2-35b. Use a radius of 0.1 unit. For the arc on the right, use a start angle of 0 and an end angle of 90. To indicate the arc center, select ALONGL from the status window, select the top line of the rectangle near its right end, and enter 0.1.

Press F10 to get ready for the other arc. Press Return to accept the radius of 0.1 that Cadkey suggests. Use start and end angles of 90 and —90. Cadkey is still set to place the arc center by measuring along a line. Select the top line of the rectangle near its left end and enter 0.1.

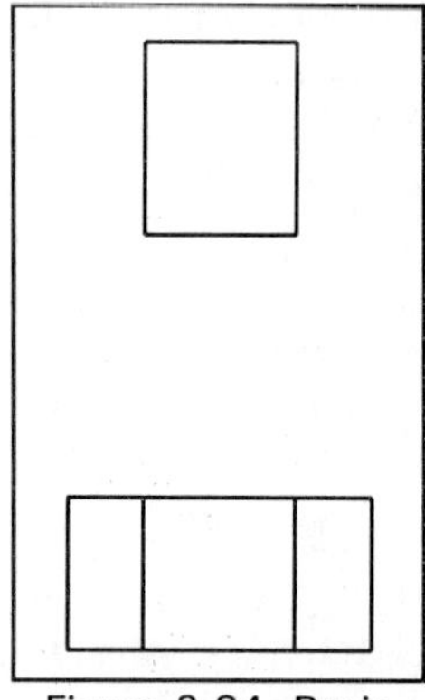

Figure 2-34 Basic configuration

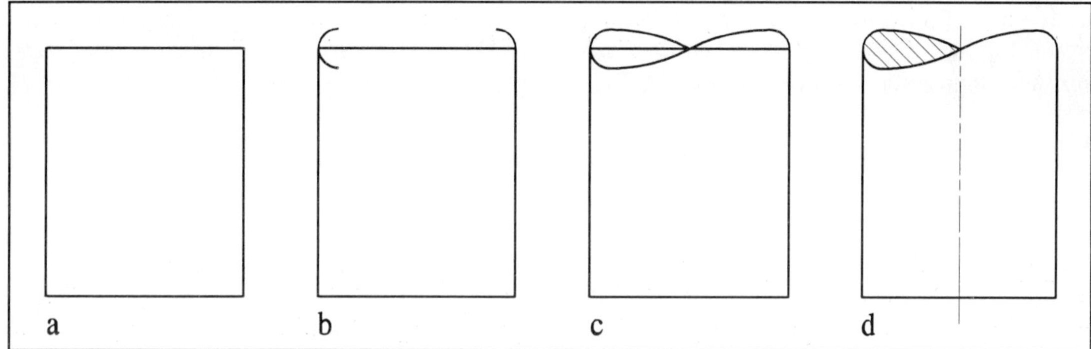

Figure 2-35 Steps in creating a cylindrical break line

CREATE—ARC—ROUND draws an arc through a point and tangent to an entity at the end of the entity. Use this to add the last three arcs (Figure 2-35c). For the tangent entity, select one of the arcs you just drew. For the arc termination point, select CENTER from the menu options window and select the top line of the rectangle. Then specify whether the arc should turn clockwise or counterclockwise as it goes from the tangent entity to the point. You may want to select the wrong alternative deliberately, just to see the flourish with which Cadkey responds. You can easily use ^Q to delete the results. Delete also the top line of the rectangle.

Crosshatching

The next step is to crosshatch the area between arcs as in Figure 2.35d. Use DETAIL—X-HATCH—BRICK. Press Return to accept the 45° line angle and enter 1/20 as the distance between hatch lines. Use WINDOW to specify the area to be crosshatched. Be sure the window encloses the area you want but does not completely enclose any other entities. Select YES (or press Return) to indicate your selection is complete. The area should now be crosshatched as in Figure 2-35d. Note that crosshatch lines are thin even though Cadkey is set to use thicker lines for other entities.

Get Cadkey ready to add the centerline in Figure 2-35d. Press Alt-Y and reset the line thickness to the thinnest choice. Press Alt-T and select the centerline pattern, the next-to-the-bottom choice. If SNAP is not already on, turn it on. You probably need to press PgDn twice to reduce the SNAP distance from 1/2 of a unit to 1/8 of a unit. Then use CREATE—LINE—ENDPTS—CURSOR to draw in the centerline. Just indicate the endpoints. Cadkey supplies the long-short-long line pattern between these ends.

As you press Alt-A to get all the drawing on the screen, watch the centerline. It gets shorter, but the individual segments stay the same length. There just aren't as many segments. The crosshatching reacts differently to the change in scale. The number of lines stays the same and the lines are spaced more closely.

Use Alt-W to put a window around the lower rectangle. Then, still using CREATE—LINE—ENDPTS—CURSOR, add the centerline shown in Figure 2-36a.

Dealing with Crosshatching Problems

The next step is to crosshatch the two areas that bracket the hole (Figure 2-35c). Select DETAIL—X-HATCH—BRICK. Use a 45° line angle and a 0.1 line spacing. Put a window around the left area as in Figure 2-36a. Cadkey is less cooperative than before. Instead of seeing crosshatching, you see **Invalid data... press RETURN**. Press Return to clear the error message; then go to the main menu.

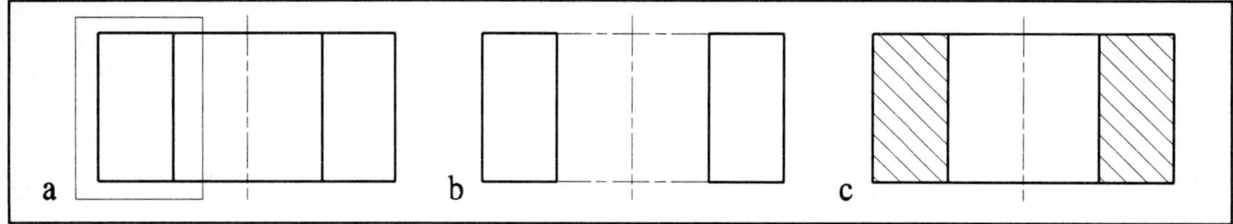

Figure 2-36 Sectioning the lower rectangle

The horizontal lines are the problem. The lines that bound an area to be crosshatched cannot extend beyond the edge of the boundary, and these do. The BREAK commands provide the remedy. These commands, which work much like the TRM/EXT commands, let you break a single entity into two or more segments. Select EDIT—BREAK—DIVIDE. Choose the top horizontal line as the entity to break and the two inner vertical lines as the breaking entities.

Something else went wrong. The line *should* look the same as before, but it has a weak midsection (Figure 2-36b). Cadkey is still set to construct thin centerlines, and one of the rules of the BREAK command is that the segment broken out is redrawn according to current settings.

One way to repair the damage is to delete the offending segment and redraw it properly, but another approach is more instructive. Without making any changes, use the same BREAK command on the lower horizontal line.

To correct the line type, select CONTROL—ATTRIB—L-TYPE—CHANGE, pick the solid line from the menu options window, select SINGLE, and select the two thin lines. To correct the line width, press F10 twice, select L-WIDTH—CHANGE, pick the next-to-the-thinnest line, select SINGLE, and select the two lines. Your drawing should again look like Figure 2-36a.

As before, select DETAIL—X-HATCH—BRICK. Use a 45° angle and a 0.1 spacing. Select WINDOW, and again place it as in Figure 2-36a. Because Cadkey ignores all entities not completely enclosed by the window, the lines you just operated on pose no problem. Press Return to tell Cadkey the selection of boundary lines is complete, and the crosshatching appears as in Figure 2-36c. Select WINDOW again and repeat the ritual to crosshatch the other area.

Dimensioning

Figure 2-37d shows the dimensions to add. There are at least two ways to do this, and the most direct is the least convenient. You could have constructed the shaft, for example, with a 1.9988 diameter, assigned tolerances of +0 and —.0007, and asked Cadkey to give you limit dimensions. But it's easier to start with what Cadkey gives you and change it later.

In that spirit, use DETAIL—DIMENSN—HORIZTL. Cadkey thoughtfully sets the selection menu option to ENDENT, almost always the best choice. Pick the two lower corners of the cylinder. Indicate the position of the dimensioning text by putting the cursor where you want the center of the number to fall. In the result (Figure 2-37a), the number is wrong, the arrows should be on the outside to avoid crowding, and the lettering should be smaller for the same reason. Cadkey asks, **Accept dimension ? (YES)**. Select NO. Don't press F10 or Esc.

Select **DH=0.300000** (DH means dimension height) in the status window. You probably have to use **--more--** to find it. Enter 0.2 to reset this lettering height. Now find **ARR:IN**, which says that the arrows are inside the two extension lines. Select this entry to change it to **ARR:OUT**.

Again select the dimensioning text position and select YES to accept the dimension. Add the dimension for hole diameter, as in Figure 2-37b. Now the numbers may be wrong, but number heights and arrow directions are correct.

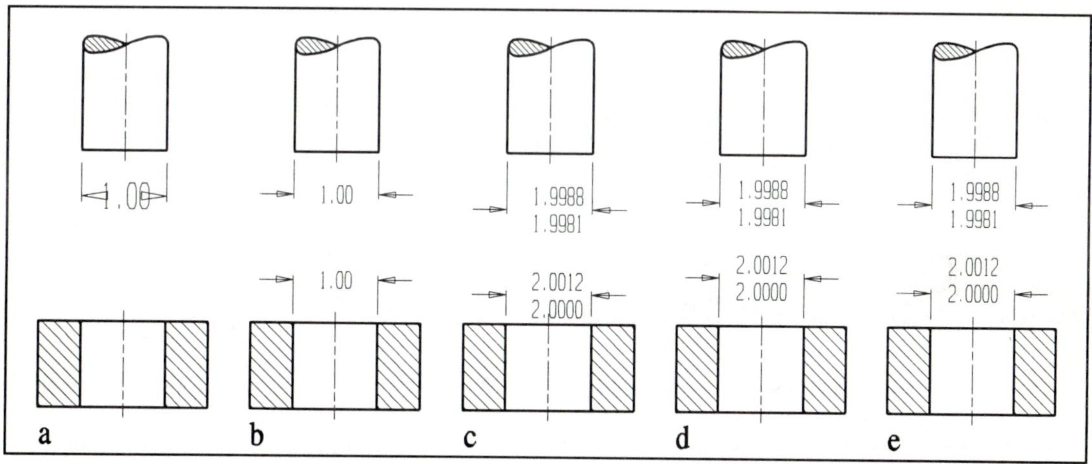

Figure 2-37 Dimensioning using the basic hole system

Editing the Dimensions

You constructed a shaft one unit in diameter, but the final dimensions call for a shaft two units in diameter. The purpose of this inconsistency is to emphasize how much freedom you have to alter dimensions. (This same freedom lets your instructor assign several hole-and-shaft problems without making you create a new drawing each time.)

To change the numbers, use DETAIL—CHANGE—EDIT TX to call Cadkey's TEXT EDITOR. Select the shaft dimension (the selection point is the lower left corner of the number). Press Backspace twice to delete the two zeros; then type in .9988 to make the number 1.9988. Press Return to start a second line of text and type in 1.9981. Press F6 (SAVE TX) to replace the original dimension with the one you just changed.

Edit the hole dimension. Delete 1.00, type in 2.0012, press Return, type in 2.0000, and press F6. Now the numbers are right but the added digits have left the dimensions badly positioned (Figure 2-37c). What happened here is that the first number of the dimension, not the center of the array, stays in the same place.

Press F10 to back up a step and select TXT POS. If SNAP is not still on, press ^X to turn it on and make it easier to center the text. Select the shaft dimension. (The position for selecting it is now the lower left corner of the *first line* of numbers). A rectangle appears and moves with the cursor to show the area the text will fill. You may need to press PgDn once or twice to get finer control over the vertical position. Press the mouse button when you think the position is right. Because Cadkey expects you to want another chance, it moves the text to the new position, but it does not remove the rectangle. The rectangle continues to move as you move the cursor. Each time you press the mouse button, Cadkey again moves the dimension to wherever you have the rectangle. Press F10 when you are satisfied. Then select the hole dimension and adjust its position.

Figure 2-37e shows a problem you may encounter. The arrows for the hole dimension are centered on the bottom number rather than on the pair of numbers. The explanation is that a blank line has crept into the dimensioning text. Somebody hit Return after typing in 2.0000. The hole dimension has one blank line below the numbers, and Cadkey has neatly centered the arrows on the complete array of lines, including the blank one.

Use DETAIL—CHANGE—EDIT TX to fix this. The prompt line shows **Enter text:2.0012**. Press the down arrow and it shows **Enter text:2.0000**. Press the down arrow again and it shows just **Enter text:**, indicating a blank line. Press F1 (DEL LN) to delete this line and F6 to save the text. The dimension disappears briefly; then it reappears with the arrows properly centered. If you think you may still have irregularities due to blank lines, select the dimension again for editing, use the arrow keys to run up and down the lines of text, and press F1 whenever you see a blank line.

Wire-Frame Drawing of a Gear

In this exercise you create a wire-frame drawing of the gear in Figure 2-39. Load the **blank** file.

Use CREATE—CIRCLE—CTR+DIA to construct the center hole. Make it one unit in diameter and KEY IN its center as XV = YV = ZV = 0. You will add the keyway for this hole later.

Layout of Gear-Tooth Contour

Use CREATE—ARC—CTR+RAD to draw an arc for the face of one gear tooth. Make the radius 3.23, the start angle —5, and the end angle 5. KEY-IN the center as XV = YV = ZV = 0. Press Alt-A to enlarge the drawing, which looks like Figure 2-38.

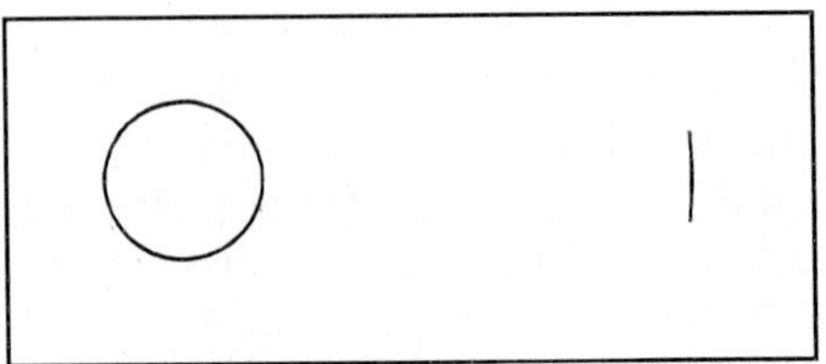

Figure 2-38 Arc for the face of the right-hand gear tooth

Press F10 to back up one step and enter a new set of parameters. Draw two more arcs. The parameters for these arcs are:

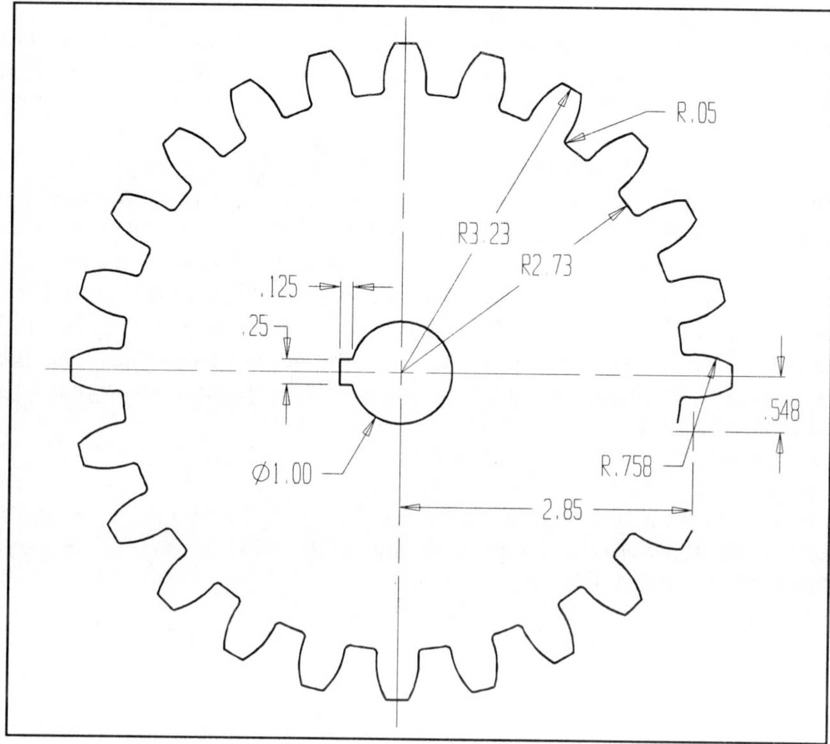

Figure 2-39 Spur gear

Radius:		2.73	.758
Start angle:		3	−110
End angle:		12	−50
Center at	XV =	0	2.85
	YV =	0	.548
	ZV =	0	0

At this point, the arcs (Figure 2-40) look carelessly drawn. Because there is no easy way to predict exactly where each arc should start and end, the start and end angles were just guesses. Later, you can easily trim the arcs to the proper lengths.

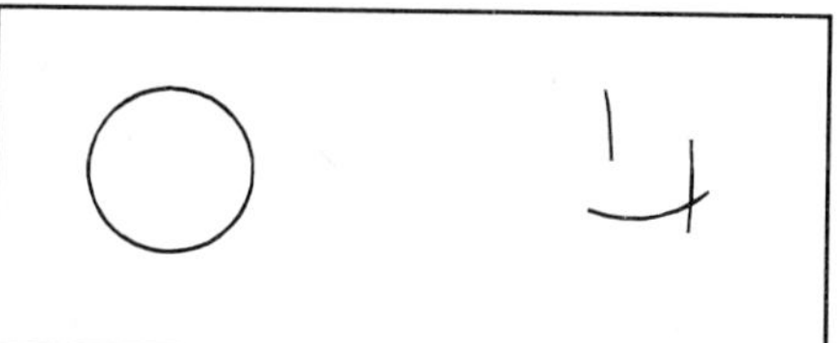

Figure 2-40 Addition of two arcs

You may or may not yet recognize the configuration that is taking shape. The lower, nearly horizontal arc represents the bottom side of a gear tooth. In a real spur gear tooth, this side, although resembling a circular arc, would have a complex shape. To simplify this exercise, this side is approximated by a simple arc; however, the next step treats the side as you would treat it if you had drawn it in painstaking detail. Instead of constructing the shape again for the top side of the tooth, you would use the MIRROR command to copy the shape already generated.

With CREATE—LINE—HRZ/VRT—HORIZTL—CENTER, create a horizontal line through the center of the circle. Figure 2-41 shows this line.

Select X-FORM—MIRROR—COPY—SINGLE to set up the MIRROR command. The line for the mirroring plane is the line you just drew, and the entity to copy is the arc you drew last—the one that is nearly horizontal. Select it and press Return. Using ENDENT, select the two ends of the horizontal line. Figure 2-41 shows the mirrored entity.

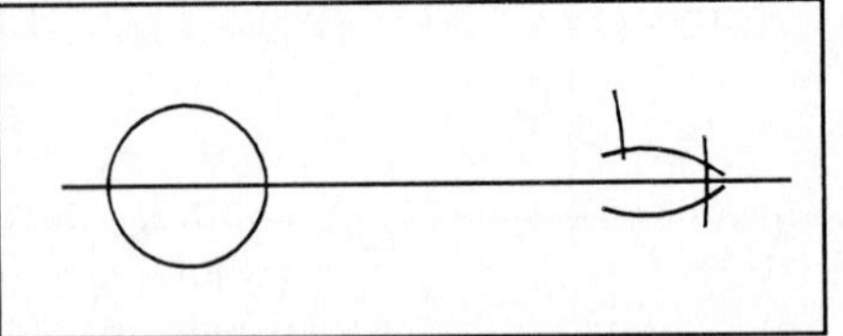

Figure 2-41 MIRROR adds side of tooth

You are not finished with the horizontal line, but it tends to get in the way and you may want to trim it to the length shown in Figure 2-42.

You need to copy the bottom side again, this time to generate the lower edge of the next gear tooth. Use X-FORM—2D ROT—COPY—SINGLE (CADKEY Light 1.5) or X-FORM—ROTATE—COPY—SINGLE (CADKEY Light 4.0). Select the bottom arc and press Return. Press Return again to accept the default value of 1 for the number of copies. Indicate the CENTER of the circle as the rotation origin.

The angle you want is the angle between two gear teeth. Because the gear has 24 teeth, you could calculate 360°/24 = 15° and enter 15. Instead, enter 360/24 and let Cadkey calculate the angle. Figure 2-42 shows the arc copied in this rotated position.

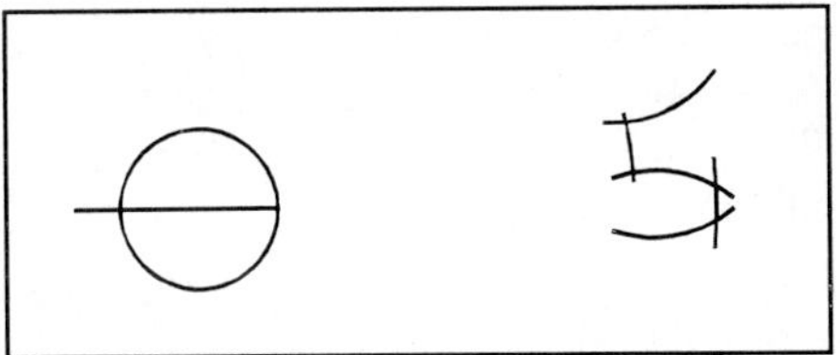

Figure 2-42 2D ROT or ROTATE creates one side of the adjacent tooth

Figure 2-39 calls for rounded corners at the base of the gear teeth. Use CREATE—FILLET—ARC—TRIM to add arcs with a radius of .05.

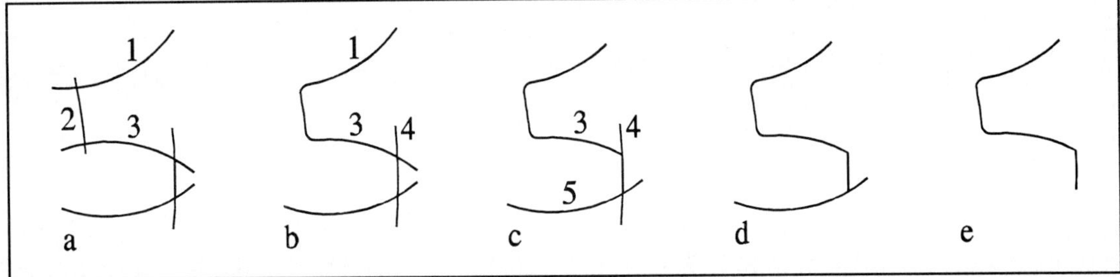

Figure 2-43 Trimming the lines for a representative gear tooth

As you recall from the tutorial on Trimming and Extending, when you use a FILLET to round a corner you can get strange results unless you are careful about where you place the cursor. Select the arcs labeled 1 and 2 in Figure 2-43a; then select arcs 2 and 3. A safe way to select each is to put the cursor near the midpoints of the arcs rather than close to the corner you are rounding.

Select EDIT—TRM/EXT—MODAL. For the trimming entity, select the vertical arc (4 in Figure 2-43b). Then select the arcs marked 1 and 3, trimming them to the lengths shown in Figure 2-43c.

Press F10 twice to back out of the MODAL routine; then pick DOUBLE from the menu. The history line at the top of the screen shows that your position in the menu system is EDIT—TRM/EXT—DOUBLE. Pick the vertical arc (4) as the entity to trim; then pick arcs 3 and 5 as the first and second trimming entities. The result (Figure 2-43d) is beginning to look less like oriental writing and more like a gear tooth. With ^Q, delete the lowest arc to obtain the shape in Figure 2-43e.

Copying the Gear-Tooth Pattern

The arc you just deleted was needed to trim the face of the gear tooth, but it became surplus because it duplicates the top arc. To avoid double lines in the final drawing, you want only one sample of each arc. You now have two arcs that represent gear-tooth sides, one arc for the face, one arc for the root, and two small arcs for the rounded inside corners. By making 23 copies of these arcs, you will generate a drawing that shows all 24 teeth.

This is a good time to use ^F to SAVE your file. GEAR (or, perhaps, A:\GEAR, depending on your computer setup) is an appropriate file name. If the copy command goes wrong, you can use FILES—PART—LOAD to retrieve the file as it was before the copy command.

Select X-FORM—2D ROT—COPY—WINDOW (CADKEY Light 1.5) or X-FORM—ROTATE—COPY—WINDOW (CADKEY Light 4.0). This lets you select the arcs by putting a window around them. Enter 23 for the number of copies.

For the rotation origin, choose CENTER from the selection menu and select the circle. (Or choose KEY-IN and specify XV = YV = ZV = 0. Or use SNAP.)

For the rotation angle, enter either 360/24 or 15.

Press Alt-A to see the whole gear, which should look like Figure 2-39 without the dimensions and without the keyway.

The Keyway

Press Alt-W and put a window around the circle. This will enlarge it to what Figure 2-44a shows and make it easier to draw the keyway.

Select CREATE—LINE—PARALEL—AT DIST, enter .125 for the distance, and select the horizontal line. Move the cursor anywhere above the line and press the mouse button. Cadkey creates a line parallel to the one you selected and spaced .125 from it. Select the original horizontal line again, move the cursor anywhere below the line, and press the mouse button to generate another line.

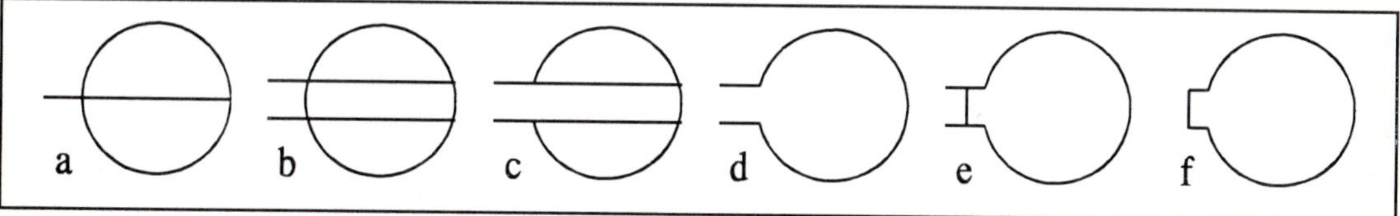

Figure 2-44 Steps in constructing the keyway

With ^Q, delete the center horizontal line. The drawing should now look like Figure 2-44b.

Select EDIT—TRM/EXT—DOUBLE to cut a small arc out of the left side of the circle. Select the circle anywhere on the portion you want to keep (near the top, for example). Then select the two lines as trimming entities. A gap appears as in Figure 2-44c.

With F10, back up a step; then select MODAL. Trim the two lines to the lengths shown in Figure 2-44d.

From the main menu, select CREATE—LINE—ENDPTS—ALONGL. Select one of the lines where it intersects the circle. You don't need to worry about accidentally selecting the circle. Even though you put the cursor closer to the circle than to the line, ALONGL will not let you select anything but a line. Enter 0.125. Select the other line and again enter 0.125. This adds the vertical line shown in Figure 2-44e.

Select EDIT—TRM/EXT—MODAL, and trim the two horizontal lines where they cross the vertical one. Figure 2-44f shows the finished keyway.

Alt-B should restore the earlier view that shows the entire gear. If it does not, use Alt-A.

Extension to Three Dimensions

In order to watch the extension to three dimensions, press Alt-V and switch to view 7. You probably need to press Alt-A to get all of the drawing on the screen. Select COORD in the status window to switch its setting from VW to WLD.

As before, press ^F to save your drawing. Cadkey responds with **Enter part file name (gear):**, where the word in parentheses is the file name you last used in saving or loading your drawing. (If you used upper-case letters, so will Cadkey.) Press Return to accept this default file name. The message **File already exists, replace it?** appears. You will probably answer YES, in which case Cadkey first saves the current drawing and then erases the one you saved earlier. If you answer NO, Cadkey prompts you for a different file name.

Select X-FORM—TRANS-R—JOIN—ALL DSP—ALL (CADKEY Light 1.5) or X-FORM—DELTA—JOIN—ALL DSP—ALL (CADKEY Light 4.0). Make 1 copy with dX = 0, dY = 0, and dZ = .75. The reason for choosing Z as the coordinate to vary is that the pattern for the gear was laid out in the top view, where the coordinates you see are X and Y. Z is therefore the coordinate that sets thickness. See the inside front cover for an illustration of world coordinates.

If all goes well, Cadkey will copy your drawing, add join lines, and give the drawing in Figure 2-45. (If the isometric view shows no change, you may still be in VIEW coordinates. The joined copy is there, but its angle is wrong, and in the isometric view the copy coincides with the original. If this happened to you, see TROUBLESHOOTING.)

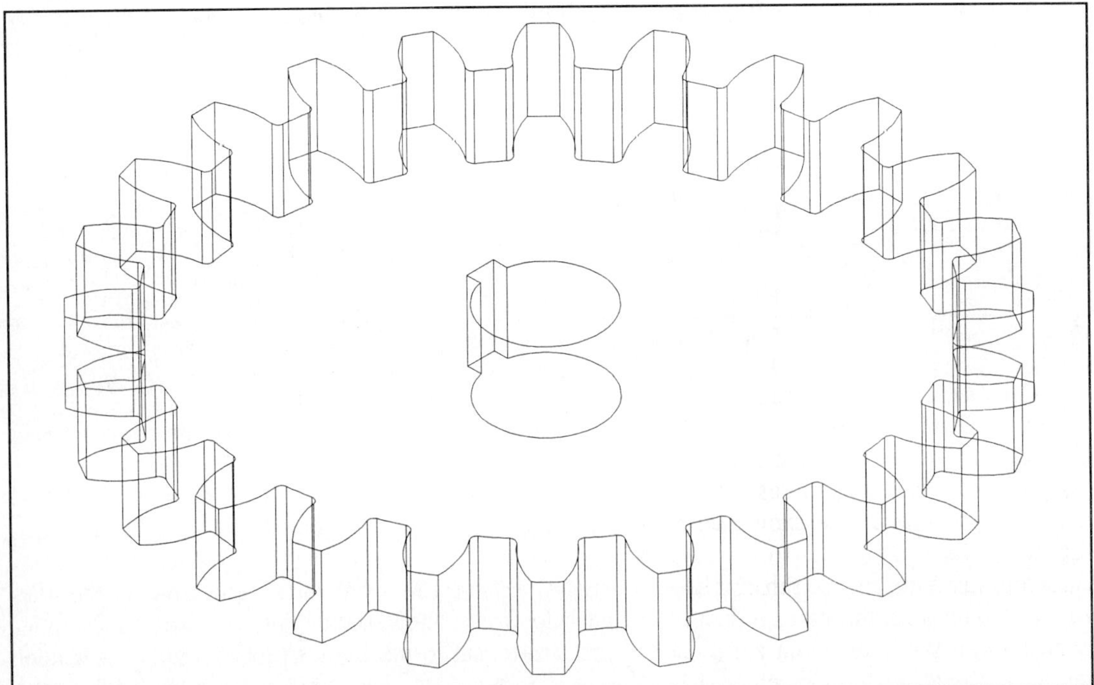

Figure 2-45 Wire-frame drawing of a spur gear

If you feel ambitious, you may want to remove hidden lines to obtain the pictorial view in Figure 2-46. Before you start, be warned that the process is more tedious than educational. You also need to add some tangent lines (use 2D mode). The easiest way to add them is to create a temporary horizontal line and use the PRP TAN option to construct the tangents.

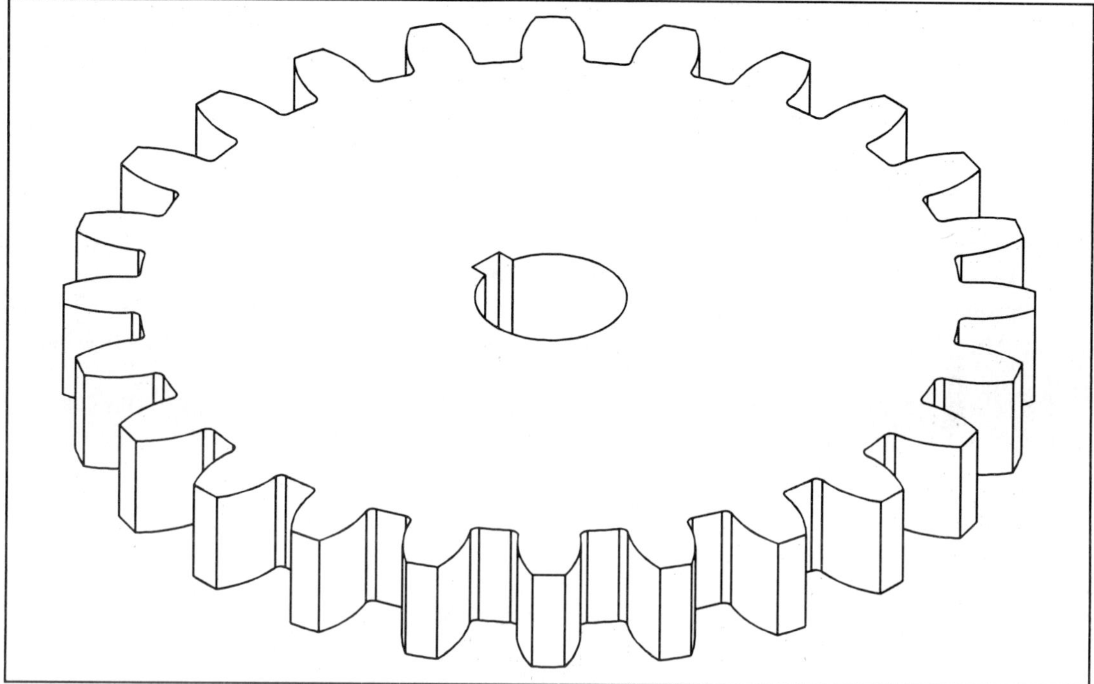

Figure 2-46 Pictorial view of gear

Bolthead Pictorial

This exercise is included because it shows applications of several position-menu options. The bolthead you will draw is for a bolt of unit diameter, but you can scale it up or down to use for any bolt size. In the last part of this exercise, you create a PATTERN and use it to add the bolthead to a separate drawing.

When getting a problem ready to present in class, many instructors will work it three or four times to find the method that leads most smoothly to the correct answer. This approach makes the classroom presentation easy to follow and it makes the instructor look good. But there are other effects. It fails to show the unexpected obstacles that one can encounter in unfamiliar problems, and it also fails to demonstrate how skilled problem solvers handle such situations. Watching someone bungle through a problem is often more instructive than watching the smooth presentation. What follows, however, is the smooth, well-rehearsed approach. Most Cadkey operators doing this problem for the first time would create more construction lines and would have more to do in the final cleanup operation. Nevertheless, you need to be careful. Students report that this exercise offers more opportunities than usual for things to go wrong.

Setting up

Load the **blank** file. Use DISPLAY—VWPORTS—AUTOSET to put Cadkey in its four-viewport mode. Select the four-viewport option from the menu options window and designate the upper left viewport as the primary one.

Starting the Bolthead

Use CREATE–LINE–N-GON to construct a hexagon. Choose:

number of sides = 6
rotation angle = 0
"radius" of hexagon = .75
option = FLAT
center position: With the cursor in view 1 (top left), KEY-IN XV = YV = ZV = 0.
group entities? NO

Set DEPTH (D in the status window) to 2/3 and switch the construction mode (CONST in the status window) to 2D.

Use CREATE–CIRCLE–THREE-P–CENTER to construct a circle tangent to the sides of the hexagon. In the top (upper left) view, select any three sides. Cadkey draws a circle that, in the top view, passes through the centers of these three sides, but a glance at the isometric shows that the 2D construction mode has placed the circle at the current depth of 2/3, above the hexagon in space (Figure 2-47). To double the size of the image in all views, press Alt-D and press Return.

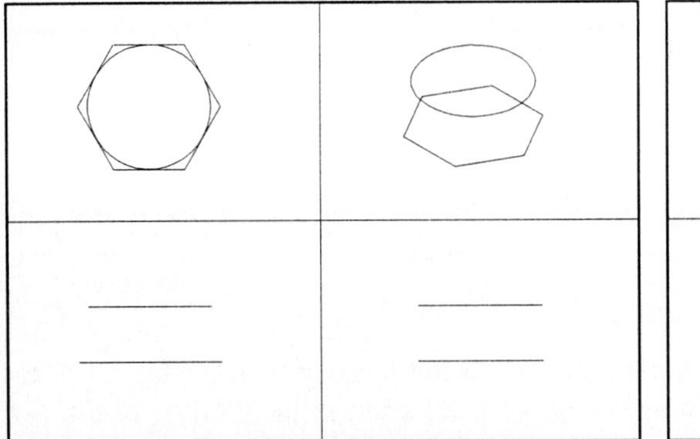

Figure 2-47 Hexagonal base and top circle for bolthead

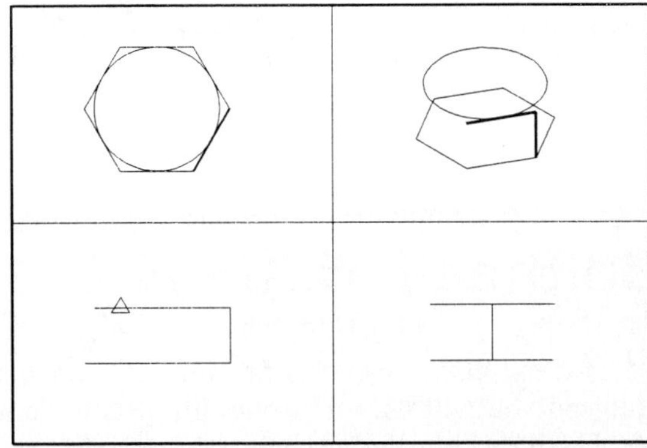

Figure 2-48 Addition of construction line and vertical edge

Still working in the top view, use CREATE–LINE–ENDPTS–ENDENT to add a line that, in this view, coincides with the lower right side of the hexagon—the side shown darker in Figure 2-48. As the isometric shows, this creates a line at a depth of 2/3–at the same depth as the circle and tangent to it.

Switch back to 3D construction mode.

In the isometric, still using CREATE–LINE–ENDPTS–ENDENT, draw a vertical line from the right end of the tangent line you just drew to the hexagon corner below it. You may have some difficulty positioning the top end of the line, but by now you should know some tricks that will help. Figure 2-48 shows this line.

Cutting the Chamfer

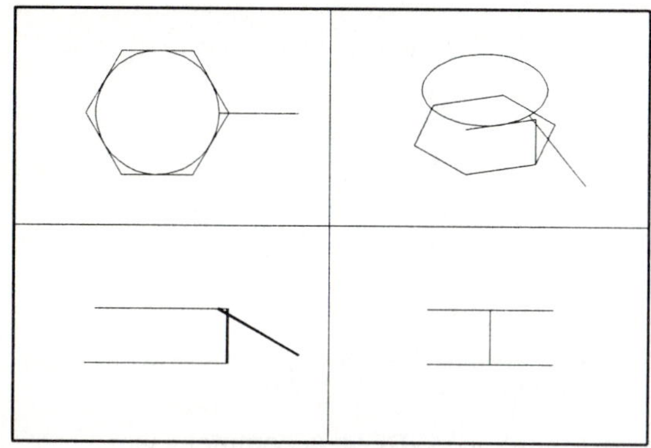
Figure 2-49 Setting the angle of the chamfer

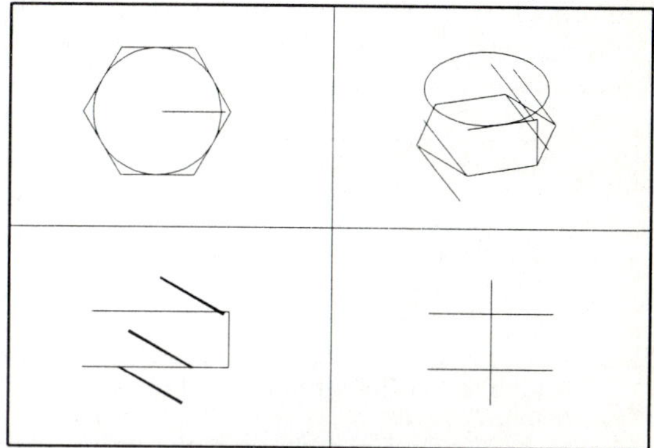
Figure 2-50 Alternate construction for 30° trimming entity

Trimming this vertical line to just the right length takes a little doing. A 30° chamfer gives boltheads their characteristic shape. To set this angle, create a 30° line, working entirely in the front (lower left) view. Use ENDENT to start the line from the "end" of the circle (its 0° point). Select the circle where it shows on edge, putting the cursor on the left half of the circle, in the position suggested by the triangle in Figure 2-48. This position keeps Cadkey from selecting the tangent line instead. Shift to POLAR in the menu options window. In the modified position menu that appears, select ENDENT and select the circle again. This specifies the 0° point of the circle as the polar origin. Specify —30 as the angle and 1 as the distance from this origin. Figure 2-49 shows what the front view should look like. The line is longer than it needs to be, but only its angle is important.

If this construction gives you trouble—if Cadkey seems to be in a bad mood—there is another way to get the line you need. Select CREATE—LINE—ANGLE, enter —30, and select the bottom line in the front view, near the center. This catches either the front side or the back side of the hexagon and creates a —30° line attached to one end or the other. As the isometric view in Figure 2-50 shows, the resulting line could show up in any of four places. Any one of these four lines will work. Use CREATE—LINE—PARALEL—THRU PT to draw a line parallel to the —30° line and passing through the endpoint of the circle.

With EDIT—TRM/EXT—FIRST, trim the top off of the vertical line, using the —30° line as the trimming entity. You can do this in either the front view or the isometric view. Then, with ^Q, delete the —30° line you worked so hard to construct. (The objective of this exercise is to make a pictorial view of the isometric. If the objective were the front view, you would need to trim and retain this —30° line, but it does nothing for the pictorial.)

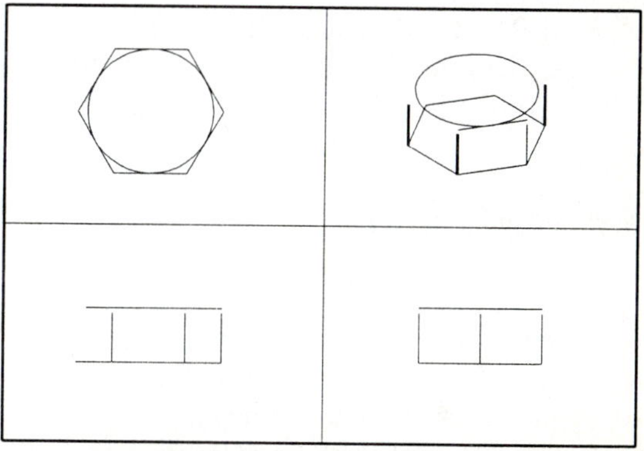
Figure 2-51 Vertical lines trimmed and in place

Use CREATE—LINE—PARALEL—THRU PT to copy the vertical line three times. In the isometric view, select the line, choose ENDENT from the position menu, and select the

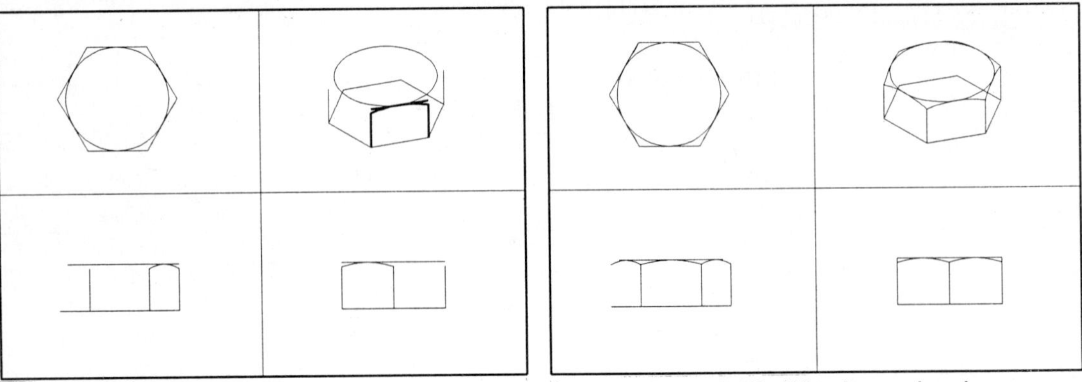

Figure 2-52 Construction of first arc

Figure 2-53 Wire-frame drawing

corners of the hexagon to give the result shown in Figure 2-51. For a complete wire-frame drawing, you would make five copies, but the visible lines are all you need to create.

Using CREATE—ARC—THREE-P, draw the arc shown in Figure 2-52. Working in the isometric view, use ENDENT to select the top of a vertical line, CENTER to select the middle of the tangent construction line, and ENDENT to select the top of the next vertical line.

Delete the construction line. If you accidentally delete the wrong entity, use ^U to restore it; then try again.

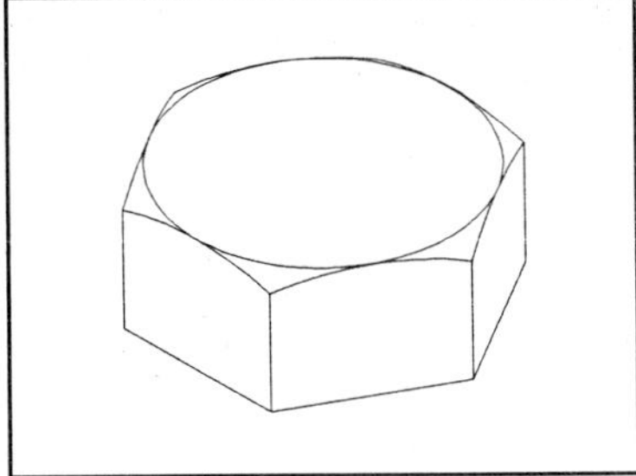

Figure 2-54 Bolthead pictorial

To generate five more arcs and create the view shown in Figure 2-53, use X-FORM—2D ROT—COPY—SINGLE (CADKEY Light 1.5) or X-FORM—ROTATE—COPY—SINGLE (CADKEY Light 4.0). Select the arc. Specify 5 copies. With the cursor in the top (upper left) view, select the rotation origin, using KEY-IN to enter coordinates of 0, 0, 0. Enter 60° for the rotation angle.

To convert this wire-frame drawing to the pictorial view in Figure 2-54, delete three hidden lines.

Creating a Pattern

With ^V, or by selecting COORD in the status window, switch the coordinate system from COORD=VW to COORD=WLD. Use FILES—PATTERN—CREATE—ALL DSP—ALL to make a PATTERN of this bolthead. Specify the isometric as the view in which to select all entities. Leaving the cursor in the isometric view, specify X = Y = Z = 0 as the base position. When you enter a file name of eight characters or less—**bolthead** will do—Cadkey creates the pattern.

An Application

Clear the screen to get ready to draw an object that needs the bolthead pattern. You can either use FILES—PART—LOAD to load your **blank** file or use DELETE—ALL DSP—ALL.

In view 1, the top view, use CREATE—ARC—CTR+DIA to create two arcs with diameters of 5 units. Specify the start angle as —135 and the end angle as 45. Use KEY-IN to specify XV = YV = ZV = 0 (or X = Y = Z = 0) as the center of the first arc and XV = 0, YV = 0, and ZV = 3 as the center of the second.

With CREATE—CIRCLE—CTR+DIA, create a circle with a diameter of 5 and a center at X = 0, Y = 0, and Z = 3.25.

With CREATE—POLYLIN—N-GON, create a regular polygon with ten sides. The rotation angle could be anything—0° is fine. Use CORNER as the way to specify the radius, and enter a radius of 2. Put the center at X = 0, Y = 0, and Z = 3.25. The point to using POLYLIN—N-GON rather than LINE—N-GON is to make the polygon a single entity rather than ten separate ones. This bookkeeping detail makes the polygon easier to delete when you are finished with it.

Use Alt-V to switch to view 7 (or, if you are still in the four-viewport mode, just start working in the isometric). With CREATE—LINE—ENDPTS—ENDENT, put sides on the cylinder. Draw these vertical lines from the end of one arc to the end of the other, being careful not to select the circle. (If you wonder why to avoid the circle, try selecting it. Doing so shows you where the 0° point of a circle lies in the isometric view, and you can easily delete the line that goes to it.) Use EDIT—TRM/EXT—MODAL to extend the two vertical lines to the circle. Figure 2-55 shows the result. With ^F, save the drawing (the next step adds many entities).

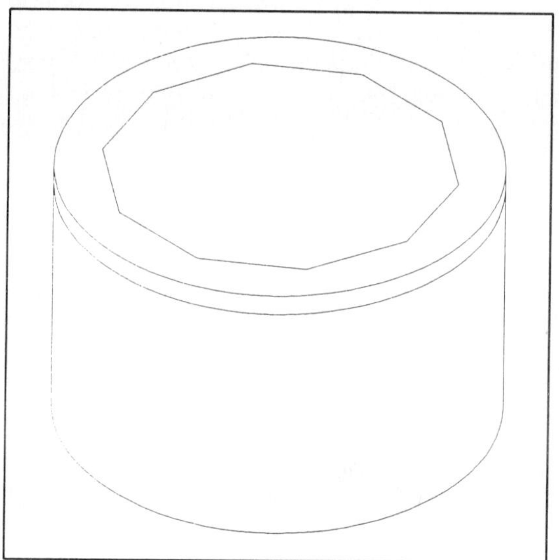

Figure 2-55 Cylindrical container

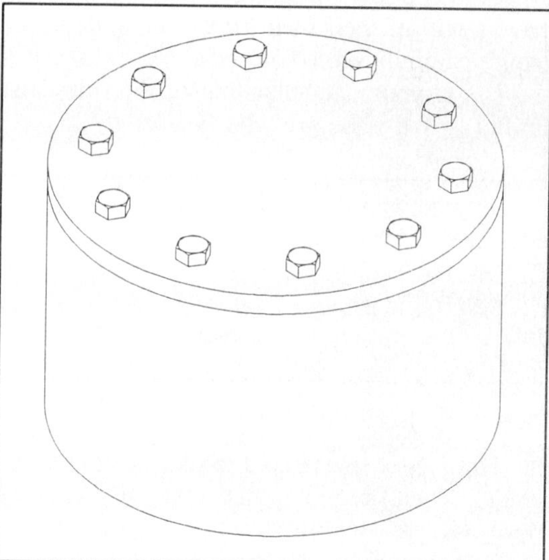

Figure 2-56 Container with bolts added

Retrieving the Pattern

Bolts will keep the lid from slipping off the top of the container. Retrieve the bolthead pattern with FILES—PATTERN—RETRIEVE and respond to a series of prompts:

- Enter the file name you used for the bolthead pattern.
- Group the entities or not, as you wish. If you didn't save your drawing, YES is the safer choice. It makes it easier to delete mistakes—see DELETE for details.
- Select CUR-LEV to put the entities on the current LEVEL.
- Enter a scale factor of .25 to provide quarter-inch bolts.
- Enter a rotation angle of zero.

Indicate the pattern base position by choosing ENDENT and selecting corners of the polygon. Each time you select a corner, Cadkey puts a bolthead there. When you finish, delete the polygon. You delete all of it by selecting just one side. Figure 2-56 shows the final result.

The questions on page 24 concern the rules for trimming and extending arcs. I assume you found answers to these questions before looking back here.

When you extend an arc, the end that Cadkey extends depends on which half of the arc you put the cursor on, not on which end of the arc is closer to the trimming entity (the boundary line). How near or how distant the boundary is makes no difference.

When you trim an arc—when the boundary and the arc cross one another—Cadkey, with one exception, trims the arc at the boundary, regardless of where on the arc you put the cursor.

The exception occurs because there are two places where an arc can intersect a straight line. When you select the line as the trimming entity, the results depend on where you put the cursor. Cadkey uses whichever intersection point is nearest the cursor. If, in the example you have been working with, you pick the right-hand point—not the point where the arc and the line cross, but the point where they would cross if you extended the arc—Cadkey extends the arc to that point. Following the rule for extending arcs, Cadkey decides which end of the arc to extend by noting which half of the arc you put the cursor on.

To inexperienced users, and even to some moderately experienced ones, arcs often seem to have a will of their own. It can be quite upsetting, when you have a drawing you care about, to trim a carefully placed arc or circle and see it jump to the wrong position. The exercise in Figure 2-57 tests your understanding of the rules just stated. It also lets you build confidence in your ability to show the arc who is master.

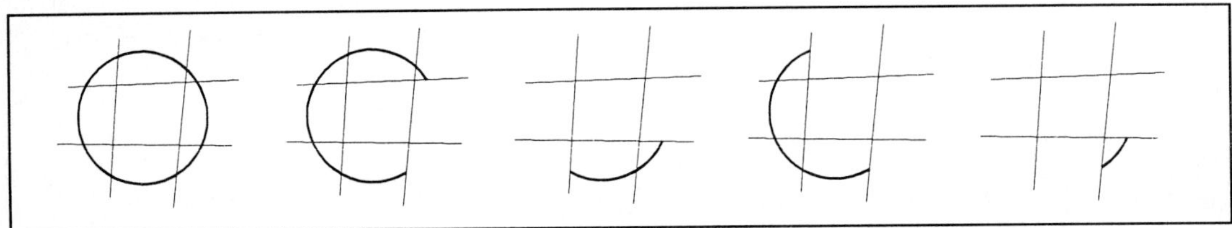

Figure 2-57 Trimming and extending an arc

Draw four lines and a circle. Use DETAIL—TRM/EXT—DOUBLE to cut a bite out of the circle. Then, by repeatedly using DETAIL—TRM/EXT—FIRST, move the arc to various angular positions. Keep shifting its location until you can consistently get it to go where you want it.

Chapter 3

Reference

This chapter describes all CADKEY Light commands. Topics appear in alphabetical order. When a topic could logically appear under more than one heading, both are included, with a cross reference to guide you to the main description.

Words in upper case indicate either the command names that you select from menus, for example, CREATE, LINE, ENDPTS, and ENDENT; or the headings of sections you can find elsewhere in this chapter, for example, LEVELS and STATUS WINDOW. Section headings are capitalized as a shorthand way of telling you where to find more information. STATUS WINDOW in the footnote of the inset tells you where to look if you wonder what the term status window means.

Not every repetition of a command name or topic heading appears in capitals. Once a term has been identified in this way, it is capitalized again only when doing so seems to make the discussion easier to follow.

About half of the topics in this chapter give you specific instructions on executing a command or series of commands. Each of these topics includes an outline, extracted from the Cadkey menu system, showing the steps that lead to the command of interest. The inset shows a sample menu outline.

```
6 DISPLAY
   2 PAN              Alt-P
   3 ZOOM
      1 HALF          Alt-H
      2 DOUBLE        Alt-D
      3 SCALE*        Alt-S
      4 WINDOW        Alt-W
      5 AUTO          Alt-A
      6 BACK-1        Alt-B
   4 VIEW*            Alt-V
```

*SCALE and VIEW are labeled S and View in the STATUS WINDOW.

The only way you can initiate most commands is to go through Cadkey's menu system, but there are exceptions, and the inset shows how menu outlines point out these exceptions. For example, it shows that you can initiate the SCALE command in three ways:

1. Use Cadkey's menus.

   From the main menu, press F6 to select DISPLAY, F3 to select ZOOM, and F3 to select SCALE. Or make these same selections by using the cursor in the MENU OPTIONS WINDOW.

2. Use the IMMEDIATE MODE COMMAND Alt-S.

   You can execute immediate mode commands from any point in the menu structure, and most of the time you can do this even when you are in the middle of another operation. Cadkey interrupts that operation, executes the immediate mode command, and returns you to the first operation at the point where you left off.

3. Move the cursor into the STATUS WINDOW and select S.

   The status window (on the left side of the screen, below the menu options window) shows current settings of several parameters, for example, the scale of the drawing. The status window lets you control any parameter it lists. To select the parameter you wish to change, use the cursor just as you use it to select items from the menu options window.

ALEV

ALEV is a STATUS WINDOW entry that shows which level is active and also lets you change the active level. The active level is the one being used for current construction. Don't confuse level with DEPTH, which is Cadkey's third dimension. See LEVEL for details.

Angular Conventions

Angles are measured in degrees and can be either positive or negative; thus 90° and —270° denote the same angle. Angles can indicate angular positions, as in the diagram on the left in Figure A-1, or they can indicate how much something is rotated, as in the diagram on the right.

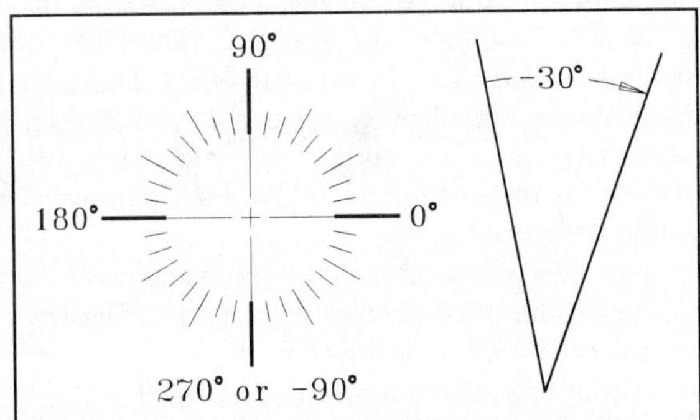

Figure A-1 Angular conventions

Positive angular rotations are counterclockwise. This explains why (1) the 30° angle in Figure A-1 is negative and (2) the angle you specify for *slanted letters* is negative (unless you want to be unconventional in which way you slant them).

There is one exception to the counterclockwise rule: Crosshatching at a 45° angle gives lines that slope upward to the left. In other words, the lines are rotated 45° clockwise from the horizontal rather than 45° counterclockwise.

Append

This command, used for editing text, adds a blank line following the one displayed on the prompt line at the bottom of the screen. See TEXT EDITOR for a description of this command and of other commands in the same menu.

Arc

The first three ARC commands draw an arc with a given center. "Center" means the center of curvature, not the middle of the curved line.

CTR+RAD or **CTR+DIA**: Enter a value for radius or diameter. Then enter the arc's start and end angles, using standard polar coordinate conventions: 0° at 3 o'clock, 90° at 12 (see

Figure A-1). Entering 0 and 10 gives a 10° arc. Because the arc is drawn counterclockwise, entering 10 and 0 gives a 350° arc. Finally, specify the arc center.

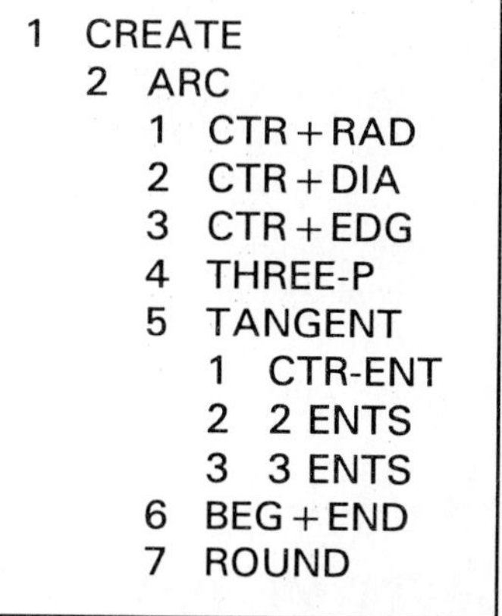

CTR+EDG: As with CTR+RAD, enter the start and end angles. Specify the arc center plus any point on the arc or on an extension of the arc. (The arc does not need to reach to the edge point you select.)

THREE-P: Specify the start point, any point on the arc, and the end point.

TANGENT draws an arc tangent to one, two, or three entities. All three options first ask for the start and end angles. **CTR-ENT** asks for the tangent entity and the center position. **2 ENTS** asks for the arc radius and for the two tangent entities. **3 ENTS** asks for three tangent entities. (See also FILLET—ARC, another command that provides tangent arcs).

If you have problems getting this command to do what you want, see **Notes on Tangent Arcs** at the end of this section.

BEG+END: Enter the included angle of the arc, in other words, the arc length in degrees. Specify the positions of its start and end points. Cadkey draws the arc counterclockwise from the start point to the end point.

ROUND draws an arc tangent to a line or arc, starting at an end point of that line or arc, and ending at a point you select. Select the existing line or arc near the desired end point. Specify whether, in going from the tangent entity to the termination point, the arc should curve clockwise or counterclockwise. One choice gives an arc that is a smooth extension of the given line or arc; the other choice, an arc that starts with a sharp 180° turn. ROUND can also draw an arc tangent to the "end" of a circle, which is the 0° location.

Notes on Tangent Arcs

You can construct a tangent arc even though the arc does not touch the entity or entities to which it is tangent. If the arcs do not touch, Cadkey treats them as though they were extended to reach the points of tangency. In Figure A-2, TANGENT—2 ENTS created a 180° arc centered at the small cross and tangent to two existing arcs. None of the arcs reach the points of tangency. The construction is such that extensions of the arcs, shown here by dashed lines, satisfy the tangency requirements.

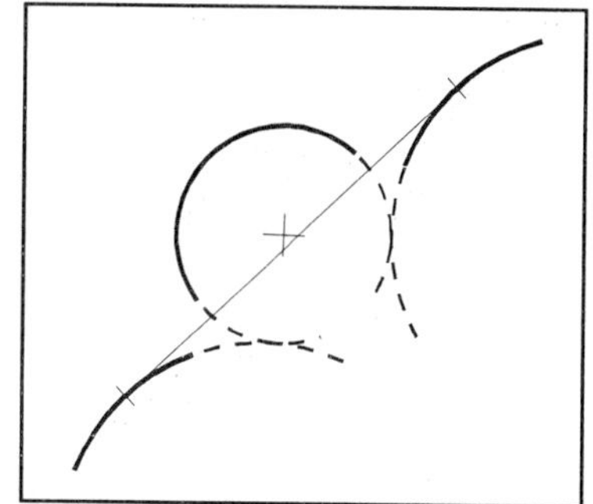

Figure A-2 Creating an arc tangent to two arcs

When you select the two existing tangent arcs, use care in placing the cursor. Figure A-2 shows a line tangent to these two arcs, and two short markers show where this tangent line ends. If, when you select these arcs, you place the cursor at points beyond the ends of the tangent line, Cadkey gives you a **solution not found** error message.

There can be as many as eight ways (Figure A-3) to draw a large-radius arc tangent to two circles. When you select the circles, place the cursor carefully, near where you expect the tangent points to be, to let Cadkey know which possibility you have in mind.

Although you can draw arcs tangent to segments of POLYGON and POLYLINE entities, you get an **Invalid entity combination** error message if you try this in 3D construction mode (see 2D/3D). Switch to 2D mode.

If you use any segment of a POLYGON or any *internal* segment of a POLYLINE as a tangent entity, the point of tangency must lie on the segment, not on an extension.

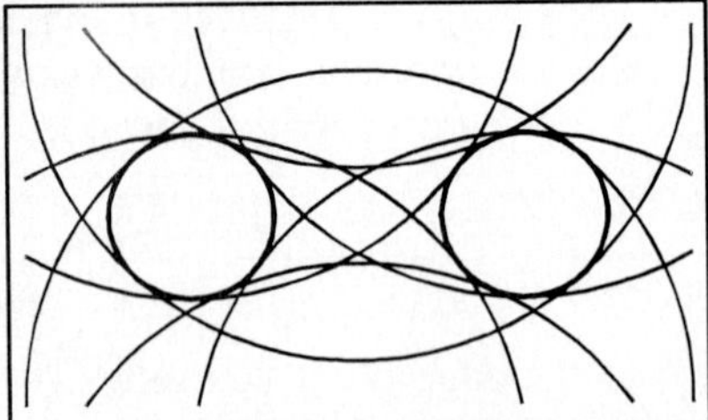

Figure A-3 Eight tangent arcs

Arrow Keys

Ordinarily the arrow keys have no effect—Cadkey was designed to be used with a mouse or a digitizing tablet. But if you don't have one of these devices, you can configure Cadkey (see Chapter 4) to let the arrow keys move the cursor. The space bar takes the place of the mouse button for indicating position. With a little ingenuity you can construct anything without a mouse that you can construct with one, but unless you use Cadkey only occasionally and only for simple constructions, you will probably conclude that a mouse is a necessity.

The arrow keys move the cursor in steps. The step distance is not a neat number like half an inch or 10 mm, but a seemingly random one that depends on your computer setup. Each time you press PgUp, the step distance doubles. Pressing PgDn cuts it in half. Pressing PgDn three times cuts the initial step distance in half three times, to 1/8 of its initial value.

To get more accurate control over cursor position, use the SNAP commands. You can set the vertical and horizontal snap distances to the values you need; and, with snap on, the cursor will move only to points on the snap grid. PgUp and PgDn, which would let you vary snap distance if you had a mouse, control step distance instead. In other words, with snap on, pressing PgDn two or three times doesn't shorten the distance between allowable cursor positions. Instead, it makes you press the arrow key more often to get from one position to the next.

Arrows

The ARROWS command determines whether dimension lines and the associated arrowheads will be **IN** (between extension lines) or **OUT** (outside of extension lines). The default is IN. See ARROWS/WITNESS LINES—CONTROL.

Arrows/Witness Lines—Construction

The ARROWS and WITNESS commands create lines like the leaders and witness lines that Cadkey supplies with DIMENSIONS. These commands are less versatile than the LINE command. You can, for example, draw lines too long and trim them to the right length, but you cannot do this with arrows or witness lines. Getting arrows and witness lines just where you want them often requires special techniques, some of which will be described shortly.

If the LINE command is easier to use than WITNESS, why bother with WITNESS? There are three reasons, not always compelling. (1) The lines used in dimensioning appear only in the view in which they are drawn. Witness lines drawn in view 2 do not clutter the isometric. (2) Editing is simpler if all lines are the appropriate type. (3) When you are trying to select the corner of an object as a construction point or a point to dimension to, there is no danger that ENDENT will accidentally pick up the end of a witness line (see LIMITATIONS, below).

```
3 DETAIL
  4 ARR/WIT
    1 ARROWS
      1 ENDPTS
      2 STRING
      3 PARALEL
      4 PERPEND
    2 WITNESS
      1 ENDPTS
      2 STRING
      3 PARALEL
      4 PERPEND
```

ARROWS draws a line with an arrowhead. The length of the arrowhead is equal to the lettering height for dimensions.

ENDPTS lets you specify the end points of the line. The arrowhead is at the end you select last.

STRING draws a chain of arrows, each pointing to the arrow that follows.

PARALEL draws an arrow parallel to and equal in length to an existing line, and through a selected point. The head of the arrow is on the end that was selected last when the reference line was drawn.

PERPEND draws an arrow from a selected point, perpendicular to a selected line, and with the arrowhead touching the line or an extension of the line.

WITNESS draws lines without arrowheads, using the same commands and rules used for arrows.

Limitations

With ordinary dimensioning, Cadkey supplies a gap that spaces witness lines half a letter height from the object. WITNESS does not automatically supply this gap.

Because arrows and witness lines are not considered LINES by Cadkey, they cannot be used in subsequent construction. If you are using ENDENT to specify a position or if you are selecting an entity as part of a TRIM/EXTEND operation, Cadkey ignores all arrows and witness lines, telling you **entity not found** when you try to select one. Consequently, if you want to draw an arrow or a witness line parallel to or perpendicular to some reference line, you cannot use another arrow or witness line as the reference.

Techniques

ENDPTS—ALONGL (see LINE) provides a way around the limitation of not being able to use arrows and witness lines as reference lines. To create the witness line in Figure A-4, select the side of the rectangle near the point marked by the small triangle. If you use a negative number with ALONGL, you specify a position beyond the end of the line. For a full-size drawing, distances of —1/16" and —5/8" would put the endpoints in the right places.

To put an arrow in the right place, you can use a similar trick. You can't use PERPEND to draw the arrow from a point to the witness line, but you can use PERPEND to draw it from a point to an extension of the side of the rectangle.

SNAP gives you another way to create the witness line and the arrow in Figure A-4. Unless a corner of the object already coincides with a point on the snap grid, use SNAP—ALIGN to bring them together. SNAP then gives you control over the positions of dimensions, arrows, and witness lines with respect to the corner of the object and therefore with respect to one another. This makes it easier for you, when you assemble the elements that make up a dimension, to line them up accurately with the drawing you are dimensioning as well as to line them up with one another.

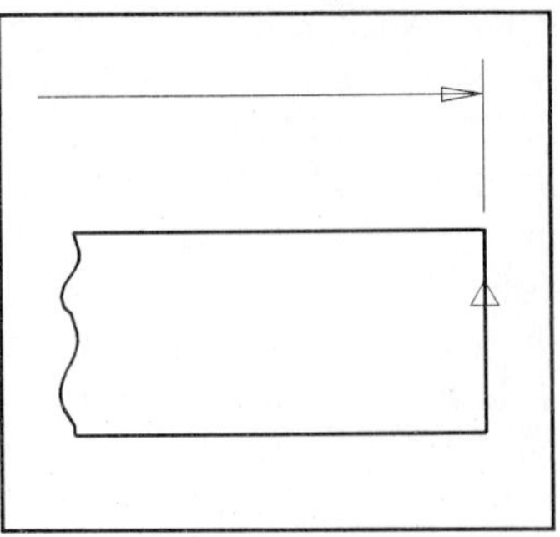

Figure A-4 Construction techniques

One more technique is to use the more flexible LINE command to draw construction lines where you want arrows or witness lines. Then use ENDENT to draw arrows or witness lines over these lines. If you put the construction lines on a separate LEVEL, you can easily use DELETE—LEVEL to get rid of them when they have served their purpose. Or you can use the MASKING MENU, described under SELECTING ENTITIES, to delete the lines while leaving the arrows and witness lines intact.

Arrows/Witness Lines—Control

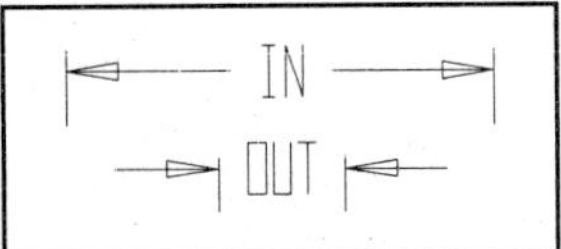

Figure A-5
ARROWS options

ARROWS lets you choose whether dimension lines and the associated arrowheads will be IN (between witness lines) or OUT (outside of witness lines). See Figure A-5.

Also see DIMENSIONING for illustrations of how this choice affects dimensions of arcs and circles.

WITNESS and **LEADER** invoke commands that let you eliminate one or both extension lines (Cadkey calls these witness lines) or dimension lines (Cadkey calls these leaders or arrows). As Figures A-6 and A-7 show, the WITNESS commands and the first four LEADERS commands work the same way:

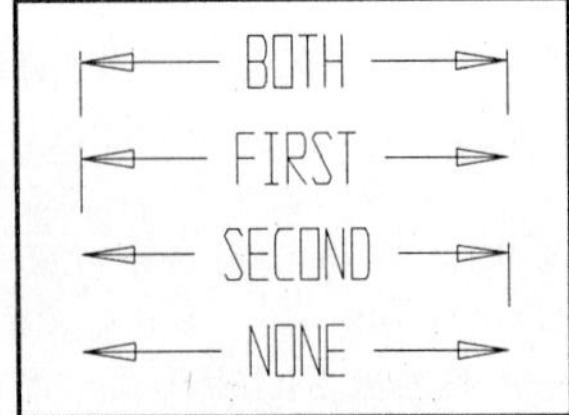

Figure A-6
WITNESS options

BOTH is the default condition. Cadkey draws both witness lines or both leaders when it creates dimensions.

FIRST gives the first witness line or leader. If the first point you pick to dimension is on the left and the next

```
3 DETAIL
  9 SET
    1 ARROWS
      1 DIRECT
        1 IN*        ^A
        2 OUT*       ^A
    2 WIT/LDR
      1 WITNESS*     ^B
        1 BOTH
        2 FIRST
        3 SECOND
        4 NONE
      8 LEADER*
        1 BOTH
        2 FIRST
        3 SECOND
        4 NONE
        5 SOLID
        6 1ST SOL
        7 2ND SOL
        8 NO ARRS
```

*The STATUS WINDOW lists these commands as ARR, WIT, and LDR.

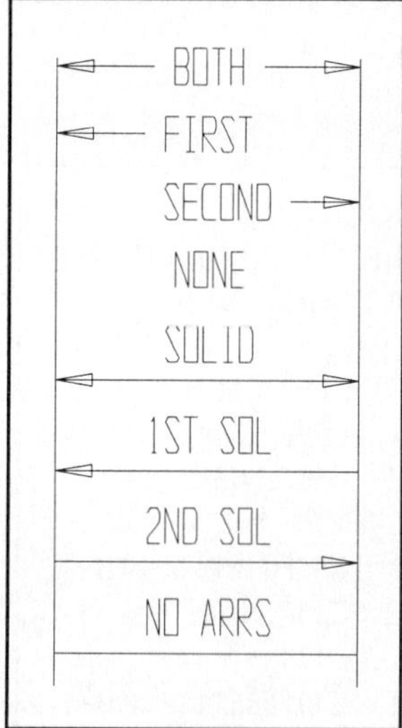

Figure A-7
LEADER options

is on the right, Cadkey draws the left witness line or leader, as Figures A-5 and A-6 show. If you pick the point on the right first, Cadkey draws the right witness line or leader.

SECOND gives one witness line or one leader, putting it on the side of the dimension point you pick second.

NONE omits both witness lines or both leaders.

The last four LEADER options—**SOLID** through **NO ARRS**—not only let you select which arrow shows; they also let you choose a different style for the leaders—one in which the line is continuous rather than broken to leave room for the dimension. With solid leaders, horizontal dimensions appear above the leader; vertical dimensions, to the left of the leader.

Applications

Figure A-8 shows a drawing in which one of these commands is necessary and another is desirable. Cadkey drew each dimension with both witness lines and both leaders.

Cadkey shortened the stems of the leaders for the 1.00 dimension to avoid crowding the number, but those for the .50 dimension are the normal length. The left leader of the .50 dimension and the right leader of the 1.00 dimension overlap. The longer stem of the .50 leader pokes into the 1.00 dimension. The .50 dimension should have been constructed with the left leader omitted.

Double witness line are not always problems. In the screen display or in a printout you see no clue that the line is double. Although plotters draw the line twice, many plotters track well enough that the double line is not significantly heavier than single ones. If you look closely at Figure A-8, you see places where the plotter did quite well. The witness line between the 1.00 and .50 dimensions is double, but only slightly heavier than the others; and you can barely see that the density of the top left witness line is not uniform. But the plotter did not do as well with the top witness line on the right side of the drawing. This line shows a variation in density that would be out of place in a drawing where appearance is important.

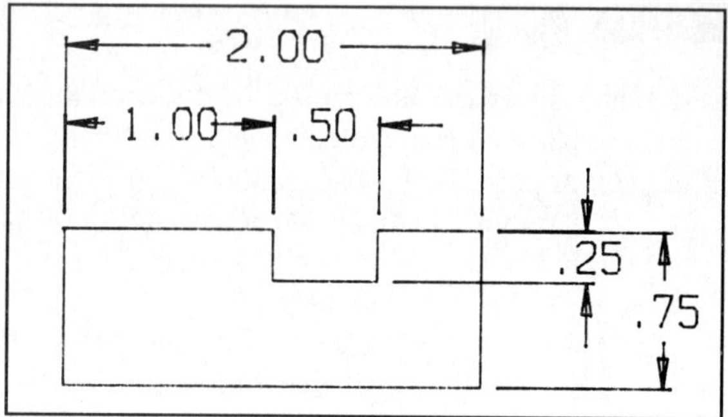

Figure A-8 Dimensions with double lines

Related Commands

The CHANGE commands let you change existing dimensions. You can change the direction (IN or OUT) of leaders, and you can add or remove witness lines. But you cannot add or remove a leader from an existing dimension. To change a leader, you must delete the dimension and reconstruct it with the correct leader configuration.

Attributes

ATTRIB appears twice in Cadkey's menus. **CONTROL—VERIFY—ATTRIB** (not discussed here—see VERIFY) shows what COLOR, LINE TYPE, LINE THICKNESS, etc. you have assigned to a selected entity. **CONTROL—ATTRIB**, discussed here, lets you set these same attributes.

The five properties governed by the CONTROL—ATTRIB commands are COLOR, LINE TYPE, LINE WIDTH, PEN NUMBER, and whether POLYLINES or POLYGONS show in outline form or as filled areas. For the first four of these five attributes, Cadkey offers two choices: CURRENT and CHANGE. The fifth attribute, the OUTLINE/FILLED choice, operates in CHANGE mode only.

CURRENT assigns the attributes to be used for subsequent construction. A menu appears, from which you can select the new attribute. For example, you might specify that arcs, lines, etc. be drawn as dashed lines or colored red. CURRENT does not affect entities already created.

CHANGE changes the attributes of the entities you select but has no effect on entities created later.

```
7 CONTROL
  1 VERIFY
    1 ATTRIB
  2 ATTRIB
    1 COLOR*
      1 CURRENT Alt-X
      2 CHANGE
    2 L-TYPE*
      1 CURRENT Alt-T
      2 CHANGE
    3 L-WIDTH*
      1 CURRENT Alt-Y
      2 CHANGE
    4 PEN #*
      1 CURRENT Alt-Z
      2 CHANGE
    5 OUT/FIL
      1 OUTLINE
      2 FILLED
```

*The STATUS WINDOW lists these commands as COLOR, L-TYPE, L-WID, and PEN. It operates only in CURRENT mode.

Color

COLOR assigns the color used to display entities on the computer screen. Use the cursor to select your choice from the stack of fifteen colored rectangles that Cadkey displays (the sixteenth color is the background color), or press Return and key in the color number.

A particular color on the screen does not necessarily call for the same color on the plotted output. The code number that specifies a red line on the computer screen could be used to instruct a plotter to use a green pen or a pen that draws a thicker-than-normal black line. Or it may be PEN # that determines the pen selection, in which case COLOR has no effect on the plot. See the notes that follow on Pen Number for an explanation.

Line Type

L-TYPE displays samples of four line types:

1. Solid
2. Dashed
3. Centerline
4. Phantom

Use the cursor to select the type you want, or press Return to invoke a menu of line types.

If you are fussy about centerlines, you may want to make your own from regular line segments rather than to select centerline as a line type. When two centerlines cross at the center of a circle, traditional drafting practices call for two short segments at the intersection. Because Cadkey has no way to know just where the short segments of centerlines should fall, the results it gives you are random (Figure A-9). Plots or printouts add to the uncertainty, differing from what you see on the screen (usually they look better).

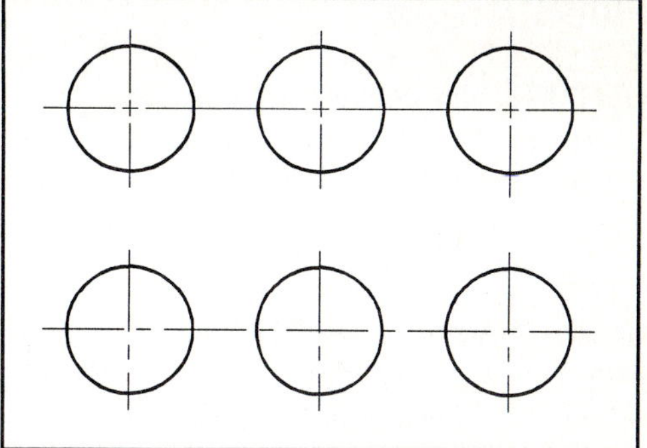

Figure A-9 Traditional centerlines (top) and those generated by computer (bottom)

Line Width

L-WIDTH lets you set line widths for lines, arcs, circles, and polylines. Notes, dimensions, crosshatching, and POLYGONS are not affected. Cadkey specifies width as an odd number from 1 to 15 (Figure A-10). To assign a new width, pick a sample from the on-screen display or press Return and enter a number.

Figure A-10 Line widths on a dot-matrix printer (left) and on a laser printer (right).

Actual line thickness depends on the resolution, measured in dots or pixels per inch, that your equipment provides, and what you see on the screen is not what you see in a plot or printout. Figure A-10 compares a nine-pin dot-matrix printout with a laser printout. The same pattern on an ancient CGA monitor showed all but the top three lines overlapping. A VGA monitor showed the three heaviest lines overlapping.

If you plan to plot rather than print your drawing, you may want to use a thicker pen rather than multiple strokes to get wider lines. To control widths in this way, use PEN # or COLOR.

Pen Number

PEN # assigns a pen numbers to each entity. This is a code number that tells a plotter which pen to use to draw the entity. Numbers 1 through 8 may be used to call for pens of varying colors and thicknesses.

Or you can use COLOR rather than PEN # to control the plot. The two sets of numbers control plots in the same way—they are simply code numbers, and whenever you start a plot, Cadkey asks which set you want to use for pen selection. COLOR offers fifteen choices instead of eight, an advantage if your plotter uses more than eight pens. Another advantage of COLOR is that the colors on the screen make it easier to confirm, as you create each entity, that the code number you assigned is the one you intended.

Filled Areas

OUT/FIL can convert a closed boundary to a solid area of color. It can also do the reverse, a useful operation when a filled area obscures a region where you need to do some editing. If you fill a figure whose lines cross one another, Cadkey creates interesting patterns (Figure A-11).

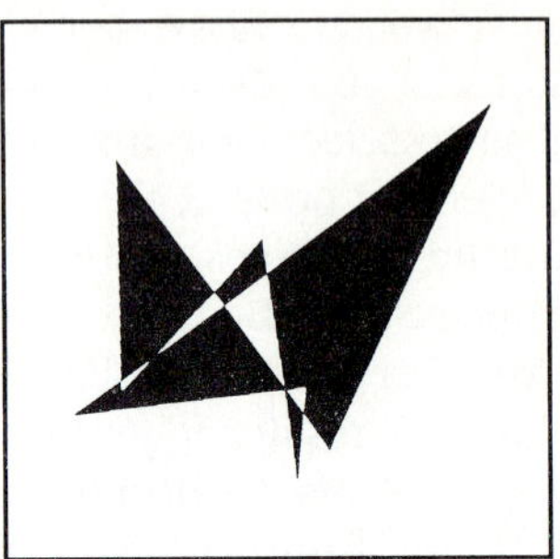

Figure A-11 Filled entity

There are two restrictions: (1) Cadkey fills only POLYLINES and POLYGONS. (2) Unlike the other ATTRIB commands, OUT/FIL operates in CHANGE mode only. It alters existing entities but cannot control future construction.

You can fill POLYGONS in either of two ways. You can use the OUT/FIL command to fill existing POLYGONS, or you can fill them when you create them. But closed polylines don't give you this choice. Cadkey creates them only in outline form; therefore the only way to fill them is to create them as outlines and then use OUT/FIL.

OUTLINE, the reverse operation, converts a filled figure to an outline. As one step in this operation, Cadkey has you choose the color of the outline.

If you elect to fill a POLYGON when you create it, or if you use OUT/FIL to fill a figure constructed earlier, Cadkey displays an 8 x 32 matrix of 256 color samples. With either procedure, you can use the cursor to select the color you want, or you can press Return and enter your color selection by number. (The color in the upper left corner is zero, and the first column includes zero through seven. As you move to the right, columns start with 8, 16, 24, 32, etc. The last color sample, on the lower right, is number 255.)

If you want to change the color of an already-filled area, use the OUT/FIL command in the same way that you would use it if you were filling an unfilled entity.

A distant relative of the OUT/FIL command lets you create BOLD letters that are either filled or in outline form. See LETTERING.

Axes

Cadkey's AXES are a set of arrows in the lower left corner of each view, labeled to show the orientations of the coordinate axes in the WORLD coordinates X, Y, and Z (see COORDINATES). Cadkey does not need to show VIEW coordinates because these are always the same—XV is to the right, YV is up, and ZV is toward you.

```
6 DISPLAY
  8 AXES
    1 DISP VW
      1 ON
      2 OFF
    2 CONST VW
```

DISP VW—ON displays the gnomon that shows the directions of the axes.

DISP VW—OFF eliminates the gnomon to give you a clearer screen.

CONST VW is a command in professional versions of Cadkey that provides a second gnomon. In CADKEY Light 1.5, the menu shows this command, but it is not functional. The CADKEY Light 4.0 menu omits this command.

For the eight predefined views, the axes give you the same information that you see on the inside front cover of this handbook.

Cadkey shows an oblique axis as solid if it projects toward you; dashed if it projects away. In view 7, for example, the X axis is toward you, down, and to the right; the Y axis, away from you, up, and to the right. See the inside front cover for an illustration.

The gnomons do not distinguish an axis that points directly toward you from one that points away from you, but you can use the **right-hand rule** to find these directions. This is a rule engineers use in vector analysis. It is also the rule you use to remember which way to turn a screw with a screwdriver: If the curled fingers of your right hand point in the direction you turn the screw, your extended thumb shows the direction—in or out—that a right-handed screw (the ordinary kind) will move. In a right-handed set of axes, let the curled fingers of your right hand show the direction you would have to rotate the X axis to make it coincide with the Y axis. Your thumb then points in the Z direction. If you aren't familiar with this rule, check it against the drawings on the inside front cover.

Break

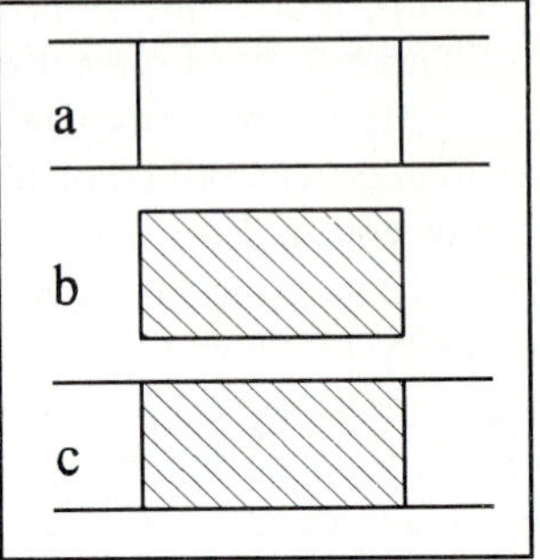

Figure B-1 A problem in crosshatching

Cadkey cannot crosshatch the rectangular area in Figure B-1a because the two horizontal lines extend beyond the edges of the area they enclose. If you trim away the ends of these lines as in Figure B-1b, there is no problem.

But there is a way to crosshatch the area without deleting the ends of the horizontal lines. You can BREAK the two horizontal lines; that is, you can cut each of them into three segments butted end to end. This makes all four boundary lines just the right length. Because the troublesome ends are now separate lines, you don't have to include them when you select the lines that enclose the area you want to crosshatch. Cadkey can now crosshatch the area, as Figure B-1c shows.

Overview

The BREAK commands can divide a LINE, ARC, CIRCLE, or POLYLINE into two or three parts. (POLYGONS are not affected; POLYLINES sometimes give strange results.) The part broken away disappears briefly; then it reappears as a separate entity, usually leaving the drawing looking as though nothing happened. Variations on the break routine can make the part broken away disappear or reappear in a different form, for example, as a line of a different thickness.

If you are familiar with the TRIM/EXTEND commands, you will find the BREAK commands easy to use. The **entity to break** corresponds to the **entity to trim**. The **breaking entity**, like the **trimming entity**, defines the boundary at which the change occurs.

To find where a break should occur, Cadkey will, if necessary, use an imaginary extension of the breaking entity (the boundary line), but it will not extend the entity to break. In other words, the break commands resemble just the TRIM part of the TRIM/EXTEND commands.

Where TRIM/EXTEND trims away parts of entities, BREAK converts these parts to new entities having properties determined by Cadkey's current settings for COLOR, LINE TYPE, LINE WIDTH, PEN NUMBER, and LEVEL. (See ATTRIBUTES for the ways to set the first four of these attributes; LEVELS for ways to set the fifth.) If Cadkey is currently set to produce wide lines, and if the active level is 4, the part broken away returns on level 4 as a wide line.

Command Summary

```
2 EDIT
  2 BREAK
    1 FIRST
    2 BOTH
    3 DOUBLE
    4 DIVIDE
    5 MODAL
```

With FIRST, BOTH, DOUBLE, and MODAL, select the entity to break by putting the cursor on the segment that is to keep its present attributes. The part on the other side of the break will have attributes assigned by Cadkey's current settings, which may or may not be the same as those of the original entity.

FIRST breaks one line, arc, or open polyline.

BOTH breaks two entities (lines, arcs, or open polylines) where they intersect.

DOUBLE puts two breaks in a line, arc, circle, or polyline. It is the only break command you can use with circles or closed polylines. The segment that retains its present attributes is the middle segment of a line or arc and the selected part of a circle.

DIVIDE puts two breaks in a line, arc, or open polyline. The parts that retain their present attributes are the two outer segments.

MODAL breaks a series of lines, arcs, or open polylines, with all the breaks along a single trimming entity.

Rules for POLYGONS and Polylines

You can use a segment of a POLYGON entity as a breaking entity, but the segment must intersect the entity to be broken. Although Cadkey will use an extension of a line or arc to find a break location, it will not use an extension of a POLYGON segment.

Because the shape of a POLYGON is fixed, you cannot use it as an entity to break.

The rules for POLYLINES depend on whether the polyline is open or closed. (A *closed* polyline is one in which the last segment ends at the start point of the first.) Open polylines usually behave as you would expect, but if you use a closed polyline as the entity to break or as the breaking entity, you will find the rules stricter than those for TRIM/EXTEND.

When you use a segment of a *closed* polyline or an *internal* segment of an open polyline as a breaking entity, the segment must intersect the entity to be broken. But you can use an extension of the free end of an open polyline.

DOUBLE is the only command that can break a closed polyline, and it divides the polyline into three entities rather than two. If the closed polyline is one you created as a STRING, the extra break point occurs where the start of the polyline meets the end. If the closed polyline is a RECTANGLE or an N-GON, the extra break is at the right or left end of the bottom segment.

DOUBLE can give you an occasional surprise. In one instance, a broken-out segment kept its old attributes rather than conforming to Cadkey's current settings, and it gave an **Entity not found** error message in response to attempts to delete it with ^Q. (DELETE–SELECT–WINDOW got rid of it.)

Applications

The introduction to this section shows how the break commands can make CROSSHATCHING easier. Figure B-2 shows a second application—conversion of a three-dimensional wire-frame drawing to a view that distinguishes between visible and hidden lines.

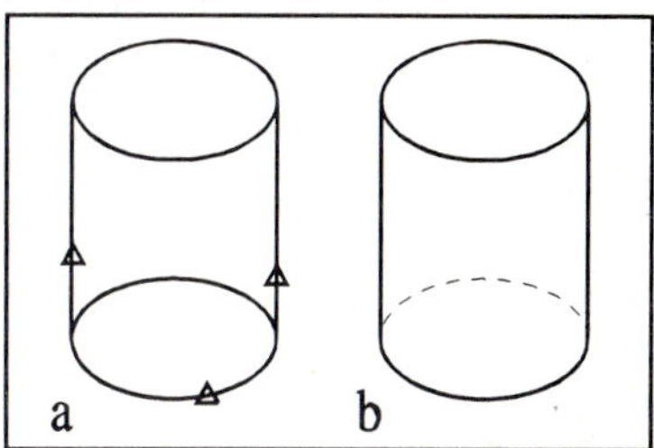

Figure B-2 A BREAK application

To convert the drawing in Figure B-2a to Figure B-2b, you must first get Cadkey ready to draw thin, dashed lines. Use ^Y to reset the current line width to 1 (the line width in Figure B-2a is 3), and use ^T to set the line type to DASHED (see ATTRIBUTES).

With these changes made, use EDIT—BREAK—DOUBLE, to generate the dashed segment. Select the lower ellipse as the entity to break and the two vertical lines as the breaking entities. Small triangles show the selection points. The equivalent operation with TRIM/EXTEND would have deleted the back half of the ellipse; here, it converts it to a thin dashed line.

Figure B-3 shows a third application—one that uses LEVELS. When you make the active level hidden, the similarity of the break and trim operations is striking. The difference is that the parts you trim away are not lost forever but are stored on the hidden level. Suppose you use ^L to set the active level to 99 and then you hide level 99 with DISPLAY—LEVELS—REMOVE. Newly created entities, including segments created by the break command, don't show because they appear on a hidden level. With this setup, BREAK makes parts of entities disappear, just as TRIM/EXTEND would. But the missing parts still exist and you can use DISPLAY—LEVELS—ADD to restore them. See LEVELS for details on removing and adding levels.

(You can use DISPLAY—LEVELS—MOVE to create a similar illusion—that you are deleting entire entities, just as if you were using ^Q.)

These two commands—BREAK and MOVE—removed hidden lines from the isometric in Figure B-3a, producing the pictorial view in Figure B-3b. To make pictorial views like this one, you have to remove hidden lines and hidden parts of lines. Then, when you switch to another view, you find it is incomplete, as is the top view in Figure B-3c. This is the same incomplete view that DELETE and TRIM would have produced; but in this case, you can use DISPLAY—LEVELS—ADD—99 to restore the missing lines as in Figure B-3d.

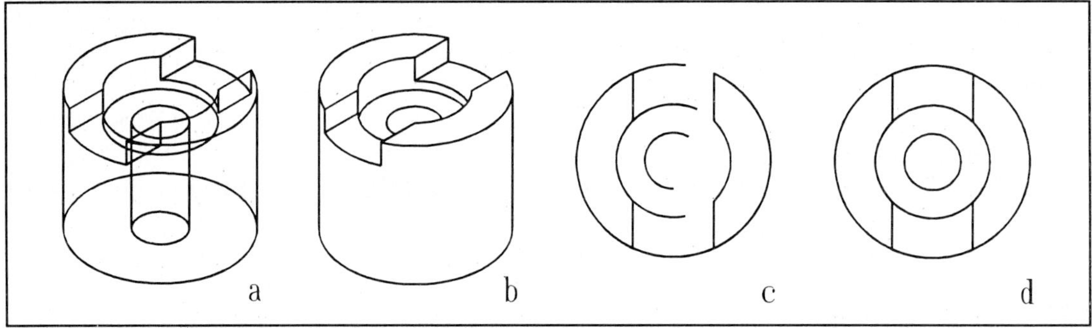

Figure B-3 Effects of using the BREAK command to remove hidden lines.

Precautions

An arc or a circle used as a trimming entity can, in general, break another entity in either of two places. With an arc as a breaking entity, it's easy to forget that the second point can be on an extension of the arc. Place your selection points near where you want the break to occur.

If you use a level to hide entities, remember to change the active level back to a visible one when you finish. Otherwise, as you continue to work on your drawing the entities you create will be invisible, and you will wonder why Cadkey seems to be ignoring all of your commands.

By Type

BY TYPE is an option Cadkey sometimes offers you when you select entities. You can also use Alt-M to make it appear. It limits Cadkey's choices to certain types of entities, thereby making it easier to keep Cadkey from selecting entities you don't want selected. For more detail, see Basic Type Masking under SELECTING ENTITIES.

CADUTIL

Each new professional version of Cadkey includes a corresponding version of CADUTIL, a utility for converting part and pattern files generated by earlier versions of Cadkey to files that the current version can read. The version most likely of interest to you is the one that comes with CADKEY 4.0 and also with CADKEY Light 4.0, enabling these programs to read files from earlier versions.

CADKEY Light 1.5 is based on CADKEY 3.5, a professional version of Cadkey. These two versions produce compatible files; that is, either version can read files created by the other.

CADKEY Light 4.0 is based on and is compatible with CADKEY 4.0, the professional version introduced in 1991. Neither of these programs can read CADKEY Light 1.5 or CADKEY 3.5 files directly; however, they can read these files after the CADUTIL program converts them. The reverse is not true. There is no CADUTIL program to convert a Cadkey 4.0 file to a CADKEY 3.5 file.

CADUTIL operates in DOS. If the file CADUTIL.EXE and the file you wish to convert are on the same disk and in the same directory, switch to that drive and directory and enter **cadutil**. CADUTIL tells you to **Press RETURN to convert all files in the current directory, or any other key for help**. After you press Return, CADUTIL responds with **Warning: You have decided to convert files without making backup copies of the files first... is this what you really want ? (Y/N)**. The reason for this warning is that your file, once converted, will no longer work with the Cadkey version you used to create it. If this is your only copy of the file, you probably want to enter N, which automatically exits CADUTIL. This time, enter **cadutil /b**, where the /b asks CADUTIL to make a backup. CADUTIL converts the file, but it also keeps and renames your original file, giving it the extension .BRT if it is a part file or .BTN if it is a pattern file.

If CADUTIL.EXE and the file you want to convert are in different directories, you need to add a path designation. For example, if your file is in drive A:, switch to whatever drive and directory CADUTIL.EXE is in and type **cadutil a:** (or **cadutil a:\ /b** if you want a backup).

To convert just one file in a directory that contains several files, include the name of the file in your command. Appropriate entries are of the form **cadutil filename**, **cadutil a:\filename**, or **cadutil a:\filename /b**. These are the options you are most likely to need, but CADUTIL offers others. Check the help file for information.

CADKEY, Inc. has decided that sharing a CADUTIL.EXE file is not a violation of their license agreement with holders of professional versions of Cadkey. If, for example, you have CADKEY Light 1.5 at home and your school has CADKEY Light 4.0 or CADKEY 4.0, your instructor is free to let you copy its CADUTIL program.

Calculator

Whenever you are to key in a value, Cadkey's on-line calculator lets you enter either a pure number or an algebraic expression. For example, if you want to set DEPTH to the square root of 2, you can key in sqrt(2). Even when Cadkey seems to call for an integer, you can substitute an algebraic expression: When the COPY command asks you for the number of copies, you can key in sin(60)+1+7/8. Cadkey calculates 0.86603 + 1 + 0.875 = 2.74103, drops all digits behind the decimal point, and gives you two copies. (You also get two copies if you key in 2.74.)

You write mathematical equations as you would write them in the C programming language. You could write a sum as 1.23+4.56. The basic algebraic operations are:

addition:	a+b
subtraction:	a—b
multiplication:	a*b
division:	a/b
nth power of a:	a^n

Type the symbol for exponentiation, ^, as you would type any other character. The symbol ^ does not imply use of the Ctrl key.

In complex expressions, the sequence of operations follows the rules of algebra: Functions such as sin(x) are evaluated first, then exponents, then multiplication and division, and finally addition and subtraction.

As in algebra, you can use parentheses to override this sequence: In (a+b)*(c+d), addition comes first, multiplication second. Parentheses also help if you aren't sure what sequence of operations Cadkey will use. Mathematically, 2*3/4*5 is ambiguous. Cadkey calculates it as ((2*3)/4)*5. If you want (2*3)/(4*5), use parentheses to be sure this is what you get. The first pair is unnecessary, but there is no penalty for too many parentheses.

Other algebraic functions are:

a mod b (the remainder after division):	a%b	4.1873%2 = .1873
absolute value of x:	abs(x)	abs(—3.98) = 3.98
x rounded down to the nearest integer:	floor(x)	floor(3.98) = 3
		floor(—3.98) = —4
x rounded up to the nearest integer:	ceil(x)	ceil(3.18) = 4
		ceil(—3.18) = —3
x rounded to the nearest integer:	floor(x+.5)	floor(2.7+.5) = 3

One way you can test the calculator is to use ^D to call for a new DEPTH, select VALUE from the menu, and enter a mathematical expression. The result appears after D in the STATUS WINDOW.

Cadkey's trigonometric and hyperbolic functions use angles in degrees. This is conventional for trigonometric functions, but for hyperbolic functions the usual units correspond to radians, not degrees. Conventionally, sinh 2 = 3.626860. Cadkey gives sinh(2*180/3.141593) = 3.626860, where the added factor is $180/\pi$, the radians-to-degrees conversion factor. If you can remember that $180/\pi$ is 57.29578, use sinh(2*57.29578) to enter the function.

sine of x:	sin(x)
cosine of x:	cos(x)
tangent of x:	tan(x)
arc sine of x:	asin(x)
arc cosine of x:	acos(x)
arc tangent of x:	atan(x)
arc tangent of y/x:	atan2(y,x) or atan(y/x)
hyperbolic sine of x:	sinh(x)
hyperbolic cosine of x:	cosh(x)
hyperbolic tangent of x:	tanh(x)

The remaining transcendental functions are:

square root of x:	sqrt(x)	
hypotenuse = sqrt(x^2+y^2):	hypot(x,y)	hypot(3,4) = 5
natural logarithm of x:	log(x)	
base 10 logarithm of x:	log10(x)	
e to the x power:	exp(x)	

The professional versions of CADKEY incorporate a large number of other functions in the on-line calculator. There, they can be used in macros. When CADKEY Light was derived from these professional versions, some of these other functions were carried over, even though CADKEY Light has no macro capability. Consequently, these functions are primarily of entertainment value. You could, for example, use @dimht/@lwidth to set the drawing scale to a value equal to the lettering height for dimensions divided by the line width setting. There are almost forty of these functions, most of which identify Cadkey's current settings. These are examples of this type of function.

depth setting:	@depth
drawing scale:	@scale
view:	@view
pen number:	@pen
configuration setting (0 = inch, 1 = mm):	@units
line width:	@width
line type (0 = solid; 1 = dashed, etc.):	@type
note text angle (in radians):	@noteang

Centerline

You can use CONTROL—ATTRIB—L-TYPE to generate the long-short-long pattern of centerlines. Choose between the CURRENT option, which assigns the centerline pattern to new construction, and the CHANGE option, which changes existing entities to the centerline pattern. Although a line, arc, or circle created in this pattern may contain many segments, Cadkey treats it as a single entity. See ATTRIBUTES.

Chain

CHAIN is a SELECTION MENU option (see SELECTING ENTITIES). It lets you select a series of entities that are connected end-to-end without having to select them individually. The chain can contain both lines and arcs.

The command for *generating* a chain of segments connected end-to-end is STRING (see STRING). A string can contain straight-line segments but not arcs. The string may be a series of LINE entities, a series of ARROWS or WITNESS LINES, or a single POLYLINE or POLYGON entity.

Another kind of string is a SKETCH line. See POLYLINE.

Chamfer

Chamfers are narrow beveled surfaces at corners of objects. They are often added to machined parts to eliminate sharp edges. Rounded corners are another alternative to sharp edges.

See FILLET for a discussion of both ways of eliminating the sharp corner where two entities meet.

```
1  CREATE
   6  FILLET
      1  ARC
      2  CHAMFER
```

Change

DETAIL—CHANGE offers a large number of commands that can change existing entities. These commands save you the trouble of deleting and replacing entities you need to modify.

DETAIL—SET (see SET) offers a similar group of commands for the parameters that control new construction. Suppose you want to write a dimension as 3 3/4 rather than 3.75. You can either use DETAIL—SET—DIM REP—FRACTIN to make this choice before you create the dimension or use DETAIL—CHANGE—DIM REP—FRACTIN to change the dimension after you have created it.

Neither set of commands encroaches on the other's territory. The CHANGE commands do not affect new construction and the SET commands do not affect existing entities.

This section includes more than just the commands Cadkey includes in the CHANGE menu. DETAIL—UPDATE, DISPLAY—LEVELS—MOVE, and CONTROL—ATTRIBUTES appear here because they also change existing entities.

The SET—CHANGE commands cover many topics. To hold the notes that follow to a reasonable length, and to avoid duplication of details recorded elsewhere, these notes are mostly outlines rather than complete discussions of the CHANGE options. You will find much more detail under headings such as ATTRIBUTES and LETTERING. These and similar topics are primarily concerned with the SET commands, but the SET commands control the same attributes that the CHANGE commands let you change.

Text Attributes

The **TXT ATT** commands let you change the style of text in existing NOTES, LABELS, or DIMENSIONS. Cadkey lets you make several changes at once, changing letter height, aspect ratio, etc. Whether you make one change or several, you finish by pressing F8 to indicate you are DONE and then select the entities to be changed. See LETTERING if you need more detail on the text attributes discussed here.

Until you exit the TXT ATT routine, Cadkey remembers the changes you made. Suppose you want to switch the font of one note from BOX to BOLD and change the letter height in another note. After you change the first note to bold, you press F10 to get back to the TXT ATT menu, select HEIGHT, enter the height you want, and press F8 for DONE. The text of the second note comes out at the new height, but because you selected bold earlier, the newly selected text is also bold. To clear earlier settings, press F10 not once but twice to exit the TXT ATT menu; then reselect TXT ATT. See the note that follows under DONE for details on why this happens.

FONT lets you choose whether the font will be BOX or BOLD. The default is BOX.

HEIGHT lets you reset letter height.

NOT ANG rotates a NOTE, using the lower-left corner of the first line as the center of rotation. NOT ANG does not rotate LABELS or DIMENSIONS.

ASPECT changes the width-to-height ratio of characters.

MIRROR produces a mirror image of the text in a NOTE but does not affect LABELS or DIMENSIONS. Cadkey asks if you really want to do this. Select YES or NO.

SLANT produces slanted letters. With Cadkey's angular conventions, positive angles are counterclockwise; thus the angles you would ordinarily use for slanted letters are negative. Cadkey accepts angles from -31° to 31°. The standard for slanted engineering lettering is —22°.

FILL fills the spaces between the double lines of BOLD text. It has no immediate effect on BOX text, but if you specify that box text be filled and if you later convert that text to bold, Cadkey remembers and gives you bold filled text.

DONE is your final choice, necessary before you can select the text entities to change. Cadkey then invokes the selection menu (see SELECTING ENTITIES) to let you choose these entities.

When you have selected the entities to change and pressed Return, Cadkey makes the changes. It then returns you to the selection menu, so that if you wish you can select more entities, perhaps using a different selection method (for example, SINGLE instead of WINDOW) to change more text the same way as before. If, instead, you press F10, Cadkey takes you back to the TXT ATT menu but keeps your earlier choices in effect. You may add to them or revise them before again pressing DONE. Or you can start fresh by pressing F10 again to exit the TXT ATT routine and then pressing F1 to reenter it.

TXT POS moves text. Cadkey draws a rectangle, and as you move the cursor this rectangle moves with it to show the area the text will fill. You press the mouse button at the new location, and Cadkey recreates the entity. The rectangle remains, so if you are not happy with the position you selected, you can immediately revise it. Press F10 when you are satisfied. Cadkey then asks you to select another entity to move.

For a dimension with separate + and — tolerances, the new text position will be higher than the moving rectangle indicates.

```
3 DETAIL
  7 CHANGE
    1 TXT ATT
      1 FONT
        1 BOX
        2 BOLD
      2 HEIGHT
      3 NOT ANG
      4 ASPECT
      5 MIRROR
      6 SLANT
      7 FILL
      8 DONE
    2 TXT POS
    3 EDIT TX
    4 DIM VAL
    5 DIM REP
      1 DECIMAL
      2 FRACTIN
      3 FT / IN
      4 DEGREES*
      5 DEG / MIN*
    6 WITNESS
      1 BOTH
      2 FIRST
      3 SECOND
      4 NONE
    7 ARROWS
      1 DIRECT
        1 IN
        2 OUT
    8 TOLER
      1 VALUES
        1 POS TOL
        2 NEG TOL
        3 BOTH
      2 TYPE
        1 NONE
        2 +/—
        3 LIMIT
    9 DIM SCL
```

*CADKEY Light 1.5 does not offer these two options.

MOVE (see MOVE/COPY/JOIN) is a related command. For a note, MOVE and TXT POS accomplish the same thing, but TXT POS does it more conveniently. For a label or dimension, the processes differ. MOVE moves the entire entity. For a label, TXT POS moves the text but leaves the point of its arrow where it was before. For a dimension, TXT POS moves the text and rearranges the arrows and witness lines so the distance marked by the dimension is the same as before.

EDIT TX lets you change or add to the text of a NOTE, LABEL, or DIMENSION. See the note that follows on DIM VAL for more information or see TEXT EDITOR for complete details.

Dimension Values and Formats

DIM VAL lets you enter a new value for a dimension. The value you enter is subject to Cadkey's current settings for leading and trailing zeros and number of decimal places. If you enter 0.2250, you may see .23 on the screen. DIM VAL does not change tolerances.

See TEXT EDITOR, DIMENSIONING STANDARDS, and (under DIMENSIONING STANDARDS) DIM MOD for other ways to change dimensions. The TEXT EDITOR, which you can invoke with the EDIT TX command just described, lets you change the text and format of existing dimensions. Even if you delete all numbers and enter a word or words, Cadkey keeps the dimension-line arrows neatly positioned with respect to the center of whatever area the revised text fills. The section on DIMENSIONING STANDARDS tells you how to reset the number of decimal places and specify whether Cadkey shows leading and trailing zeros. The DIM MOD command changes the procedure for creating dimensions, letting you edit the text of dimensions as you create them.

DIM REP (Dimension representation) lets you change the form of existing dimensions:

DECIMAL changes dimensions from fractional to decimal form. It also asks you to specify how many decimal places to show. In CADKEY Light 4.0, DECIMAL also converts angular dimensions in degrees, minutes, and seconds to decimal form.

FRACTIN changes dimensions to fractional form, for example, 3 5/16. You choose whether to show distances to the nearest unit or to the nearest half, 4th, 8th, 16th, 32nd, or 64th.

FT / IN changes dimension units to feet and inches, for example, 6' – 3 5/8". As with FRACTIN, you specify how precisely Cadkey writes the fractional inch part of the dimension.

DEGREES is a CADKEY Light 4.0 option that changes the form of angular dimensions to degrees and decimal fractions of a degree. You can set the number of decimal places by your choice under DECIMAL. CADKEY Light 1.5 does not need this option because it always uses this format.

DEG / MIN, an option not available in CADKEY Light 1.5, changes angular dimensions to degrees, minutes, and seconds.

WITNESS first has you select a dimension; then it asks which witness lines to show. Your options are BOTH, FIRST, SECOND, and NONE. FIRST is the witness line on the end you selected first when you created the dimension. If you guess FIRST and the wrong line disappears, simply select SECOND and Cadkey will correct the layout.

The usual reason for removing a witness line is that two dimensions start at the same point, making their witness lines overlap. You can confirm that you removed one of the overlapping lines because Cadkey temporarily erases both in the overlap region. REDRAW restores the line that remains.

See ARROWS/WITNESS LINES—CONTROL for more information, including the reason for not just leaving both witness lines.

ARROWS offers one option: DIRECTION. Cadkey asks you to select a dimension, tells you the current arrow direction, and asks which direction you want. Use this command when the arrows are IN (between witness lines) and you want to move them OUT to avoid crowding the dimension. See ARROWS/WITNESS LINES—CONTROL for more information.

ARROWS does not let you remove an arrow from an existing dimension. To make this change you must delete the dimension and replace it with the dimension as you want it.

TOLER lets you add or delete tolerances or change values of existing ones. See TOLERANCES for definitions of terms and information on the forms tolerances can take.

VALUES lets you change the magnitudes of existing tolerances. Selecting **POS TOL** or **NEG TOL** lets you change only one of the two tolerances; **BOTH** lets you change both. When you enter a negative tolerance, include the minus sign; for example, enter —.02.

TYPE lets you remove, add, or change the form of tolerances. **NONE** removes tolerances or replaces limit dimensions with single values, +/— adds ± tolerances or changes limit dimensions to ± tolerances, and **LIMIT** produces limit dimensions. Any dimension that already has tolerances assigned keeps the same tolerances in the new format; for example, 1.50 ± .05 converts to limit dimensions of 1.55 and 1.45. If you add tolerances where there were none, they get their values from the SET commands (see TOLERANCES).

When you use TYPE to add ± tolerances, Cadkey does not observe the DBL-UP option (see TOLERANCES), but uses separate lines for the positive and negative tolerances. A trick gets them on one line: Back up twice; then follow TOLER—TYPE— +/– with the VALUES—BOTH routine, entering the appropriate tolerance values.

DIM SCL (dimension scale) multiplies dimensions by the scale factor you enter. Tolerances are unaffected. A dimension of 3.00 ± .01 and a scale factor of 2 yields 6.00 ± .01. If you later assign a scale factor of 3 to the same dimension, it becomes 9.00 ± .01, not 18.00 ± .01. In other words, the scale factor is applied to the original dimension, not to an intermediate value produced by an earlier DIM SCL assignment.

You cannot apply DIM SCL to angular dimensions or to dimensions that you have keyed in or have modified with EDIT TX; however, you can use EDIT TX to revise the values that these dimensions show.

Related Commands

UPDATE changes NOTES, LABELS, and DIMENSIONS to conform to most of the SET command options. The options that are updated and that apply to lettering (and therefore to all three types of entities) are height, font, slant, and fill. Cadkey does not update character aspect ratio, note angle, or placement points. See LETTERING for notes on these parameters.

The other parameters UPDATE can change affect only DIMENSIONS:

Decimal, fractional, foot/inch, degrees, or degrees/minutes representation
Precision (number of decimal places, or whether fractional inch dimensions show to the nearest 1/2", 1/4", etc.)

Scale
Leading and trailing zeros
Tolerance format (NONE, +/-, or LIMIT)
Tolerance values

UPDATE offers an alternate way to execute most of the CHANGE functions. Use the SET commands to specify lettering styles and dimensioning formats; then execute UPDATE to change notes, labels, and dimensions to the desired forms.

SET offers an array of commands that establish parameters for lettering and dimensions. See SET for a summary of the parameters these commands affect and for references to more detailed information. The descriptions of what the SET commands do also tell you what the CHANGE and UPDATE commands do.

```
3 DETAIL
  8 UPDATE
  9 SET
6 DISPLAY
  6 LEVELS
    4 MOVE
7 CONTROL
  2 ATTRIB
    1 COLOR
    2 L-TYPE
    3 L-WIDTH
    4 PEN #
    5 OUT/FIL
```

CONTROL—ATTRIB controls parameters that could logically be included in the already overloaded SET and CHANGE commands. See ATTRIBUTES for details on these commands. The first four let you either assign attributes to be used in future construction or change existing entities. OUT/FIL changes only existing entities.

COLOR controls the colors of entities. You can also use it later, when you plot a drawing, to assign the plotter pens used to draw these entities.

L-TYPE specifies whether lines are solid, dashed, etc.

L-WIDTH controls thickness of lines.

PEN #, like COLOR, can be used to assign plotter pens.

OUT/FIL determines whether polylines and POLYGONS show as outlines or filled areas.

TRIM/EXTEND, **BREAK**, **MOVE** and **LEVELS—MOVE** also let you make changes, but these are not closely related to the CHANGE commands and are not discussed here.

Circle

```
1 CREATE
  3 CIRCLE
    1 CTR+RAD
    2 CTR+DIA
    3 CTR+EDG
    4 THREE-P
    5 TANGENT
      1 CTR-ENT
      2 2 ENTS
      3 3 ENTS
    6 TWO-PTS
```

CTR+RAD or **CTR+DIA**: Key in a value for the radius or diameter; then select the position for the center.

CTR+EDG: Select the center position; next, the position of a point on the circumference.

THREE-P: Select three points on the circumference.

TANGENT: **CTR-ENT** creates a circle with a given center and tangent to a given line, arc, or circle. **2 ENTS** creates a circle of a given radius tangent to two entities. **3 ENTS** creates a circle tangent to three entities. When one or more of these entities is an arc or circle, there are usually two or more possible tangent circles. (See ARC if you want to see a configuration that allows eight tangent circles.) To get the circle you want, select points near where the points of tangency should fall.

If a point of tangency does not fall on a line or arc, Cadkey selects the appropriate point on the extension of that entity.

If you have trouble with these TANGENT commands, see ARC. A subsection titled Notes on Tangent Arcs covers a number of technical details.

TWO-PTS: The two points are the ends of a diameter.

Color

CONTROL—ATTRIB—COLOR (see ATTRIBUTES) controls the color of entities. Choose any of fifteen colors. Cadkey lets you either assign the color for subsequent construction or change the color of existing entities.

See also the OUTLINE/FILL command, also discussed under ATTRIBUTES. This command lets you produce solid areas of color.

Configuration

CONFIG.EXE is a program that configures Cadkey for the type of monitor, mouse, printer, and plotter your computer uses. It also takes care of several bookkeeping functions, such as whether Cadkey works in inches, millimeters, feet, centimeters, yards, or user-defined units. The results of the configuration process are stored in the file CONFIG.DAT.

Control

CONTROL is one of the eight options in the main menu. MISC might have been a better name for it. Among other things, it lets you change LINE WIDTH, measure a distance, set the construction mode (2D or 3D), set the coordinate system (VIEW or WORLD), set LETTERING parameters, or use a SYSTEM COMMAND to temporarily exit to DOS.

Coordinates

Cadkey uses two coordinate systems, VIEW (VW) and WORLD (WLD). These are simply bookkeeping systems, and which one you choose affects three-dimensional construction only when you key in coordinate values.

VIEW coordinates are fixed with respect to the *screen*, with XV to the right, YV up, and ZV toward you.

7 CONTROL	
4 COORDS	
1 VIEW*	Alt-V
2 WORLD*	Alt-V

*The STATUS WINDOW lets you toggle between COORD:VW and COORD:WLD.

WORLD coordinates are fixed with respect to the *object*; therefore they look different in different views. In the top view, they are the same as VIEW coordinates. Thus, X increases toward the right side of the object; Y, toward the back; Z, toward the top. The inside front cover shows world coordinates in Cadkey's eight standard views.

The cursor tracking window, below the status window, normally shows the values of XV and YV last used to select a point. But you can use ^T to show cursor position continuously, showing it in either coordinate system. See CURSOR TRACKING.

Copy

See MOVE/COPY/JOIN for ways of copying all or part of a drawing, either to move it to a new location or to repeat it. See LEVEL for the way to move parts of a drawing from one level to another.

PATTERN (see FILES) provides copies that can be saved for later use and be retrieved into any drawing, not just the one containing the original.

CREATE–LINE–PARALEL copies a single line. The copies are parallel to the original and equal to it in length. See LINE.

Crosshatching

3 DETAIL
5 X-HATCH

XHATCH, the crosshatch command, lets you fill closed areas with any of these seven patterns. Crosshatching is also called section lining, and it usually indicates a cutaway view of an object.

1 BRICK or IRON

2 STEEL

3 COPPER

4 ALLOYS

5 ALUMINUM

6 RUBBER

7 MARBLE

The first of these patterns is widely used as a general-purpose pattern for cross sections. CADKEY Light 1.5 calls it BRICK; CADKEY Light 4.0 calls it IRON.

Select one of the seven patterns for crosshatch style; then follow the prompts:

Enter angle for hatch lines (45) = > You would expect the angle in these examples (rotated 45° counterclockwise from the horizontal) to be 45°, but, in an exception to Cadkey's ANGULAR CONVENTIONS, it is —45°.

Enter distance between hatch lines (0.25 = > The scale of the drawing affects this spacing. If you want lines 0.1" apart on a half-size drawing, enter 0.2. When the line spacing is uneven, the distance you enter is the spacing of the closest lines. For example, the STEEL and BRICK patterns in these examples have the same values of spacing.

Choose option—select the entities that bound the area you want to crosshatch.

Selection OK ? This option appears when you use CHAIN as the selection method. CHAIN can take off on a wrong path, and if it does you can select NO and start over.

Selection complete ? (YES) If you respond with NO, Cadkey lets you select additional entities singly; thus you could select most of the entities with WINDOW or CHAIN and add a few more entities at this point to complete your selection.

Three Rules

Crosshatching shows only in the view you use when you create it.

To DELETE crosshatching (or to select it for any other purpose), put the cursor on the first or last crosshatch line. This is not always easy to do. The selection point is usually so close to the boundary that you are apt to select one of the boundary lines instead. If other methods fail, one that always works is to use TYPE MASKING (see SELECTING ENTITIES) to limit Cadkey's selections to crosshatching.

Even if the boundary looks continuous in the current view and Cadkey is in 2D mode, the boundary of the area to be crosshatched must be continuous in space.

Solutions to Problems

You probably need to read no further to get through most crosshatching problems, but if you run into difficulties, read on. It helps to have a fuller understanding of what the XHATCH command will and will not do.

Figure C-1 shows a series of examples. Figure C-1a shows a rectangle with a side that extends beyond the boundary. If you try to crosshatch this rectangle, Cadkey tells you, **Invalid data... press RETURN**. One solution is to use EDIT—TRM/EXT—FIRST to trim the line to the correct length.

Figure C-1b shows a gap in the boundary line. To crosshatch this area, you would first have to close the gap, again with EDIT—TRM/EXT—FIRST.

Figures C-1c through g show the results you can expect when you use a WINDOW to select the entities that bound the area you want to crosshatch. The rectangles drawn with thin lines represent the windows.

In Figure C-1c, the centerline is a problem. This is not one of Cadkey's centerlines (Cadkey offers a centerline LINE TYPE—see ATTRIBUTES); instead, it is three separate line entities. This type of centerline is a little more trouble, but it usually looks better. Because Cadkey selects only those entities that the window completely encloses, it ignores the two longer parts of the

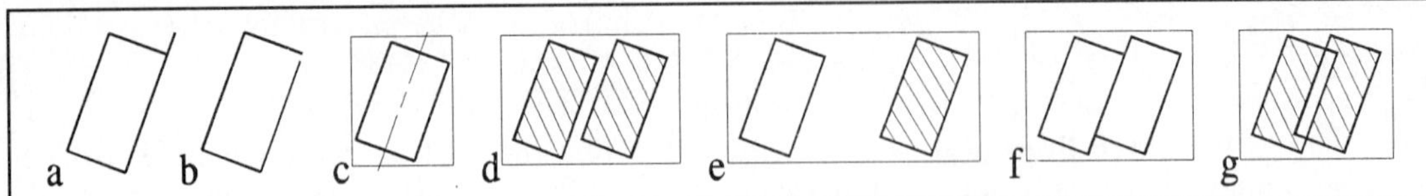

Figure C-1 Crosshatching a rectangular area

centerline; but the short line in the middle remains to give problems. Cadkey does not know how to crosshatch it. If the line were Cadkey's centerline line type, the three segments would be only a single entity, the window as shown would exclude it, and the line would be no problem. When, as in this case, only one line is giving you trouble, you can DELETE it with ^Q, create the crosshatching, and use ^U (undelete) to restore the line.

Figure C-1d shows that you can use a window to crosshatch more than one area. The result is a single crosshatch entity. Consequently, you could not delete the crosshatching from one rectangle without deleting it from both, and to select it for deletion you would have to select the first or last line of the entire array, not just the first or last line within one rectangle.

Figure C-1e shows that you cannot always crosshatch multiple boundaries in one crosshatch operation. The rule is that at least one crosshatch line must appear in both areas. In this example, if you extended the bottom crosshatch line, it would not cross the rectangle on the left. You could, however, crosshatch both areas at once by using a different angle for the crosshatch lines. The angle used here is 60°. An angle of —30° would give two or three section lines that appear in both rectangles.

Figure C-1f shows that you cannot use a window to crosshatch two areas when parts of their boundaries coincide. Cadkey would, however, crosshatch the areas one at a time if you selected them separately. You could crosshatch both in one step if you removed the common boundary, drew in the crosshatching, and then replaced the boundary.

Figure C-1g shows that you can use a window to crosshatch areas that overlap. It also shows that the result can be strange. Move on to Figure C-2 to see how XHATCH works in situations like this one. Figure C-2a shows a window enclosing six concentric circles. When Cadkey finds a closed boundary, it crosshatches everything within that area until it comes to another closed boundary. Then it stops crosshatching until it finds a third closed boundary. As it continues inward, it alternates between crosshatched and open areas.

Figure C-2b and Figure C-3 show Cadkey's response to more complex drawings. In Figure C-2b, the window eliminates most of the detail by completely enclosing only a few entities. Figure C-3 shows the alternating pattern you get with a window that encloses everything. Cadkey can handle as complex a drawing as you want to give it, provided only that each entity is part of a closed figure.

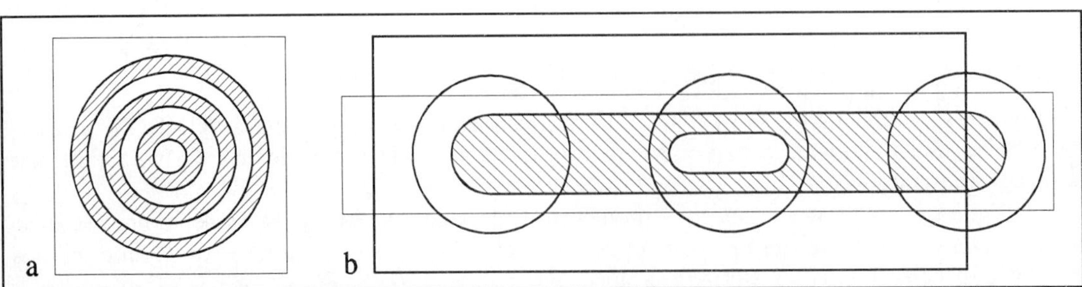

Figure C-2 Crosshatching across multiple boundaries

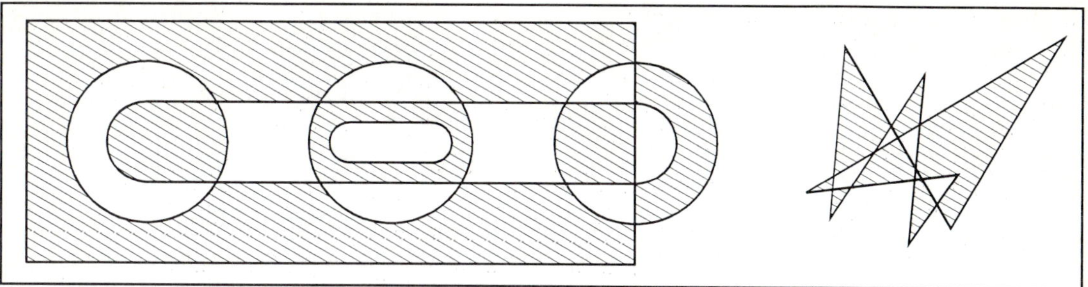

Figure C-3 Crosshatching unusual configurations

An Application

Figure C-4a shows a half section of a bearing. To be complete, it needs the crosshatching you see in Figure C-5b.

Recall that Cadkey refuses to section an area if any of the entities forming the boundary extend outside its limits. In Figure C-4a, the areas to be sectioned have six places where boundary lines extend too far. These are the six horizontal segments shown thinner in Figure C-4b. Four more horizontal lines—the ones that meet the small half circles—present no problem. Although they touch the boundary, they are not parts of it.

There are several ways you could take care of these lines. Four possibilities are:

1. DETAIL—TRM/EXT—DIVIDE (see TRM/EXT), by cutting segments out of the middles of lines, would take care of five places where the lines give trouble. DETAIL—TRM/EXT—FIRST, by cutting a line shorter, would remove the sixth segment—the second from the top. Although Figure C-4b shows these troublesome segments as fainter lines, these procedures would eliminate them completely.

   Use the WINDOW shown in Figure C-5a to select the entities that form the boundaries to be crosshatched. Although the four heavy lines that cross the right edge of the window might seem to be a problem, they are not. Because a window doesn't select entities unless it completely surrounds them, Cadkey ignores these four lines.

   If you generate the centerline pattern using the centerline line type, it is a single entity, not completely enclosed, and Cadkey ignores it. If you laboriously create it as three separate line entities, you must deal with the center segment. As already noted in connection with Figure C-1c, you could use ^Q to delete it, crosshatch the areas, and use ^U to restore it. You could temporarily hide it on another LEVEL (an option worth the trouble when there are several problem lines rather than just one). Or you could wait until you are ready to construct

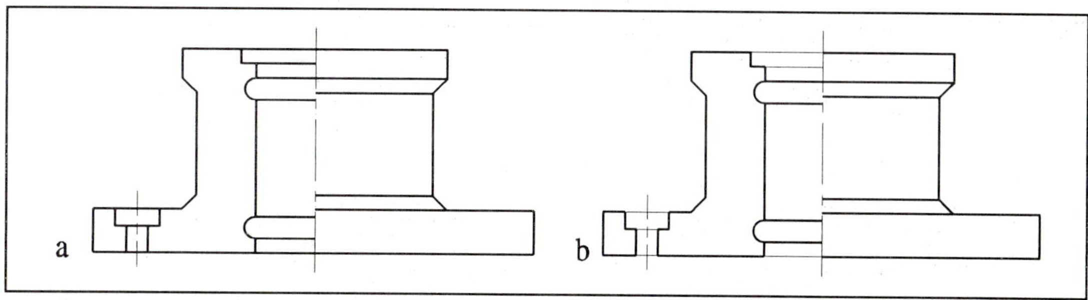

Figure C-4 Steps in crosshatching a half section

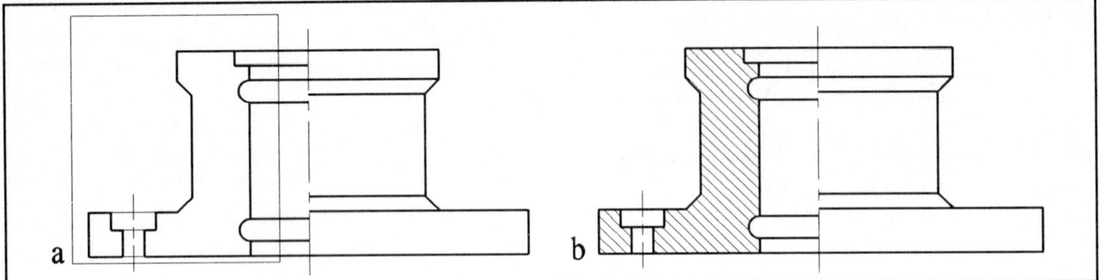

Figure C-5 Steps in crosshatching a half section (continued)

the window, use Alt-M to invoke TYPE MASKING (see SELECTING ENTITIES), select L-WIDTH, pick the width you used for the boundary lines, press Return, select DONE, and construct the window. This last procedure keeps Cadkey from selecting the thin lines usually used for centerlines.

Finish the drawing by using TRM / EXT—FIRST to extend the horizontal lines, filling the gaps you created earlier.

2. Use the procedure just described, but instead of creating a window, use SINGLE to select, one at a time, the entities in the two boundaries. Or, to save time, use CHAIN (see SELECTING ENTITIES) to select the larger boundary. After Cadkey selects the chain, it asks, **Selection complete ? (YES)**. Respond with NO, and Cadkey lets you pick more entities singly, giving you a chance to add the shorter boundary on the left.
3. If you section the two areas one at a time, you could BREAK the entities shown thinner in Figure C-4b rather than deleting segments from them. BREAK usually leaves the appearance of the drawing unchanged, but it cuts the lines, converting the problem segments into separate entities. This makes it easy to draw windows that exclude not only the horizontal segments but also the centerline.
4. Another way to use BREAK is to send the broken parts of entities to an unused LEVEL. See BREAK for the way to make the segments disappear and then to restore them when the crosshatching is complete.

Cursor

CURSOR is the name of the crosshairs that move across the screen. It is also the name of the default option in the POSITION MENU, which allows points to be selected solely by the position of the cursor. (Most careful construction involves other options—see POSITION MENU.)

This discussion covers miscellaneous information, admonitions, and advice.

Active Area

To select an entity, you don't need to place the cursor directly on the entity. You can put it anywhere within 1/2" of your target. Cadkey responds in one of two ways. In the first, Cadkey searches its DATABASE for entities that pass within 1/2" of the center of the cursor and selects the one that is closest.

Selection Trap

The second of Cadkey's responses occurs when you place the cursor within 0.1" of an entity. A circle 0.2" in diameter, centered on the cursor, is called the selection trap. When Cadkey finds an entity in this area, it interrupts its search of the database and selects that entity.

The selection trap is designed to save you time. It lets Cadkey select the entity without searching its entire database. But if you don't understand what is happening, the selection trap can also cause frustration. When two or three entities are close to one another and you try to select one, Cadkey may repeatedly insist on picking another. If three entities are within 0.1" of the cursor, Cadkey picks the first one it runs across, regardless of which entity is nearest the cursor.

If you understand what Cadkey is doing, the cure is often easy. Suppose you want to delete the short vertical line in Figure C-6 but Cadkey wants to pick the arc. The problem is that the line and arc are so close that putting the cursor on the line gets both line and arc inside the 0.1" selection trap. If Cadkey finds the arc first, it selects it, even though your cursor is nearer the line.

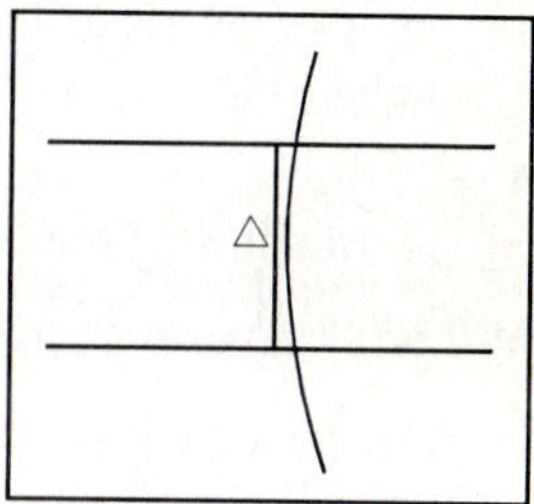
Figure C-6 Selection technique

The solution is to put the cursor to the left of the line, where the small triangle is. If you position the cursor carefully, you can get the line inside the selection trap (for faster selection) but put the circle out of range.

Selection Techniques

Selection problems have several other cures. (1) Because the database lists entities in the order you created them, Cadkey normally favors selection of the entities you created first. But by using Alt-R (or selecting DB in the STATUS WINDOW) you can reverse the direction in which Cadkey reads its database and give priority to entities created more recently. See DATABASE SEARCH for more detail. (2) You can use a WINDOW to expand the region giving trouble and space the entities more widely. (3) If, for example, you want to delete some POINTS, you can use TYPE MASKING (see SELECTING ENTITIES) to limit selections to points and prevent deletion of other entities. (4) If your drawing is three dimensional, switching to another VIEW may space the entities more favorably. (5) If you have used more than one LEVEL, it may help to use level masking (see SELECTING ENTITIES).

It's not always good to position the cursor accurately. Although the selection trap can speed Cadkey's response, it can also deceive you. Most accurate construction requires techniques such as ENDENT (see POSITION MENU) to make Cadkey snap precisely to specific points on the drawing. But it's easy to forget to check the position menu, and you may sometimes find yourself using CURSOR when you intended to use ENDENT. If you habitually put the cursor a visible distance from the point you want, you will immediately notice Cadkey's failure to snap to the object as you intended, and you can back up a step to make corrections. But many beginners carefully place the cursor on the point they're selecting, unaware that they could be creating a drawing full of small errors.

Often you can enjoy the benefits of the selection trap but avoid its risks. With ENDENT, for example, you can place the cursor close to an entity but not close to the end you are selecting. This puts you close enough to the entity for rapid selection, but far enough from its end to see the selection point snap to the point you want.

Cursor Tracking

```
6 DISPLAY
   9 CURSOR
      1 TRACKING    ^T
         1 OFF
         2 VIEW
         3 WORLD
```

The cursor tracking window appears in the bottom left corner of the computer screen. When cursor tracking is off, this window shows, in VIEW coordinates, the x and y values of the last point you selected. Pressing **^T** gives you three choices:

OFF retains the default setting. If you want to know the coordinates of some point on the screen, you can see them by pressing the mouse button, even though Cadkey is not asking you to specify a position.

VIEW gives you a continuous display in VIEW coordinates, letting you see the XV and YV coordinates of the cursor as you move it around the screen.

WORLD gives a continuous display of the WORLD coordinates X, Y, and Z.

The cursor tracking window sometimes shows the words MENU AREA, STATUS WINDOW, or BREAK FUNCTION, depending on where the cursor is. The first two terms are obvious enough. The third, BREAK FUNCTION, refers to the **break window**, the area where you see Alt-E EXIT, F10 BACK-UP, and Esc ESCAPE. Break window is a term you can safely ignore. Because it is easier to think of these commands as parts of the menu options window, the term break window appears only one more time in this handbook—in Chapter 4, Configuration and Installation, under Set Color Options.

Database

Cadkey keeps a record of every entity you create. For a line, this record includes the coordinates of the end points, the line type (solid, dashed, etc.), line thickness, color, pen number, plus things you probably don't care about, such as the view you were using when you created it. This record of entities is called the database. You can see it piecemeal by using CONTROL—VERIFY—ATTRIB and CONTROL—VERIFY—COORD (see VERIFY).

Database Search

5 FILES
  7 DB DRAW
    1 BACK* Alt-R
    2 FORWARD* Alt-R

*Selecting DB in the STATUS WINDOW toggles between DB:FWD and DB:BACK.

DB DRAW controls how Cadkey reads its DATABASE—its list of the entities you have created. In FORWARD mode it starts with the first entry. In BACK it starts with the last. You see its action when you REDRAW the screen. FORWARD draws entities in the order in which you constructed them. BACK reverses the sequence.

A more subtle effect, but a more practical one, is what happens when you select an entity. Suppose you draw some lines and use ENDENT to put POINT entities at the ends of the lines. Later you try to select one of the points. With DB in forward mode, Cadkey selects the line. The point and the end of the line are equally close to the cursor, and in case of a tie Cadkey gives priority to the entity it finds first. If you set DB to BACK, Cadkey reads the database from back to front, it finds the point first, and it selects the point instead of the line.

Decimal Places

3 DETAIL
  9 SET
    3 DIM REP
      1 DECIMAL
        1 n.
        2 n.n
        3 n.nn
        4 n.nnn
        5 n.nnnn
        6 n.nnnnn
        7 .nnnnnn

DECIMAL sets the precision Cadkey assigns to decimal dimensions and their tolerances. You can use up to six decimal places.

You can configure Cadkey to drop trailing zeros, in which case the full number of decimal places will not always show. See DIMENSIONING STANDARDS for details.

A command similar to DECIMAL lets you set the precision of fractional dimensions. Both DETAIL—SET—DIM REP—FRACTIN and DETAIL—SET—DIM REP—FT/IN let you choose whether fractional-inch dimensions and their tolerances will be rounded to the nearest 1/2", nearest 1/64", or some value in between. See DIMENSIONING STANDARDS.

Defaults

When you start Cadkey, it is ready to use 3D construction mode, to crosshatch with lines at a 45° angle, and, depending on its CONFIGURATION, to draw circles 1" or 20 mm in diameter. Such choices are called DEFAULTS. You often see these defaults when Cadkey asks you to enter a number. For example, when you create a circle you see:

Enter diameter (1) =>

If you want a diameter of 2, enter 2; but if you want a diameter of 1, all you need to do is press Return to accept the default value of 1.

Cadkey often changes its default values to what it thinks you might want. If you enter 2 for the diameter of the circle, the next time you create a circle Cadkey will suggest 2 as the default value.

Some defaults are not obvious. When you key in a location using view coordinates, Cadkey's first prompt is:

XV =

Although the prompt line does not show a default value, there is one: zero. To enter zero as the value for XV, press Return without entering any number.

You can modify some of Cadkey's default settings by using the CONFIGURATION program. Two that you can change are the directories Cadkey uses for storing PART and PATTERN files (see FILES). Initially, these are the subdirectories PRT and PTN in whatever directory the computer uses to house the Cadkey program. Usually the school reconfigures Cadkey to make your floppy disk the default directory for these files. One way to see where Cadkey automatically sends your files is to select FILES—PART—LST/LOAD and FILES—PATTERN—LST/LOAD and note the directory pathnames that show on the prompt line.

See Chapter 4 for other changes you can make using the configuration program.

Delete

```
8 DELETE
  1 SELECT
    1 SINGLE    ^Q
    2 CHAIN
    3 WINDOW
    4 GROUP
    5 PLANE
    6 ALL DSP
      1 ALL
      2 BY TYPE
      3 EX TYPE
  2 LEVEL
```

Usually, when you need to delete a few entities you press **^Q**, select the entities one at a time, and press Return. This procedure is like the SELECT—SINGLE option available through the menu. But more sophisticated techniques are also available:

SELECT produces the SELECTION MENU, giving you six ways (SINGLE, CHAIN, etc.) to specify which entities to delete. See SELECTING ENTITIES for descriptions.

DELETE—SELECT—ALL DISP—BY TYPE—GEOM—POINT—DONE is a convenient sequence if you have used a number of POINT entities for construction and are finished with them. **A word of caution:** Sometimes a mouse shifts as you press the button. If you use a mouse to select BY

TYPE, and if the mouse position happens to be borderline between the BY TYPE and ALL options, the cursor could move up and select ALL instead. The result: everything on the screen disappears. To be safe, use F2 instead of the mouse to select BY TYPE.

LEVEL deletes all entities on whatever LEVEL you specify, even if that level is hidden or if some entities are off the screen.

Four IMMEDIATE MODE commands, described under SELECTING ENTITIES, can help you select the right entities for deletion when Cadkey wants to pick the wrong ones. **Alt-M** invokes TYPE MASKING, which lets Cadkey select only certain types of entities; for example, it can restrict selections to points or to entities composed of dashed lines. **Alt-N** invokes LEVEL MASKING, which can limit Cadkey's selections either to one level or to all levels but one. **Alt-W** (see ZOOM—WINDOW), expands a small region of the drawing, making closely spaced entities easier to select. **Alt-R** (see DATABASE SEARCH) reverses the order in which Cadkey checks its list of entities to see which is nearest the cursor. This reversal may favor the entities you are trying to select.

As you select items for deletion, Cadkey either highlights each entity you pick or marks each choice with a small triangle. (The CONFIGURATION program controls how Cadkey marks your choices.) If you select the wrong entity, press F10 to cancel the selection. Cadkey may mark the entity with # to show that the selection was canceled. If you have problems with more than just the last selection, press F10 a second time to cancel all selections.

This activity leaves marks on the screen, and you may have marks left over from constructing entities. DELETE cannot remove this clutter. Instead, use **^R** to REDRAW the screen.

^U (undelete) restores the last entity deleted. See RECALL for (1) a way to restore all entities deleted, not just the one you deleted most recently, (2) precautions to take if you use the RECALL command, and (3) the use of DISPLAY—LEVELS—MOVE as an alternative to deleting entities, making the process of recalling them more controllable. If you accidentally delete a GROUP, undelete is not much help. ^U brings back only a single entity of a deleted group.

DEL LN and DEL END

DEL LN and DEL END are two commands for editing text. The first deletes the current line. The second deletes all characters from the cursor to the end of the line. See TEXT EDITOR for a description of these commands and of the five others in the same menu.

Depth

DEPTH is measured perpendicular to the face of the computer screen. Positive values are toward you; thus depth is the same as the VIEW coordinate ZV (see COORDINATES). New construction takes place at this depth unless you use the POSITION MENU to override the depth setting (see the note at the end of this section).

The DEPTH command sets the working depth for subsequent construction. Your selection remains in effect until you again invoke the DEPTH command.

```
7 CONTROL
  3 CONST
    2 DEPTH*      ^D
      1 VALUE
      2 POSITION
      3 OFFSET
```

*Depth is labeled D in the STATUS WINDOW.

There are three ways to specify depth:

VALUE asks you to enter the new depth coordinate.

POSITN asks you to select a location that is at the depth you want. Use ENDENT or a similar restriction (see POSITION MENU) to select a specific point on your drawing. Cadkey sets the depth to the depth of that point. This works whether Cadkey is in 2D or 3D construction mode (see 2D/3D).

OFFSET changes depth by the value you key in. If depth is 1 and you enter an offset of 3, depth is reset to 4.

If CONST is set to 2D, construction occurs at the working depth. If CONST is set to 3D, construction still occurs at the working depth except when ENDENT or a similar selection method (see POSITION MENU) pulls Cadkey to a specific point in three-dimensional space. See 2D/3D for details on how different commands respond to these construction modes.

The STATUS WINDOW shows the current depth. In views 1 through 6, you can make the CURSOR TRACKING WINDOW (see CURSOR) show depth in a different way by showing you the cursor position in the WORLD coordinates X, Y, and Z.

Detail

DETAIL is item 3 in the main menu, the selection you make if you want to create DIMENSIONS, NOTES, LABELS, ARROWS, WITNESS LINES, or CROSSHATCHING.

The SET options of the detail menu let you set or change the parameters that control the properties of this group of entities.

DETAIL is also a MASKING MENU option (see SELECTING ENTITIES) that lets you limit Cadkey's selections to one of the entity types created by the DETAIL commands.

Dimensioning

Cadkey offers a rich assortment of dimensioning options, giving you considerable freedom in how you dimension drawings. To keep this section from becoming unwieldy, it is limited to fundamentals. It's best to assimilate this material and get some practice in dimensioning before you go deeper into the subject. When you are ready for additional material, you will find it under these five headings:

DIMENSIONING—BASIC SKILLS tells how to place dimensions exactly where you want them. This is required reading after your first dimensioning session.

DIMENSIONING STANDARDS tells how to set letter height, number of decimal places shown, etc.

DIMENSIONS AND THE TEXT EDITOR tells how to extend the standard dimensioning formats to include notes and how to change numbers in existing dimensions.

TOLERANCES shows a number of ways to add tolerances to dimensions.

ARROWS AND WITNESS LINES tells how to add individually the extension lines and dimension lines (Cadkey calls these witness lines and leaders) that Cadkey ordinarily supplies automatically.

```
3 DETAIL
  1 DIMENSN
    1 HORIZTL
    2 VERTICL
    3 PARALEL
    4 RADIUS
    5 ANGULAR
    6 DIAMETR
  9 SET
    1 ARROWS
      1 DIRECT*   ^A
        1 IN
        2 OUT
```

*The STATUS WINDOW also gives access to this command.

HORIZTL and **VERTICL** are the most-used routines. They dimension the horizontal or vertical component of the distance between two points. In response to the prompts, you pick the two points to dimension between and then show where the dimension goes. (Throughout this handbook, the noun "dimension" usually refers to the **number** portion of the dimensioning array.) Cadkey then draws the entire layout, with the dimension centered on the third point, and asks whether this is what you want. If you say NO, you don't have to start over; you simply reselect the third point—the location for the dimension.

While Cadkey is waiting for you to relocate the dimension, you are free to make certain changes: If the dimension line arrows are crowding the dimension, you can press **^A** (see the discussion that follows on ARROWS—DIRECT) to move them outside of the witness lines. If you see that the letter height is wrong or that you are about to put the dimension on the wrong LEVEL, you can use the STATUS WINDOW to make changes. Then you can pick up where you left off and complete the dimension.

PARALEL dimensions the total distance between two points (Figure D-1). The dimension line is drawn parallel to the line that would connect the points.

RADIUS dimensions the radius of an arc or a circle, using a single leader. The leader is an arrow that starts with a horizontal line as long as the letter height. Cadkey asks whether to start the leader on the right or left side of the dimension.

The left side of Figure D-2 shows five radius dimensions. The two 50 mm dimensions used the arrows OUT option. The other three used arrows IN. With the arrows IN option, the dimension line starts at the arc center. (See Figure D-3 for a clearer look at the ARROWS option.) Cadkey does not provide the two small crosses that mark two of the arc centers. If you want them, you must add them separately.

The 50 mm dimensions illustrate a problem you may run into occasionally. Both dimension the same arc. The one on the left came out as expected, but the one on the right points not to the arc, but to a point on an extension of the arc, a point almost 180° beyond its end. Usually the cure is easy. Select YES to accept the dimension, then use DETAIL—CHANGE—TXT POS to move it. Try to find a position that brings the leader back to where you want it. If this doesn't work, delete the dimension and try again, this time switching the side the leader is on.

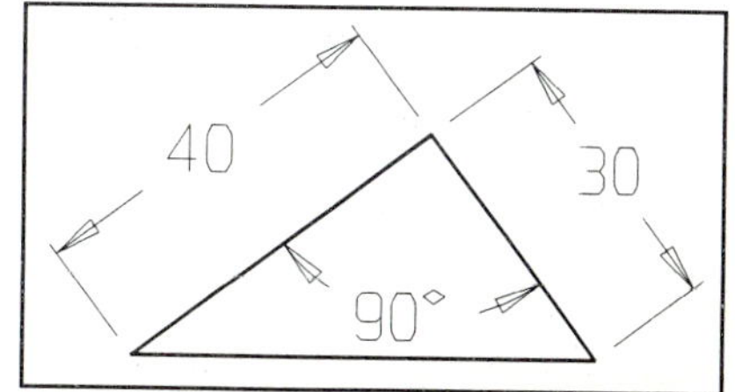

Figure D-1 Parallel dimensions

If this still doesn't work, more drastic measures will. Because Cadkey is most apt to be stubborn about the leader when the arc is only a few degrees long, you

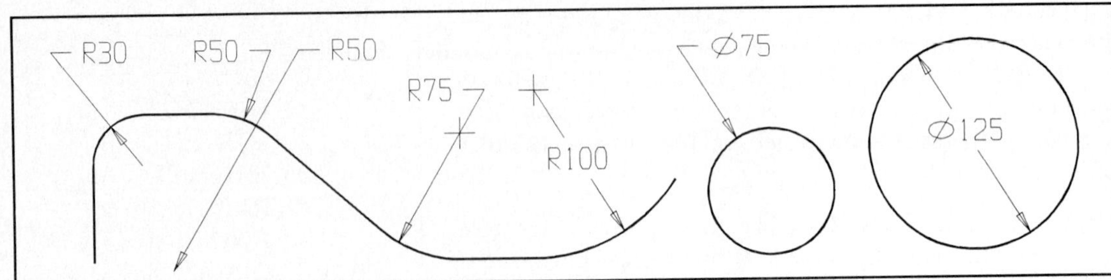

Figure D-2 Dimensions for arcs and circles

need a longer arc. Delete the dimension; then create a CIRCLE that coincides with the arc. Use the CTR+EDG option to draw it. To indicate the center of the circle, select CENTER from the position menu and select the arc. To indicate the edge, select ENDENT and select the arc again. Now apply a radial dimension to the circle. No matter where you place the dimension, the leader will behave itself. Finally, delete the circle. If you later have to use DETAIL–CHANGE–TXT POS to adjust the position of the dimension, you will have no problem. Cadkey will think it is still dimensioning the circle.

ANGULAR dimensions the angle between two lines. Two crossing lines create four angles, and Cadkey's prompt, **Select angle to be dimensioned**, asks you to put the cursor somewhere between the two segments that form the angle you want to dimension. At this point, CADKEY Light 1.5 prompts you to indicate the text position, but CADKEY Light 4.0 has you first make one more choice: INNER vs. OUTER. If you choose INNER, Cadkey does the normal thing and dimensions the angle as one smaller than 180°. If you choose OUTER, Cadkey dimensions the angle as one greater than 180°.

DIAMETR dimensions the diameter of an arc or a circle. Cadkey supplies the diameter symbol Ø. Using ^A to switch between ARROWS IN and ARROWS OUT lets you dimension diameters as shown for the two circles in Figure D-2. Other configurations are possible (Figure D-3), but these are the two that are standard for dimensioning circles. You control the angle of the line in the 125 mm dimension by where you place the dimension text. If you want the dimension line at a 45° angle, select the text position along an imaginary 45° line passing through the center of the circle. If the text is near the center of the circle, the angle is critically dependent on the text position. You may find it easiest to select YES to accept the dimension whether you like its position or not; then you can come back with DETAIL–CHANGE–TXT POS and try various positions until you get what you want.

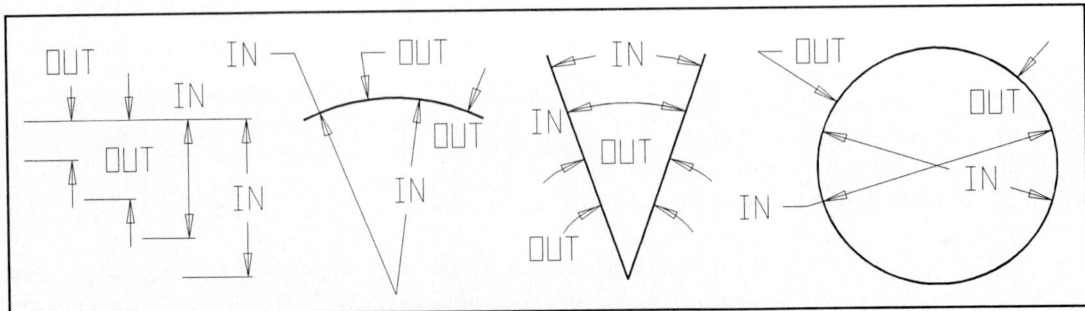

Figure D-3 Arrows IN/OUT options

ARROWS–DIRECTION–IN/OUT lets you choose whether arrows go inside or outside of witness lines or of arcs and circles (Figure D-3). ^A toggles between these two modes. Figure D-3 shows the configurations Cadkey can generate using these two options. Not all of these configurations can be recommended. When you dimension arcs and circles, you would do well to choose from the forms shown in Figure D-2.

Dimensioning—Basic Skills

Never use just the cursor to select the points marking distances to be dimensioned. Cadkey suggests the right procedure by making ENDENT the default choice in the POSITION MENU when you are to select these points. If you change this option, be sure to change it to another that selects with precision the points between which the dimension applies.

Cadkey puts small gaps—half of the lettering height—between the object and the ends of extension (witness) lines. Figure D-4a shows these gaps. Preserve them by selecting points that put the ends of extension lines next to outside corners, where they will not overlap object lines. In Figure D-4b, the selection point, shown by the triangle, is too low. Because ENDENT tells Cadkey to dimension to the bottom end of the line, the extension line goes too far down.

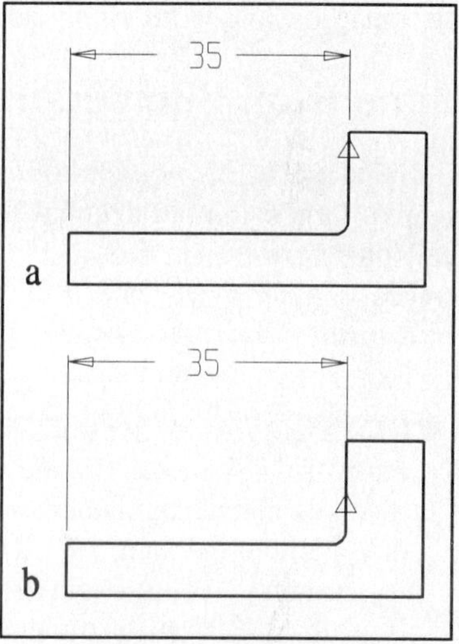

Figure D-4 Selection points for dimensions

It is good practice to space the first dimension line about 1/2" from the object and to space uniformly (usually 3/8" apart) any dimension lines that are farther out. Although the exact distances are not always important, you might want to observe them if only to demonstrate to your instructor that you have enough control over Cadkey to be able to do so. SNAP makes it easy to keep these spacings accurate. (Press PgDn twice to convert from the default snap spacing of 1/2" to a spacing of 1/8". Put the first dimension four snap increments from the object and the next dimension three more snap increments out.) If the edge of the object does not coincide with one of the snap positions, and if you feel like being fussy about the 1/2" spacing of the first line, use DISPLAY–SNAP–ALIGN–ENDENT to align the snap grid with a corner of the object.

Dimensioning Standards

The SET menu handles many of the bookkeeping aspects of dimensioning. The default settings are appropriate for most dimensioning in inches. For metric dimensions, see the notes below on UNITS, DIM HT, and ZEROS.

Your selections in the SET menu remain in effect until you change them. These selections affect future construction but do not change dimensions you have already placed on the drawing. If you want to change existing dimensions, see CHANGE and UPDATE for the procedure.

If the menu outline shown here were complete, it would be about three times as long as what you see. To keep it short, many fifth and sixth level options were left out. For example, under FRACTIN, there are six choices, letting you choose whether to have fractional dimensions rounded to the nearest 1/2", the nearest 1/4", etc. The default settings in angle brackets suggest the nature of the options you would see if the menu outline were complete.

```
3 DETAIL
  9 SET
    3 DIM REP
      1 DECIMAL                        <n.nn>
      2 FRACTIN                         <1/2>
      3 FT / IN                         <1/2>
      4 DEGREES (Ver 4)
      5 DEG / MIN (Ver 4)
    4 TEXT
      1 DIM HT*             <0.3" or 8 mm>
      3 DIM FNT*                  <1 = BOX>
      5 DIM PLC
        1 HORIZL                    <CENTER>
        2 VERTICL                   <CENTER>
        3 AUTO CEN (Ver 4)            <NO>
      8 CHR ASP*                       <0.5>
    5 TOLER                           <NONE>
    6 STANDRD
      1 ZEROS
        1 LEAD                          <NO>
        2 TRAIL                        <YES>
      2 DIM ALN                         <NO>
      3 DIM MOD                   <AUTOMAT>
    7 UNITS                           <INCH>
    9 VER DIM                           <NO>
```

*The STATUS WINDOW shows these TEXT settings, labeled DH, DF, and AS.

Values in angle brackets are Cadkey's default settings.

Three options are available only in CADKEY Light 4.0.

Dimension Representation

DIM REP lets you choose whether to give dimensions in decimal form, in fractional form, or in feet and fractional inches. After you make this choice, you specify the precision with which Cadkey writes the dimensions.

DECIMAL gives dimensions in decimal form. You can set the number of digits behind the decimal point to any number between 0 (n.) and 6 (n.nnnnnn). (This choice does not limit the precision of dimensions as stored in Cadkey's DATABASE. It limits only the precision used to show these dimensions on the screen.)

FRACTIN gives the fractional part of dimensions in numbers such as 1/2, 1/4, etc. Choose the precision you want Cadkey to use. If you select 1/2, a dimension of 11/16 is written 1/2. If you select 1/4, it is written 3/4. If you select 1/8, it is written 3/4 (not 5/8, which is equally close–Cadkey rounds up).

Fractional dimensions are not automatically inch dimensions. If Cadkey is configured for metric dimensions, it does not hesitate to dimension a distance as 20 17/64 millimeters; however, your instructor is not apt to be this liberal.

FT / IN gives dimensions in the English system at its worst–feet, inches, and fractions of an inch. As with FRACTIN, you select the precision you want, and your selection carries over into FRACTIN should you later select that dimensioning mode. Even if Cadkey is configured for other units such as millimeters, FT / IN gives distances correctly in feet and inches.

DEGREES, the default for angular dimensions, shows angles in degrees and decimal fractions of a degree. The options under DECIMAL also set the number of decimal places that angular dimensions show. In CADKEY Light 4.0, the DEGREES format is an option; in CADKEY Light 1.5 it is the only way to dimension an angle.

DEG / MIN is a CADKEY Light 4.0 option, not available in CADKEY Light 1.5. In this format, Cadkey dimensions angles in degrees, minutes, and seconds. The precision of angles shown this way is fixed—you cannot drop the seconds part of the dimension.

Size, Style, and Positioning of Numbers

The following **TEXT** commands control the size, style, and placement of the numbers used in dimensions. See LETTERING for more detail.

DIM HT sets number height and arrow length. Height is subject to the scale of the drawing, so 8 mm numbers are 4 mm high on a half-size drawing.

DIM FNT lets you select other styles such as bold fonts and slanted numbers. See LETTERING for font samples.

DIM PLC controls placement of dimensions. Normally, Cadkey finds the rectangular area that encloses the dimension and its tolerance and puts the center of this area at the cursor. But if you select VERTICL–BOTTOM and HORIZTL–LEFT from the DIM PLC menu, Cadkey will place the lower left corner of the rectangular area at the cursor.

AUTO CEN is a CADKEY Light 4.0 option. If you select YES, it centers dimensions between witness lines. In other words, for a horizontal dimension, the cursor determines how far up or down the dimension goes, but Cadkey takes control of its side-to-side positioning. This makes dimensioning go faster and look better, but it presents one problem. When you dimension a distance so short that the dimension will not fit between witness lines, Cadkey refuses to let you put it outside. For such dimensions, select NO to turn AUTO CEN off.

No matter where the *placement* point for a dimension is, the *selection* point (the point you pick to delete it, move it, etc.) is the lower left corner of the first number.

CHR ASP sets the width-to-height ratio of numbers, with higher character aspect ratios giving wider numbers. The default is 0.5. You might prefer 0.8. See LETTERING for examples.

Format of Dimensions

TOLER lets you choose whether decimal dimensions show with tolerances, what the tolerances are, and what format they appear in. See TOLERANCES for details.

STANDRD sets conventions for writing dimensions:

ZEROS determines whether dimensions use leading or trailing zeros. The defaults (showing trailing zeros but no leading zeros, for example, .500) is standard for decimal-inch dimensions. The opposite setup (for example, 0.5) is standard for metric.

LEAD determines whether numbers less than 1 have a leading zero. Setting LEAD to YES adds the zero. This command affects both dimensions and their tolerances.

TRAIL affects trailing zeros. Setting TRAIL to NO strips trailing zeros from dimensions but leaves trailing zeros on the associated tolerances.

DIM ALN determines the angle at which dimensions are written. The default, **NO**, writes all numbers horizontally (Figure D-5a). **YES** aligns them with the distance being dimensioned, printing vertical dimensions sideways and parallel dimensions at the same angle as the dimension line (Figure D-5b).

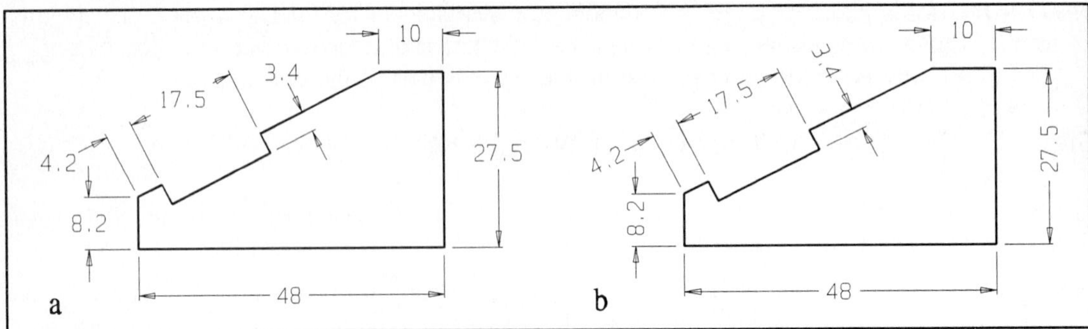

Figure D-5 Horizontal and aligned dimensioning styles

DIM MOD lets you choose between AUTOMATIC and MANUAL dimensioning modes. In automatic mode, Cadkey calculates each dimension as you create it, rounds it to the specified precision, and adds tolerances if appropriate. Manual mode lets you edit each dimension as you create it. See DIMENSIONS AND THE TEXT EDITOR for an explanation.

Other Commands

UNITS may be set to give dimensions in a variety of units. Cadkey normally dimensions in whatever units are used for construction, and the CONFIGURATION file determines whether Cadkey constructs in inches, millimeters, feet, centimeters, yards, or meters. But with the UNITS command you can use units for dimensioning that are different from those used in construction. See UNITS for more detail.

VER DIM (verify dimension) asks you, **Suppress dimension verification message ?** YES suppresses the **Accept dimension ?** prompt, letting Cadkey accept all dimensions without pausing to let you edit them. YES also suppresses the **Accept label ?** prompt (see LABEL).

Dimensions and the Text Editor

```
3 DETAIL
  7 CHANGE
    3 EDIT TX
      1 DEL LIN
      2 JOIN LN
      3 INSERT
      4 APPEND
      5 DEL END
      6 SAVE TX
      7 ABORT
```

When different dimensions require different tolerances, you can use DETAIL–SET–TOLER–LINEAR–+/––POS TOL and –NEG TOL to reset tolerances for each new dimension, but this procedure is tedious. It is easier to use one set of tolerances for all dimensions and then, with the TEXT EDITOR, change the tolerances to their correct values.

The text editor also lets you combine notes with dimensions, producing combinations like 2.75 TYP. When you create dimensions in other than standard form, you need to know some tricks to get them just the way you want them. The discussion that follows is a series of examples to show some of these techniques and to help you avoid some common problems.

The first four illustrations in Figure D-6 show the combinations to be discussed in the text that follows. The fifth illustration shows a problem discussed not in this section, but in the tutorial on BASIC HOLE-AND-SHAFT DIMENSIONING in Chapter 2. That tutorial is good preparation for what follows in this section. Although it uses fairly basic techniques, it sees you through some problems you might not expect to encounter.

A sixth procedure, the one noted in the opening paragraph, in which you simply change tolerance values without adding any text, is included in the discussion that follows on Diameter Dimensions.

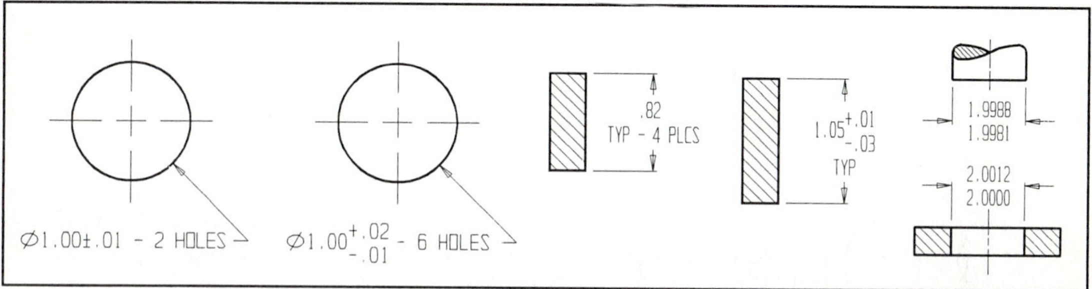

Figure D-6 Applications of the text editor to dimensioning problems

Diameter Dimensions

The dimension in Figure D-7b includes a note to show that it applies not to just one hole, but two. To add this kind of note, call the text editor with DETAIL—CHANGE—EDIT TX and select the dimension you want to change. Cadkey lets you delete, add, or change what you see on the prompt line. In this example, add - 2 HOLES to the dimension in Figure D-7a. Don't forget the space before the dash. Cadkey leaves the number part of the dimension where it was before and pushes the leader (the line with the arrow) to the right to accommodate the added characters. If this change puts the leader in an awkward position, you can move the dimension with DETAIL—CHANGE—TXT POS.

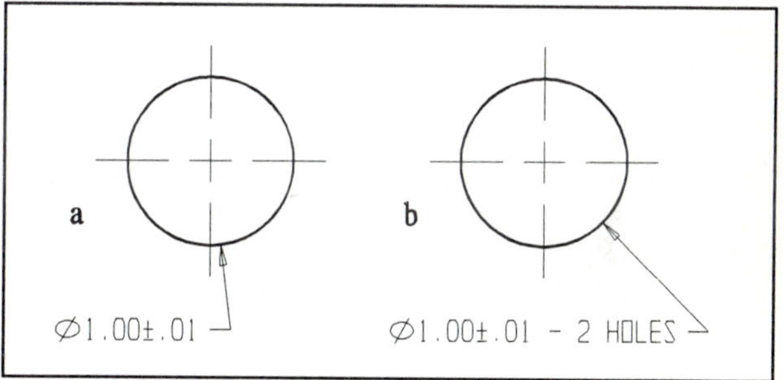

Figure D-7 Adding a note to a dimension

Had the leader been on the left, the process would have been simpler. Because the first character, ∅ in this case, does not move, adding the text would not have moved the leader.

Figure D-8 shows a more complex array of numbers. If you want to add text, the task becomes harder; but if you just need to change the numbers, you can do so easily. Use the up and down arrow keys to move from one element of the array to another, use the Backspace or Delete keys to remove numbers you want to change, and type in the numbers you want. Press F6 when you finish, and the revised dimension appears on the screen. This is the easiest way to assign tolerances individually. But note that if you want to assign separate + and — tolerances you must create the dimensions in that format first. The text editor cannot, by itself, create the layout in Figure D-8a.

If you use the text editor to add another line of text to the dimension in Figure D-8a, you disrupt the layout, and the dimension looks like Figure D-8b. Because you can't use the text editor to add text to this dimension, you must add the text separately, in the form of a NOTE.

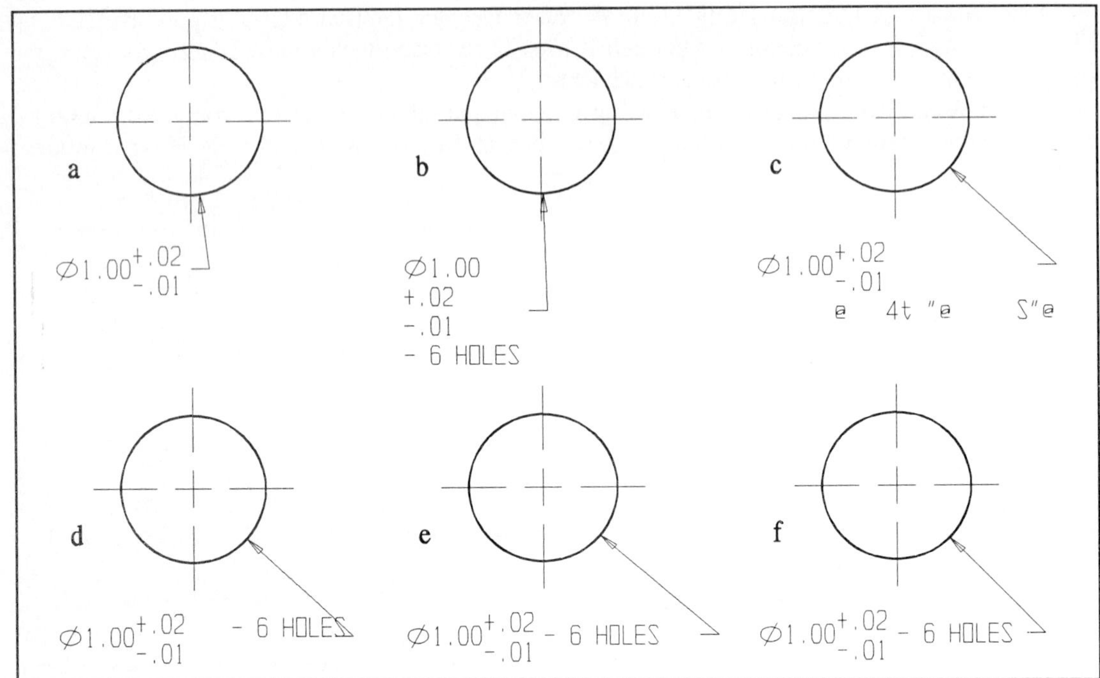

Figure D-8 Adding a note to a more complex dimensioning array

Before you add the note, make room for it by moving the leader to the right (Figure D-8c). You can do this with the text editor by adding spaces to the line containing the +.02 tolerance. A row of ordinary spaces does not work here—Cadkey strips away trailing spaces. But Alt-255 (hold down the Alt key while typing 255 on the keypad at the right side of your keyboard) gives a special kind of space. If you use this for the final space, Cadkey retains all the spaces you add.

For some reason, Cadkey occasionally adds a line of profanity to dimensions that go through the text editor. Figure D-8c preserves one such outburst. Select the dimension for editing, use the up and down arrow keys to find the offending line, and use DEL LN to remove it.

Write the note with DETAIL—NOTE—KEYIN. Key in - 6 HOLES, press F6 to end the note, and use the cursor to add it to your drawing. (See NOTE for more detail.)

It would be surprising if this put the note in the right place. Figure D-8d shows a more likely outcome. Move the note with DETAIL—CHANGE—TXT POS. Cadkey lets you choose new positions as often as you need to get the note to look right. Figure D-8e shows this result.

The problem that remains is minor. The note is in the right place, but the leader starts too far to the right. (Depending on how many spaces you used, you could have the opposite problem of the leader crowding the note.) Here, the space for the note is wider than it should be. To fix this, go back to the text editor and delete (or you may need to add) a couple of spaces from the string following +.02. This moves the leader closer (Figure D-8f), providing the final layout.

Horizontal Dimensions

If a horizontal dimension is on a single line—if, for example, it looks like 1.75±.01—adding text to change it to 1.75±.01 TYP involves nothing more than getting it into the TEXT EDITOR and typing whatever you want to add. Cadkey shortens the right leader to make room.

But if the horizontal dimension is like the diameter dimension in Figure D-8, with plus and minus tolerances shown separately, the text you add must be separate, in the form of a note; and you, not Cadkey, must shorten the right-hand leader to make room. The procedure is the same as if you were adding a note to a diameter dimension with the leader on the right. Use the text editor to add spaces (see the preceding notes on diameter dimensions for the Alt-key trick that lets you do this), and these spaces will push the leader to the right to make room for your note.

Vertical Dimensions

If the dimension has no tolerances or if the dimension and its tolerance are on a single line, the job may involve several steps, but all are easy. With the dimension in the text editor, press Return to add a new line, and type in the text you want. Figure D-9 shows an example of the process. As before, the editing of Figure D-9a to give Figure D-9b does not move the first character of the dimension; instead, the arrows move to recenter themselves around the larger dimensioning array.

Usually you get two lines of text that are poorly centered with respect to one another (Figure D9-b). The text editor can correct such problems. To get the result shown in Figure D-9c you would add four leading spaces to the first line.

To move the dimension to the position shown in Figure D-9d, use DETAIL–CHANGE–TXT POS. When you select the text to move it, remember that the selection point is the lower left corner of the first character and that the first character is a space. Place the cursor just above the letter T.

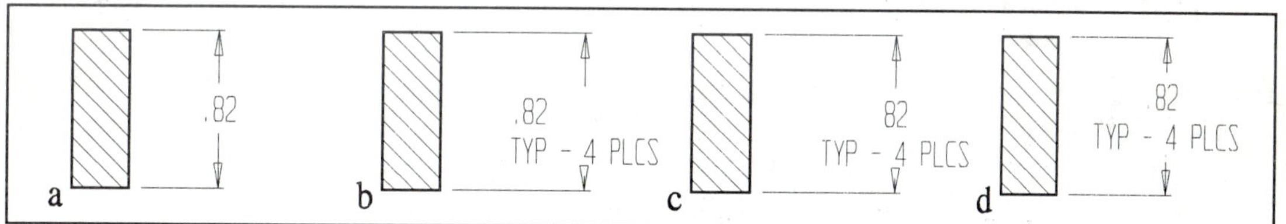

Figure D-9 Adding text to a vertical dimension

If the dimension has separate + and — tolerances—Figure D-10a shows an example—the job is harder. You cannot use the text editor to incorporate text in the dimension, because doing so would disrupt the array, as it did with the radial dimension in Figure D-8b and as you see again here in Figure D-10b. You must add the text as a separate NOTE. And you cannot get Cadkey to shorten the lower leader or remove the lower leader from an existing dimension. Instead, you must create the dimension with the lower leader missing, as it is in Figure D-10a. (If the dimension is already on the drawing with both leaders, you can't fix it but must delete and replace

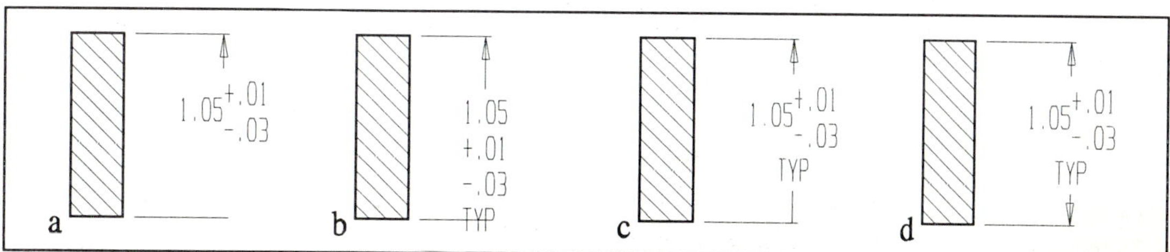

Figure D-10 Second method of adding text

it.) Use DETAIL—SET—WIT/LDR—LEADER—FIRST (or select LDR from the STATUS WINDOW) to eliminate the second leader. Add the note; then use DETAIL—ARR/WIT—ARROWS to replace the missing leader.

Add the missing arrow with DETAIL—ARR/WIT—ARROWS—ENDPTS. Draw the arrow from top to bottom—the point goes on the end you select last. See ARROWS/WITNESS LINES—CONSTRUCTION if you have trouble lining up this new arrow with the upper leader. Construction methods for arrows are much more limited than those for lines, and you need to know the rules.

One way to line up the arrow and the dimension is to use SNAP. If one point on the snap grid does not already coincide with the bottom corner that you are dimensioning to, use DISPLAY—GRD/SNAP—SNAP ALN—ENDENT to put it there. Then use snap to create the arrow and also to put the dimension in its final position. Snap not only lines up the arrow and the dimension; it also puts the point of the arrow squarely on the extension line. Figure D-10d shows the result.

Manual Dimension Mode

```
3 DETAIL
   9 SET
      6 STANDRD
         3 DIM MOD
            1 AUTOMAT
            2 MANUAL
```

Another way to use the text editor is to edit dimensions as you create them.

AUTOMAT is the way Cadkey usually creates dimensions. Cadkey measures the distance you dimension, rounds its value to the correct number of decimal places, adds the tolerances specified by the current SET parameters, and creates the dimension.

MANUAL is automatic in the sense that Cadkey still creates appropriate arrows and extension lines, but manual in the sense that you write the dimension. When you have indicated the distance to be dimensioned, Cadkey puts you in the text editor and displays a line containing a single space followed by the distance given to six decimal places. Add and delete characters as necessary to put the dimension in the form you want; then press F6 (SAVE TX) to create the dimension. Don't forget to delete the leading space.

You can't use manual to add separate + and — tolerances to a dimension. To get this format, create the dimension in automatic mode and edit it later.

DOS

DOS stands for Disk Operating System. It is a group of programs that computer operators use to manage files and to run programs stored on the disk drive(s) of the computer. While you are running Cadkey you have no direct contact with DOS, but you need to know a few things about it just to know the basics of computer operation.

This section is not meant to be a DOS manual. If reading it raises more questions than it answers, you probably need to look at a DOS user's manual or a book on DOS. Another approach is just to use other programs such as word processors and, in the process, gradually absorb the skills that will become second nature to you as you become a more experienced user.

The following discussion is useful even if it does nothing more than introduce the names of some of the concepts you will need to assimilate.

Computer Memory

Two kinds of memory are important to Cadkey users. The first is RAM, which stands for Random Access Memory. RAM holds the information currently in use by the computer. For example, it can hold the main part of the Cadkey program plus the DATABASE for the drawing you are working on. This memory is what computer salesmen are talking about when they say a particular model has one megabyte of RAM. One byte is one character–for example, one letter of the alphabet–and a megabyte is 1,048,576 (= 2^{20}) of them. RAM is volatile memory, which means that you lose it whenever you turn off your computer or whenever a power-line interruption turns off the electricity for about a second.

The second kind of memory is disk storage, which is permanent memory. Built into most present-day computers is a hard disk, which usually can store twenty or more megabytes of information. The floppy disks, 5-1/4" or 3-1/2" in diameter, that you insert in a computer hold smaller amounts of information. Double density 5-1/4" disks store 360 kilobytes (about 360,000 bytes); high density 5-1/4" disks, 720 kilobytes. Double density and high density 3-1/2" disks store 720 kilobytes and 1.44 megabytes. When you save a file (see FILES), you transfer data from RAM to a disk, where you can store the drawing that is on your computer screen.

Files and File Names

The information computers put on disks is stored in files. A special kind of file that contains instructions telling a computer what to do is called a program. The main Cadkey file, CADKEY.EXE, is an example of such a file. A file that contains any other kind of information is usually just called a file. A saved copy of your drawing would be an example.

A DOS file name consists of up to eight alphanumeric characters plus an optional extension consisting of a period followed by up to three characters. The characters may be letters, numbers, and most other symbols, but may not include spaces, extra periods, question marks, or asterisks. If you include an illegal character in a file name, Cadkey ignores your entry and asks, a second time, **Enter part file name ( ):**

Cadkey does not let you pick an extension when you name one of its files. Instead, it reserves the extension for its own use, giving PART files (see FILES) a .PRT extension and PATTERN files a .PTN extension. DRAWING.PRT would be a complete file name, but DRAWING is the name you enter. In many other programs (Word Perfect, for example) you may assign any extension you choose, using the three extra characters to make it easier to remember what each file contains.

Directories

DOS allows you to group files into a tree-like structure made up of directories, each of which may contain files as well as other directories. Cadkey's normal configuration puts PART files in C:\Cadkey\PRT. With this setup, you will find part files on disk C: and in the PRT subdirectory of the Cadkey directory. A complete specification for such a file could be C:\CAD-KEY\PRT\DRAWING.PRT. This specification is usually called the path name of the file. It shows not only the name of the file, but also the path you take to get to it.

Some rules about path names are:

1. When you type in a path name, DOS pays no attention to whether letters are upper case or lower case. You could enter cAdkEY and get the results you want.
2. Put a colon after a letter that designates a disk drive. C: is usually a hard drive; A: and B: are usually floppy disk drives.
3. Use the backslash \ to separate the elements of path names.

The DOS Prompt

A prompt is an indication by the computer that it is ready to do something and is waiting for your input. If you are currently in the Cadkey directory, the DOS prompt, also called the command line, may look like C> or like the more informative C:\CADKEY>. DOS normally uses the shorter prompt, but most computer users expand it to show the current directory. To make this change, enter **prompt PG**. To change it back, enter **prompt**. If you want to get fancy, you can make the prompt line include such things as the current time and date. See the DOS manual for details.

An Application

A commonly used DOS command, the COPY command, shows how directories are used. Suppose you want to copy a PART file from the Cadkey directory on drive C: to a floppy disk in drive A:. You would enter

```
copy c:\cadkey\prt\drawing.prt a:
```

This copy command copies the file DRAWING.PRT from disk C: to disk A:, putting this file in both places.

Often you can use a shortcut. If you are in the PRT subdirectory of the Cadkey directory, you don't need the full path name, but can make the copy by entering

```
copy drawing.prt a:
```

The directory you are in is called the default directory (you will see shortly how to get into a particular directory). It is the directory you see on the prompt line. It is also the directory DOS assumes you mean to use unless you specify otherwise. If the file you want to copy is in the default directory, DOS lets you specify a complete path name to identify the file, but it also lets you use just the file name.

The term default directory actually has two meanings. In DOS, it is whatever directory is current. In Cadkey, it means the directory normally used for a particular purpose. If Cadkey's default directory for part files is C:\CADKEY\PRT, then Cadkey will store your part file there unless you enter a path name that tells it to store the file somewhere else. In other words, when it is time for you to enter the name of a Cadkey part file you wish to store, you can enter either CADKEY\PRT\FILENAME or just FILENAME, with the same results. But if you enter A:\FILENAME, Cadkey will send your file to drive A:.

Cadkey can be reconfigured (see Chapter 4) to make A: the default directory for file storage, in which case part and pattern files will go to disk A: unless you direct them elsewhere.

A word of caution: If you already have a file called DRAWING.PRT on disk A: and you use the copy command to copy another drawing with the same name to that disk, DOS will overwrite the old file with the new one. If you have two different drawings with the same file name, you would lose the old file by copying the new one over it. Many programs, including Cadkey, warn you if you are about to overwrite an existing file. DOS does not.

More DOS Commands

CD (for change directory) changes the default directory. If you are in the main directory of the C: drive—DOS calls this the root directory—and want to get to the part-file directory, enter

cd cadkey\prt

To get back to the root directory, enter either

cd c:\ or cd \

CD does not let you change from one disk drive to another. If you are in C:\CADKEY and want to change to A:, enter A:. One idiosyncrasy—usually a convenient one—of DOS is that if you later enter C:, DOS returns you not to C: but to the last directory you used in that drive, in this case, to C:\CADKEY.

Dir gives you a list of the files and directories in the default directory. **Dir C:\Cadkey\PRT** gives you a list of the files in the C:\Cadkey\PRT directory, no matter what directory is current.

Del deletes a file. Sometimes, when you need room on a disk to store something, you can make that room by deleting files you no longer need. A sample command you could execute from the C: drive is

del a:\drawing.prt

Running Programs

The main Cadkey program is contained in the file named CADKEY.EXE. To run it, you type **cadkey**, leaving off the .EXE part. Some programs have extensions of .COM or .BAT. Again, to initiate the program, enter its name without the extension.

Batch Files

Batch files are a way of automating DOS operations that you execute repeatedly. A practical example for this handbook is one that loads the video driver for Cadkey, loads Cadkey, and, when you have finished your Cadkey session, removes the video driver from memory. You write the batch file just as you would enter the instructions by hand. The following example assumes that Cadkey is installed on drive C:, that it it is in the directory CKLight, and that the video driver is IBMVGA.EXE.

You choose the first part of a batch file name, but you must use .BAT for the extension. CADKEY.BAT is an easy name to remember; CAD.BAT, because it is shorter, makes the batch file easier to execute. This example uses CADKEY.BAT as the batch file name.

Conventional instructions for batch files have you working in DOS. You type **copy con cadkey.bat**, type the batch file instructions, press Return, press ^Z, and press Return. But an easier method, one that makes errors easier to correct, is to use a word processor to create an ASCII text file. Cadkey's TEXT EDITOR will do quite nicely.

Use DETAIL—NOTE—KEYIN to create a note similar to the one that follows. Use upper-case letters, lower-case letters, or a mixture, as you prefer. If your computer setup is different from the one assumed (for example, you may have used a different directory name), make the appropriate changes in your note.

```
C:
cd \CKLight
ibmvga
Cadkey
ibmvga -r
cd \
```

Use DETAIL—NOTE—DUMP NT to save the note. If you want to put the batch file in the main directory of disk C:, enter C:\Cadkey.bat as the file name. If you have a subdirectory for batch files and want to put it there, enter C:\batch\Cadkey.bat (or an appropriate equivalent) as the file name. If you do not yet have such a subdirectory but wish you did, check a book on DOS for information on how to create one and also for how to use the DOS PATH command.

If you need to edit the batch file at some later time, use DETAIL—NOTE—DISK to bring it back into Cadkey as a note. Edit it with DETAIL–CHANGE–EDIT TX, and use DETAIL–NOTE–DUMP NT again to put the edited version back on your disk.

To load Cadkey using this batch file, type Cadkey and press Return. The first entry in the batch file takes you to the right disk drive (important if you are using a PATH command and you are starting from, say, a floppy disk). The second entry takes you to the directory for Cadkey. The third loads the video driver and the fourth loads Cadkey. After you exit Cadkey, DOS find itself still in the middle of the batch file, which removes the video driver from memory and then returns you to the main directory of your hard disk.

Edit

EDIT is one of the entries in Cadkey's main menu. Choices in the edit menu let you (1) adjust the lengths of entities that are too long or too short (see TRIM/EXTEND), (2) divide entities into two or more segments, often leaving their appearance unchanged (see BREAK), (3) bring back entities that were deleted by mistake (see RECALL), and (4) combine entities into groups that can be handled as single units (see GROUP).

Another editing function, but not a part of the EDIT menu, is a word processor that lets you alter the text of notes, labels, and dimensions (see TEXT EDITOR).

ENDENT

For accurate drawing and three-dimensional construction, ENDENT is the most-used option in the POSITION MENU. It causes the cursor to snap precisely to the ends of existing entities. See POSITION MENU for information.

Entity

Cadkey defines an entity as one element of a drawing. LINES, ARCS, CIRCLES, POINTS, FILLETS, DIMENSIONS, POLYLINES, NOTES, LABELS, CROSSHATCHING, ARROWS, and WITNESS LINES are all entities.

The two witness lines, the two arrows, and the number that make up a DIMENSION are a single entity. Similarly, the array of lines resulting from one CROSSHATCH operation is a single entity even though it may fill several widely spaced areas. But entities that have been combined to form GROUPS are not single entities. RECTANGLES, POLYGONS, STRINGS, and SKETCH LINES may or may not be single entities, depending on how they were constructed. See POLYGONS, POLYLINES, AND LINES COMPARED for an explanation.

Entity masking (see SELECTING ENTITIES for a discussion of the MASKING MENU) restricts some operations, letting them apply to only certain types of entities. For example, masking on CROSSHATCH lets the DELETE operation select only crosshatch entities for deletion.

Error Messages

Most of Cadkey's error messages are self-explanatory. For example, if you try to use TRM/EXT—DIVIDE instead of TRM/EXT—DOUBLE to cut an arc out of a circle, Cadkey tells you,

Can only TRIM closed curve with DOUBLE option... press RETURN

Error messages which, like this one, need no explanation, are not discussed here. Also omitted are error messages you are not likely to encounter. Some of the less common error messages that are closely associated with one particular command or group of commands are discussed where the command or commands are discussed.

Break not performed, entity would be too small

If you try to use DIVIDE to break an entity into three parts and if one of the break points is an endpoint of the entity to break, one of the end segments would have a length of zero.

Cannot create file

You get this message if, when you try to save a part file or create a pattern file, you have specified a non-existent directory or have put a space or other illegal character in a file name. Avoid .,;:?=*/\+"< >.

Drive I/O error

Using AUX (or some other name reserved by DOS) as a file name will generate this error message. Select ABORT and accept Cadkey's offer to save your file. Cadkey then exits, and you probably find that your keyboard has locked up and you need to reboot (press Del while holding down Alt and Ctrl). See FILES for an explanation of what happened.

Entity not found

No entities found and **Entity not found** can be puzzling messages. You can see an entity and Cadkey can't. Usually the entity is, for the moment, at least, ineligible for selection. Assume, for example, that you want to trim a number of lines to a height of five inches. You draw a temporary horizontal line at the five-inch level, use the MODAL option of TRM/EXT to trim the lines at the boundary this line defines, and then delete the temporary boundary line. If you try to delete the line before you exit the MODAL command, Cadkey will refuse to select it. Because Cadkey has reserved this line as a boundary for the next line that needs trimming, it is temporarily off limits.

Similarly, if you have just created a dimension and have not yet responded to the **Accept dimension ?** prompt, Cadkey will not let you select that dimension.

If you have used TYPE MASKING earlier in the current routine, or if you have set LEVEL MASKING at any earlier time and forgotten to clear it, you may be blocking Cadkey from seeing the entity you are trying to select. See SELECTING ENTITIES for information on both types of masking.

POLYLINES and POLYGONS are single entities with multiple segments. If you have selected one segment and try to select another, Cadkey gives you an error message because it cannot select the same entity twice.

You cannot use ENDENT, CENTER, or a similar position menu option to snap to a point on an ARROW or a WITNESS LINE. If you try, Cadkey treats the entity as not existing. You can, however, select an arrow or a witness line to MOVE, COPY, or DELETE it.

If you use a WINDOW to select a DIMENSION or LABEL and do not enclose all of the entity, including leaders and witness lines, Cadkey will not select it.

Intersection not found

You can see where the two entities intersect one another, but Cadkey gives you an error message. If Cadkey is currently in 3D mode, the entities are probably at different depths; therefore, in space, they do not intersect. Try switching to 2D mode (see 2D/3D).

Must have a fixed plane to display axes

DISPLAY—AXES—CONST VW generates this error message. Version 3.5 of Cadkey, from which CADKEY Light 1.5 was derived, uses this command sequence, but CADKEY Light 1.5 cannot; hence the error message. CADKEY Light 4.0 does not have this command in its menu and therefore does not give you this error message.

Not a part file

This message appears when you create a file with one version of Cadkey and try to read it with an incompatible version. See CADUTIL for a possible solution.

This message can also mean that a file has become corrupted and is therefore unreadable. This problem, which occurs more often on networks than on individual computers, seems to have no solution.

Part file is in use or unavailable.

If you have tried to save a file using the name of a read-only file, Cadkey gives you this message.

System error

Something is wrong with the disk you are using. Try another.

Trim not performed, entity would be too small

If you try to use DIVIDE to trim the center out of an entity and if one of the trimming points is an endpoint of the entity to trim, one of the end segments would have a length of zero.

Write error

You get this message when you try to save a file. It means that the disk you want to save it on has too little free space to hold it. Try saving on another disk.

For a particular combination of circumstances, simply switching disks won't work: (1) Your computer is a workstation with no hard disk and only one floppy drive, (2) your drawing is complex, (3) the computer has limited RAM (random access memory—see DOS), and (4) Cadkey is configured to put overflow files on your floppy disk. When your drawing gets too big to fit in the available RAM, Cadkey stores part of the DATABASE for your drawing in these overflow files. Under these conditions, removing one floppy to put in another leaves the computer with an incomplete drawing file, and Cadkey cannot save it.

You need to transfer some files to another disk or delete files you no longer need and thus free up space on the disk. The SYSTEM COMMANDS that let you get to DOS won't work—the computer's memory is too full to handle them. Take your disk to another computer on the network.

If you are not on a network but are in trouble because your hard disk is full, the problem is more serious. Deleting entities won't free up RAM because Cadkey's DATABASE retains records of all deleted entities.

If you cannot use any of these methods for saving your drawing as a part file, you may be able to save it as a pattern file (see FILES). Pattern files require considerably less memory than part files.

TROUBLESHOOTING (see the subsection titled Sluggishness) offers related advice, directed toward preventing the problem rather than curing it after it occurs.

Exit

EXIT lets you leave Cadkey. The command is Alt-E. Although this looks like one of the IMMEDIATE MODE COMMANDS, you can execute it only from the main menu. As part of the EXIT routine, Cadkey gives you the opportunity to save your drawing.

The only way you can exit a drawing without exiting Cadkey is to load another file (see FILE). Chapter 2 suggests that you plan ahead by creating an empty file named **blank** and that you load this file whenever you finish one drawing and want to start another. An alternative, DELETE—SELECT—ALL DSP—ALL, clears the screen but does not clear Cadkey's DATABASE of the records of the deleted entities. These old records can slow Cadkey's performance and will bring back unwanted entities if you use the RECALL command. (See Cleaning up a Part File, under FILES.)

Extend

Cadkey can make a line or arc longer or shorter by extending or trimming it. You select an entity as the boundary to which the line or arc is extended or at which it is trimmed. See TRIM/EXTEND for details.

Files

FILES are drawings stored on computer disks. The two most important types of Cadkey files are PART and PATTERN files. **PART** files are records of entire drawings. (Machinists commonly call the objects they make "parts," regardless of whether they are destined to be parts of larger assemblies.) **PATTERN** files, analogous to subroutines in computer programs, are drawings you can use as parts of PART drawings. For example, you can create a pattern for a circuit element and import that pattern repeatedly into circuit diagrams.

```
5 FILES
  1 PART
    1 SAVE    ^F
    2 LOAD
    3 LST/LOAD
  2 PATTERN
    1 CREATE
    2 RETRIEVE
    3 LST/RTRV
  6 LIST FMT
    1 SHORT
    2 VERBOSE
```

Part Files

SAVE records the part file on a disk. Cadkey asks for a file name (8 characters or less; Cadkey adds the extension .PRT). The file name may include a path (see DOS): A:\Bracket stores the file Bracket.PRT on disk A:. A:\Welder\Bracket stores it in the Welder directory of disk A:.

The message **File already exists, replace it ?** usually means that you have saved an earlier version of the same drawing. Normally you press F2 for YES, replacing the now-obsolete version with the current one. But sometimes this message means you picked a name assigned to an earlier drawing. If so, you should save the current file under a different name to avoid overwriting the earlier file.

Two other ways to save a drawing are to EXIT Cadkey or to LOAD another part file. Both commands include a save routine.

Your drawing may include some entities that do not show at the moment because they are beyond the edge of the screen or because they are on LEVELS that are hidden. These entities are nevertheless included in the file you save.

Write error... press RETURN probably means the disk you are trying to write to is full. Try a different disk. If this is not possible, try saving your file as a PATTERN. A pattern file is smaller and may fit where the part file would not. If you use this approach, be sure the screen shows everything you want included. See ERROR MESSAGES for more detail.

If you see **Cannot create file... press RETURN**, you may have directed the file to a nonexistent directory. Look first for a spelling error.

System error means you have a bad disk. Select ABORT from the menu. Don't be intimidated by the message **Save part before terminating ? (YES)** that appears on the prompt line. Pressing Esc returns you to your drawing.

LOAD reads a file from disk storage and loads it into Cadkey, replacing whatever is on the screen. The filename you enter does not need to include its .PRT extension.

Before Cadkey loads the new file, it gives you a chance to save the current drawing. If you opt not to save it, it is lost when the new file is loaded.

LST/LOAD (or LIST/LD, depending on your Cadkey version) is a second way to load a PART file. Cadkey asks the name of the directory containing your files. As part of the prompt, Cadkey names the DEFAULT directory for part files, perhaps prt/. (Sometimes Cadkey is careless in typing the backslash, \, and gets the angle wrong. Don't follow that example.)

If this is the directory you want, press Return to accept this choice. Otherwise, enter the correct directory, perhaps A:\. Cadkey displays a list of all part files located there. Use the cursor to select the one you want. As with LOAD, Cadkey gives you a chance to save the current drawing before it loads the new one.

Cleaning up a Part File

As you work on a drawing, you can expect to delete a lot of entities. These entities are not permanently lost. Cadkey keeps a record of them in its DATABASE. If you want to see them again, select EDIT—RECALL—ALL—ALL (see RECALL). Cadkey will dump all of them back on your screen.

If there are many deleted entities, they can give you two problems: (1) Cadkey works more slowly. Every time Cadkey reads through its database (and it does this every time you select an entity), it must read through records of deleted entities that are mixed with the records of current ones. (2) If you ever need the RECALL operation, you might bring back far too many entities.

When you save a drawing, Cadkey does not include these records of deleted entities in the file it records on your disk. If you have done some heavy editing, and if you are fairly sure you will never want to see those deleted entities again, consider cleaning up the database by saving your drawing and then reloading it.

The first thing to ask Cadkey to do is not SAVE, but LOAD. Select FILES—PART—LOAD. Cadkey asks: **Save current part first ? (YES)**. Press Return to accept the default (YES) and save the file. The prompt line changes to **Enter part file name (filename):**, where the name in parentheses is for the current drawing. If you have not yet assigned a file name, there will be nothing inside the parentheses. If the file name is appropriate, press Return to accept it. If not, enter the name you want to use. If Cadkey tells you **File already exists, replace it ? (NO)**, read the next two paragraphs. Otherwise, you can skip them.

> A file already exists if the file name is the name of a file you have saved earlier. If the existing file is just an earlier version of the current one, you probably want to press F2 for YES and overwrite the earlier file. Cadkey saves the drawing on the screen first; then it deletes the earlier one. (This sequence assures that the earlier version of the file is not erased if something goes wrong with the SAVE part of this operation.)
>
> If the existing file is a drawing you want to keep, press Return to accept the default of NO. Cadkey again prompts you to **Enter part file name (filename):** Enter a new name for the current drawing.

The message **Saving part file... please wait** appears. Next you see **Enter part file name (filename):**. The name in parentheses is the name of the file you just saved, and the name Cadkey is asking for is the name of the file you want to load. Because they are the same, press Return to accept this default file name. The message **Loading part file... please wait** appears. Your drawing disappears; then it reappears, unencumbered by records of deleted entities.

Pattern Files

CREATE can make a pattern of an entire drawing or of any part of a drawing. The SELECTION MENU appears (see SELECTING ENTITIES), letting you specify which entities to include in the pattern. You specify a BASE POSITION, which is a position you will use to place the pattern when you retrieve it into a drawing. Finally, Cadkey asks for a file name. As with PART files, you may use up to 8 characters. Cadkey supplies the extension .PTN.

RETRIEVE asks you to make the following choices. The entry in parentheses at the end of each prompt is the default choice. If that is the choice you wish to make, just press Return.

Enter pattern file name ():

Group pattern entities ? (YES) (See GROUP. Grouping may prove convenient later—if you need to remove a bolt from an assembly drawing you can delete it in a single operation rather than deleting it line by line.)

Enter group name (): This prompt appears only if you answered yes to the preceding one.

Choose level option (CUR-LEV)

1 **CUR-LEV** puts all entities on the currently active LEVEL.

2 **ENT-LEV** puts entities on the levels they had when the pattern was created. (If part of your pattern fails to show on the screen, some of its entities may be on levels that are hidden because you have not yet used them in the current drawing. Use DISPLAY–LEVELS–ADD or DISPLAY–LEVELS–LIST to make them visible. See LEVEL for an explanation,)

3 **KEY-IN** puts all entities on whatever level you enter from the keyboard.

4 **OFFSET** asks for a level offset value, which may be positive or negative. If you enter an offset of 3, an entity that was on level 5 when the pattern was created will be placed on level 8. If you enter 0, the results are the same as if you had selected the ENT-LEV option. If any of the resulting levels are outside the legal range of 1 to 256, the entities are placed on the currently active level.

Enter scale factor (1) => You can make the copy larger or smaller than the original.

Enter rotation angle (0) => You can make the copy at any angle.

Indicate pattern base position / Cursor-indicate position You are of course free to select options other than CURSOR from the menu options window.

If you are, for example, copying the pattern of a bolt and want to make the next copy larger or smaller or show it at a different angle, press F10 to back up to the place where you can reenter the new parameters.

LST/RTRV (or LIST/RTV) gives you another way to load a PATTERN file. Cadkey asks the name of the directory containing your files and suggests whatever has been configured as the default directory for pattern files, perhaps ptn\. Press Return to accept this default or enter the correct directory, perhaps A:\. Cadkey displays a list of all pattern files located there, letting you use the cursor to select the one you want. The procedure from this point on is like that for FILES–PATTERN–RETRIEV.

List Format

LIST FMT controls the format that LST/LOAD uses to display the directories of PART and PATTERN files. **SHORT** would list a file as **BRACKET.** **VERBOSE** would list it as **BRACKET 19454 08-06-90 11:21a**, where 19454 is file size in bytes and 08-06-90 11:21a tells when you saved the file.

Notes and Problems

File names that create problems: If you make a pattern of an auxiliary view, **do not name it AUX**. Two of my students learned this the hard way as they watched the computer slowly wipe their drawings off the screen. When this happens, the computer locks up; that is, it refuses to respond to any keyboard entry. Your only choices are to (1) reboot the computer by pressing Delete while holding down both the Alt and Ctrl keys or (2) turn the computer off and then on. Either way, your drawing is lost. (You did save it recently, didn't you?)

If you are luckier (not all computer setups react the same way), Cadkey leaves the drawing on the screen but tells you **Drive I/O error** and gives you three choices: ABORT, RETRY, and IGNORE. ABORT is the only choice that helps. Select it and you see **Save part before terminating ? (YES)**. In spite of this ominous message, you may be able to press Esc and get back to your drawing; however, things are not well. Save the drawing and exit Cadkey. When you do, you will probably find that the computer, in a delayed reaction, has locked up.

This is not a Cadkey problem; the problem is with DOS. DOS reserves the names CON, PRN, LPT1, LPT2, LPT3, AUX, COM1, COM2, and CLOCK$ for device names and reacts decisively if you use them to name *any* kind of file. Fortunately, the only name in this list that you are likely to choose is AUX.

When to save: You would be wise to save your drawing regularly. You can set the CONFIGURATION program to have Cadkey do this for you (see Chapter 4), or you can make a habit of doing this yourself. Times to save are:

1. Just before operations involving many entities (COPY, for example), when a wrong move would produce results difficult to unscramble.
2. After an extensive editing session. See Cleaning up a Part File, earlier in this section.
3. Before a thunderstorm.
4. Every fifteen minutes or so (just press ^F). Most students learn this the hard way. When something goes wrong and a student loses two hours' work, you would expect, the next time the class meets, to see other members of the class saving their work regularly. This doesn't seem to happen.

Path names: In most schools (check with the lab manager) you will be expected to save your files on your own floppy disk, and Cadkey is probably configured to direct files there. If, however, the default directory is the computer's hard disk, you should precede your file names with a floppy drive address, probably A:\. It is a matter of courtesy to avoid cluttering the school's hard disk, and a file stored on your own floppy is more likely to be there the next time you need it. To confirm that your file goes to the right place, watch the lights on the disk drives.

Other File Types

An HPGL (Hewlett-Packard Graphics Language) file is one that can be read by other computer programs such as WordPerfect and PageMaker. The way to create an HPGL file is to create it as a PLOT file. See PLOT for details.

If you press Alt-F, Cadkey saves whatever is on the screen as a Dr. Halo slide file, readable by Dr. Halo and several desktop publishing programs. Files thus saved are named S1.SLD, S2.SLD, etc. After you exit Cadkey, it's a good idea to rename these files; otherwise, the next time you start Cadkey and create slide files, those you create will have these same file names and will overwrite the files you created earlier.

The file created by one version of Cadkey may not be readable by another version. See CADUTIL for a utility that can take a file from an early version of Cadkey and make it readable by a later version.

You can save a NOTE as a separate file rather than as part of a part file. See the FILE and DUMP NT options under NOTES.

Fill

To fill an entity means to replace the usual outline form with a solid area of color. Entities you can fill are POLYGONS and closed POLYLINES (see OUT/FIL under ATTRIBUTES). You can also fill the BOLD style of letters (see LETTERING). See CROSSHATCHING for another way to shade a closed area.

Fillet

Typically, metal castings have rounded inside corners, called fillets, and rounded outside corners, called rounds. Machined parts that would otherwise have sharp corners often have rounds to make them easier to handle and fillets to relieve stress concentration at inside corners. Chamfers (beveled edges) are another way to eliminate sharp corners in machined parts. Cadkey groups fillets, rounds, and chamfers under the heading of FILLET. (Pronounce Fillet as spelled, with the accent on the first syllable.)

```
1 CREATE
  6 FILLET
    1 ARC
      1 TRIM
      2 NO TRIM
    2 CHAMFER
```

ARC—TRIM is most frequently used to round the corner where two lines intersect, using an arc tangent to each line. Enter the arc radius, then select the lines. Cadkey replaces the sharp corner with the rounded one, trimming away portions of entities that extend past the arc. If the lines are too short to meet, the TRIM function extends them to meet the arc. Figure F-1a shows a corner that was rounded in this way.

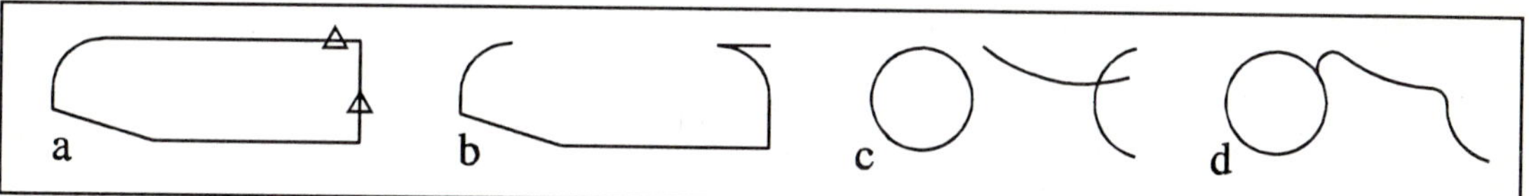

Figure F-1 A chamfer, a problem fillet, and fillets to arcs and circles

In the same way, ARC—TRIM also creates arcs tangent to any combination of lines, arcs, or circles. Figures F-1c and F1-d show a before-and-after example. Arcs and lines are trimmed where they meet the fillet; circles are left untrimmed. With a circle, Cadkey complains, "Can only TRIM closed curve with DOUBLE option... press RETURN," but as soon as you press Return it draws the fillet. (If you draw the fillet between two circles, you get the error message twice.) An arc or circle does not need to intersect the other entity before the fillet is created. It just needs to be close enough that a fillet of the specified radius can join the two entities. POLYGONS and POLYLINES give more limited results. They accept fillets only in NO TRIM mode and only if the construction mode is 2D (see 2D/3D).

When you select the entities for the fillet to join, the rules are like those for the TRIM/-EXTEND operations, and they tell you to put the cursor on the part of each entity that you want to keep. Figure F-1 shows what happens if you don't. The triangles in Figure F-1a show two selection points. The one on the right is properly placed, but the one on the top line is too near the corner. As Figure F-1b shows, Cadkey saved the wrong part of the top line. EDIT—TRM/EXT—FIRST is one way to repair the damage. For more detail on handling this problem, see the section on Trimming and Extending in Chapter 2 (look for Figure 2-24).

ARC—NO TRIM creates an arc as described for ARC—TRIM, but it does no trimming or extending.

CHAMFER creates a beveled corner instead of a rounded one, works only in TRIM mode, and works only with LINE entities.

Specify the size of the chamfer by giving the 1st distance and the 2nd distance, telling Cadkey how far back from the intersection to trim the first and second lines you select. Cadkey draws a diagonal between the ends of the two lines. Figure F-1a shows a .15 x .5 chamfer.

The FILLET—CHAMFER command differs from most in that it operates in 3D mode regardless of the 2D/3D mode setting. Because it always creates the chamfer in the plane of the two entities, it never accepts entities that do not lie in the same plane. The two FILLET—ARC commands work in a more typical manner. In 2D mode they create arcs at the current depth, and in 3D mode they create them in the plane of the entities the arcs join. See 2D/3D for details.

Grid

The visible grid is an array of regularly spaced dots that make it easier to judge distances on the screen. Because it is solely a construction aid, it does not show when the drawing is printed or plotted. Initially, it is turned off.

Cadkey also has an invisible SNAP grid (see SNAP), used to position the cursor precisely. Although the two grids coincide when Cadkey starts up, they are independent. For example, the PgUp and PgDn keys change the snap grid spacing without affecting the visible grid.

```
6  DISPLAY
   7  GRID/SNAP
      1  GRID DSP*   ^G
         1  OFF
         2  PRIM DSP
         3  ALL DSP
      2  GRID INC
      3  GRID ALN
      4  GRID=SNP
```

*The STATUS WINDOW also gives access to this command.

GRID DSP turns the grid display on and off.

OFF turns the grid off.

PRIM DSP turns the grid on. If you have selected the four-VIEWPORT display, the grid appears only in the viewport you have designated as the primary one. If you are using a single viewport, the grid shows regardless of the view.

ALL DSP turns the grid on in every viewport.

GRID INC sets the grid increments—the spacings of the grid points. You set horizontal and vertical spacings separately. These spacings are to the same scale as the drawing. If the drawing shows half size on the screen, a one-inch grid will have points spaced half an inch apart on the screen.

GRID ALN brings a point on the grid into coincidence with a selected point. Typically, you would use ENDENT or a similar positioning technique to select a specific point on the drawing.

GRID=SNP: (SNAP is a function that makes the cursor snap to an invisible snap grid, which may or may not coincide with the visible grid.) GRID=SNP adjusts the spacing and position of the visible grid to make it coincide with this snap grid. (See also SNAP for the opposite process: SNAP=GRD fits the snap grid to the visible grid.)

If no grid appears, its points may be too closely spaced. There is a limit, set by the CONFIGURATION program, to the number of grid points Cadkey will show in each viewport. As you reduce drawing SCALE and the points become more closely spaced, you reach a point where Cadkey refuses to draw the grid.

Group

Grouping a collection of entities lets you handle the entities as a unit. Suppose you have drawn an office layout and need to remove a desk. Suppose also that the entities for each desk have been grouped. You press ^Q to initiate the DELETE command and select one entity in the desk. Cadkey responds with:

Entity belongs to a group – choose selection option (GROUP)

1 GROUP
2 SUBGRP
3 ENTITY

Choosing GROUP (by pressing F1 or by pressing Return to accept the default) marks every desk for deletion. Choosing SUBGRP marks one desk. Choosing ENTITY marks only the line you selected. If you hit F2 and then hit Return, the desk disappears.

You can create groups in two ways. First, certain Cadkey routines (PATTERN is the most useful of these) offer you the option of creating a group. Second, the MAKE command lets you group whatever set of entities you select.

You see the first method when you create a regular polygon using the LINE—N-GON command. Cadkey asks:

Group entities (NO) ?

If you choose YES, Cadkey responds:

Enter group name ( ):

You might enter **polygon**. (Cadkey accepts only the first eight characters: If you enter tetrahedron, the assigned name would be tetrahed.) If you now create a second polygon, the prompts [with the assumed responses in brackets] become:

Enter group name (polygon):	[Return]
Group already exists... create subgroup #2 ?	[YES]

The GROUP Commands

2 EDIT
  5 GROUP
    1 MAKE
    2 ADD TO
    3 DEGROUP
    4 DELETE
    5 LIST

MAKE groups existing entities. If you assign a group name already in use, Cadkey adds a subgroup to the existing group. Otherwise, Cadkey creates a new group. Select the entities to be included by using any option in the SELECTION MENU. If the entities already belong to a group, Cadkey removes them from that group when you assign them to the new one.

After you select the entities to include in the group, Cadkey returns you to the selection menu, letting you select additional entities, which Cadkey adds to the same group and subgroup. Press F10 if you want the next set of entities you select to go in a different subgroup.

ADD TO adds entities to an existing subgroup. Enter the group name (which you probably know) and the subgroup number (which you probably do not know). CONTROL—VERIFY—ATTRIB (see VERIFY) gives you this data.

Occasionally LIST or the VERIFY command will show a subgroup number of zero. With this number, ADD TO will not work. The cure is to use the MAKE command on the group to give it a respectable subgroup number.

DEGROUP lets you remove one or more entities from a subgroup without deleting them from the drawing. If you remove all entities, the subgroup nevertheless remains, like an empty file folder.

DELETE removes the group name from the list provided by the LIST command and degroups the affected entities without deleting the entities.

Two other commands—DELETE from the main menu and ^Q—not only delete the entities in a group or subgroup, but also remove the affected group or subgroup from Cadkey's list.

LIST shows you a list of group names plus the number of subgroups in each group. Such a list can, for example, tell you how many desks, partition panels, etc. you have in an office layout.

Some Rules

Each group may contain up to 256 subgroups.

If you COPY a hexagon that is a subgroup, you do not create a new subgroup. Cadkey Light 1.5 expands your single subgroup to include two hexagons. CADKEY Light 4.0 does not put the copy in any group. To make the copy a new subgroup, follow COPY with the MAKE command.

The connecting lines that the JOIN command produces do not belong to any group.

The subgroups of a single group do not all have to be alike. The group DESK could even include one subgroup representing a wastebasket.

Some Advice

In the opening example, pressing F2 to delete a desk from an office layout selects in one stroke all the entities for that desk. But pressing F1 by accident would select *all* the desks, and if you are careless you could watch half your drawing disappear. To be safe, watch the prompt line. It lets you see what is happening before it is too late: **Select entity #65** means that Cadkey has selected 64 entities; and if you have eight desks, each with eight entities, Cadkey just selected them all. Pressing Esc or pressing F10 twice lets you cancel all 64 selections and start over.

If you accidentally delete a group or subgroup, the RECALL command can help you retrieve it, but not as a unit. When entities are deleted, the record showing which group and subgroup they belonged to is lost. Your only choices are RECALL—ALL, which recalls every entity deleted since the file was last loaded, and RECALL—LAST, which recalls only a single entity. SAVE your drawing before you try the RECALL—ALL option. It may dump so many entities that you'll prefer retrieving your incomplete but uncluttered version. See RECALL for other suggestions.

Immediate Mode Commands

To initiate an immediate mode command, press the appropriate letter key while holding down the Alt key or the Ctrl key. The obvious advantage is convenience. A less obvious but more important advantage is that you can execute these commands from any point in the Cadkey menus without having to back out of work in progress.

An example: During a MOVE operation, because an area of the drawing is crowded, you have trouble selecting one of the entities to be moved. Alt-W lets you draw a WINDOW around the problem area, expanding it to fill the screen. You make the selection, press Alt-B to restore the drawing to its original size, and pick up the MOVE operation where you left off.

Some operations include steps that cannot be interrupted by an immediate mode command. While you are keying in the text of a NOTE, Cadkey will not let you use Ctrl-Q to delete an entity. It will, however, let you use Ctrl-A to change the direction of dimension-line arrows at any point in the process of creating a dimension. If you aren't sure how Cadkey is responding, watch the history line along the top of the screen. When an immediate mode command is active, you see an entry in reverse video at the end of the line.

The table on the next page lists, but does not explain, all immediate mode commands. For easy reference, the back cover of this book repeats this list. However, these commands are most useful if you don't have to look up the key combinations each time you use them. The letter is the easier part to remember. Alt-A, for example, executes AUTOSCALE, which automatically scales the drawing to make it just fill the screen. But it's easy to confuse Alt-A with Ctrl-A, which reverses the direction of dimension-line arrows. As a start, remember that all commands affecting the size and orientation of the image on the screen are Alt-key commands. Alt-X, which changes color, is another Alt-key command. Otherwise, the commands you are most likely to use, at least for the first few Cadkey sessions, are Ctrl-key commands.

Ctrl is shown as ^ throughout the book. ^A represents Ctrl-A. This is a common notation and one you should be familiar with, but it can pose a problem: One of your classmates may type ^, type A, and then wonder why nothing happens. The reason for using this notation is to make some of the commands easier to remember. The difference in appearance of ^A and Alt-A may help people with visual memory remember which is which.

```
5 FILES
  1 PART
    1 SAVE     ^F
    2 LOAD
    3 LST/LOAD
  2 PATTERN
    1 CREATE
    2 RETRIEVE
    3 LST/RTRV
```

Each word shown in UPPER CASE on the next page is the heading of a topic that gives you more detail. When you turn to that topic, you will often see a menu outline like the one on the right, showing in this case that Cadkey's menu system lets you save a file by pressing F5 for FILES, F1 for PART, and F1 for SAVE. Inconspicuously added to the menu outline, and typically not mentioned in the text, is the information that the immediate-mode command ^F does the same thing.

The STATUS WINDOW offers an alternative to over half of these immediate mode commands. This window tells you the settings of the parameters it lists (for example, whether SNAP is on or off), and it lets you change that setting by moving the cursor into the window. In the table on the next page, the right-hand column shows which commands you can access through the status window.

Ctrl-Key Commands:		Shown in Status Window
^A	reverses the direction of dimension-line ARROWS.	Yes
^B	determines which witness lines show in a dimension. See ARROWS/WITNESS LINES—CONTROL.	Yes
^D	sets the working DEPTH for three-dimensional construction.	Yes
^F	saves the drawing. See FILE.	
^G	turns the visible GRID on and off.	Yes
^L	assigns the LEVEL on which subsequent entities will be drawn.	Yes
^Q	DELETES entities.	
^R	REDRAWS the display.	
^T	turns CURSOR tracking on and off.	
^U	RECALLS (undeletes) the last entity deleted.	
^V	selects view or world COORDINATES.	Yes
^W	selects construction mode. See 2D/3D.	Yes
^X	turns SNAP on and off.	Yes

ZOOM and Related Commands—those that change the size or position of the drawing on the computer screen (see ZOOM for details):

Alt-A	Autoscale scales the drawing to fit the screen.	
Alt-B	Back-1 restores the view preceding the last zoom command.	
Alt-D	Double makes the drawing twice as large.	
Alt-H	Half cuts the drawing size in half.	
Alt-P	Pan moves the drawing up, down, or sideways.	
Alt-S	Scale changes the drawing size to the scale you specify.	Yes
Alt-V	changes to another VIEW.	Yes
Alt-W	Window expands a rectangular area to make it fill the screen.	

ATTRIBUTE Settings—those that control the appearance of lines (see ATTRIBUTES for details):

Alt-T	gives solid, dashed, etc. line types.	Yes
Alt-X	controls colors on the screen and pen selection for plots.	Yes
Alt-Y	sets line width.	Yes
Alt-Z	assigns pen numbers to be used for plotted drawings.	Yes

Other Alt Functions:

Alt-L	LINE LIMITS This command is not functional in CADKEY Light.	
Alt-M	Type masking limits the types of entities Cadkey can select for the current command. See SELECTING ENTITIES.	
Alt-N	Level masking limits the levels from which Cadkey can select in subsequent commands. See SELECTING ENTITIES.	Yes
Alt-R	reverses the direction in which Cadkey reads its DATABASE.	Yes

Alt-E EXIT (available only from main menu)

Join

JOIN makes copies of entities and adds lines linking the copy to the original. The joining lines connect the endpoints of LINES and ARCS, the corners of POLYLINES and POLYGONS, and the 3:00 o'clock points of CIRCLES. Where two entities meet, that is, where the endpoint of one entity coincides with the endpoint of another, Cadkey eliminates one of the joining lines to keep the line from being double.

To construct a figure like the one in Figure J-1, start in view 1 by creating a single twelve-sided LINE N-GON. Switch to view 2, where you see this decagon on edge, looking like a single straight line. (You may have to press Alt-A to see it.) Use X-FORM—2D ROT—JOIN if you have CADKEY Light 1.5, or X-FORM—ROTATE—JOIN if you have CADKEY Light 4.0, to produce 36 copies spaced ten degrees apart. Pick a rotation origin on an extension of the line you see in view 2. Figure J-1 shows what the result looks like in view 7.

See MOVE/COPY/JOIN for more detail on the JOIN command.

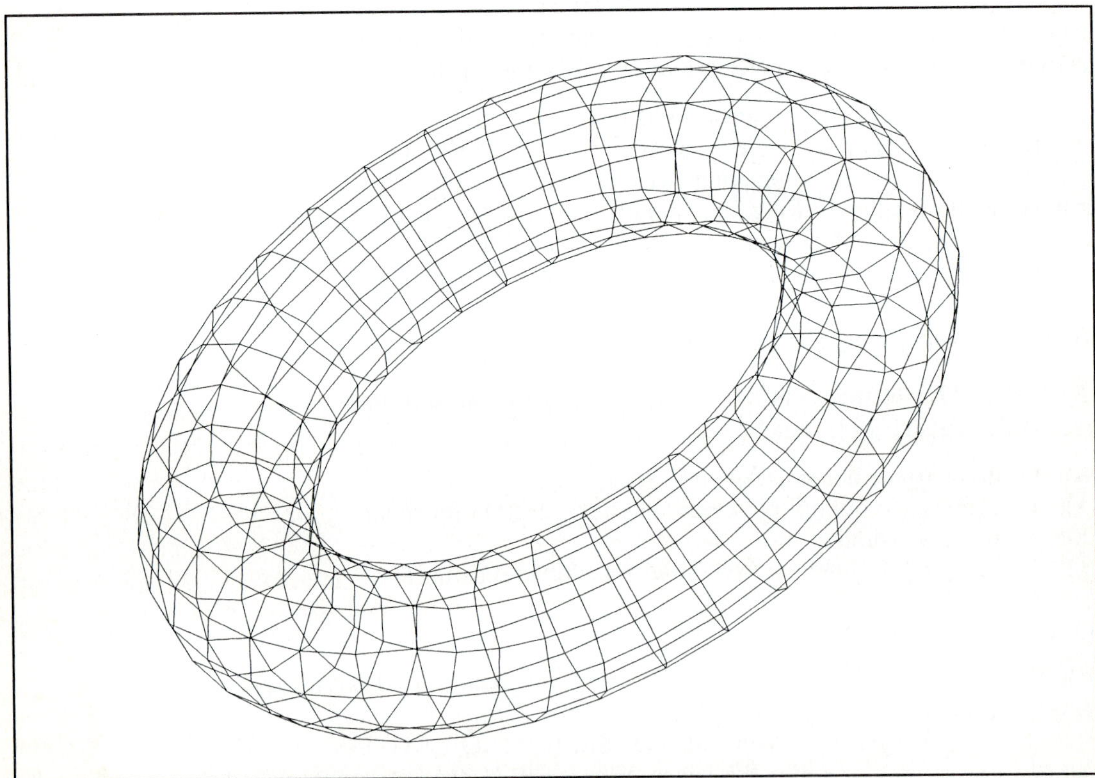

Figure J-1 Design created by the JOIN command

Label

Figure L-1 Label

3 DETAIL
3 LABEL

A label is a NOTE with an arrow. Labels may contain up to 128 characters per line and 1024 characters altogether. They show only in the view in which they were created.

To create a label, type in the text, pressing Return once to start a new line of text and selecting SAVE TX (F6) to end the label. Indicate the text position, use the cursor to show Cadkey which side of the text the leader (the arrow) should start from, and use the cursor to place the point of the leader. Cadkey asks, **Accept label? (YES)**. If you press either F2 or Return to select YES, the label is complete and Cadkey is ready to put another copy of the same label somewhere else.

If you select NO, you have three ways to make changes: You can reposition the tip. You can press F10 to back up a step and change the side where the leader starts. Or you can press F10 twice to remove the label from the screen and reposition the text.

Rules and Comments

As you type in a label, you see the menu of the TEXT EDITOR in the menu options window. Usually you can ignore all of the options except SAVE TX. The other options are most apt to be useful when you write long labels or do extensive editing.

When you place a label on your drawing, Cadkey normally puts the lower left corner of the first line of text at the cursor. You can change this alignment point; for example, you can put the center of the first line of text at the cursor. See LETTERING for ways to do this. Changing this *alignment* point does not change the *selection* point for labels. To select a label for editing, deletion, etc., put the cursor near the lower left corner of the first line of text.

Unlike NOTES, labels cannot show the text at an angle. Even 2D ROT (CADKEY Light 1.5) or ROTATE (CADKEY Light 4.0) rotates the leader but leaves the text horizontal and usually in an awkward position (see MOVE/COPY/JOIN). If you need a label at an angle, use NOTE for the text; then see ARROWS/WITNESS LINES—CONSTRUCTION for ways to add a leader.

The leader starts with a horizontal segment two letter heights long, opposite the beginning or end of the first line of text.

If the VER DIM option (see DIMENSIONING STANDARDS) is set to NO, Cadkey skips the **Accept label? (YES)** question and automatically accepts each label as you create it.

Modifying Labels

DETAIL—CHANGE—TXT POS lets you move the text of a label without changing the position of the tip of the arrow. Often it is easier to accept a label you know is not right and move it later than it is to fuss with positioning when you are creating the label.

DETAIL—SET—EDIT TX lets you change the text in an existing note. See TEXT EDITOR.

DETAIL—SET—TEXT offers several commands to control the size and style of lettering. The choices you make for NOTES apply equally to labels (see LETTERING).

DETAIL—CHANGE—TXT ATT lets you change the size and style of lettering in completed labels. DETAIL—UPDATE (see UPDATE) is another way to change text attributes.

Leader

A LEADER is a line with an arrowhead. If you want to create a straight-line leader (the type used in dimensioning), see ARROWS/WITNESS LINES—CONSTRUCTION. If you want a leader attached to a NOTE, with the leader pointing to the spot where the note applies, see LABEL.

Lettering

Three sets of commands control the size, shape, and style of the letters and the numbers used in DIMENSIONS, NOTES, and LABELS. The SET commands determine what the attributes of newly created lettering will be. CHANGE and UPDATE change the attributes of text you have already created. Although CHANGE and UPDATE come before SET in the menu outline, the SET commands are more fundamental and appear first in the discussion.

```
3 DETAIL
  7 CHANGE
    1 TXT ATT
      1 FONT
        1 BOX
        2 BOLD
      2 HEIGHT
      3 NOT ANG
      4 ASPECT
      5 MIRROR
      6 SLANT
      7 FILL
      8 DONE
    2 TXT POS
  8 UPDATE
  9 SET
    4 TEXT
      1 DIM HT        DH*
      2 NOTE HT       NH*
      3 DIM FNT       DF*
        1 BOX
        2 BOLD
      4 NOT FNT       NF*
        1 BOX
        2 BOLD
      5 DIM PLC
      6 NOT PLC
      7 NOT ANG       RT*
      8 CHR ASP       AS*
```

*These choices, labeled as shown, appear in the STATUS WINDOW.

The SET Commands

Some of the set commands apply only to dimensions; others, to notes and labels. Because CHR ASP is the only command that applies to all lettering, the size and shape of the numbers you use in dimensions are largely independent of the size and shape of the letters you use in notes and labels.

DIM HT and **NOT HT** (dimension height and note height) are subject to the scale of the drawing. If you call for letters 1/4" high, Cadkey shows them the same height as a 1/4" rectangle. If your final printout is a half-size drawing, and if you want lettering to be 1/8" tall, set dimension and note heights to 1/4".

Cadkey's default value for lettering height depends on the units chosen in the CONFIGURATION file. This height is 0.3 inch, 8 millimeters, 0.025 foot, 0.8 centimeter, 0.008333 yard, or 0.008 meter. Cadkey lets you assign any height between 0.00005 and 10000. The numbers for the height limits (not the default heights) are the same, regardless which units the configuration file calls for.

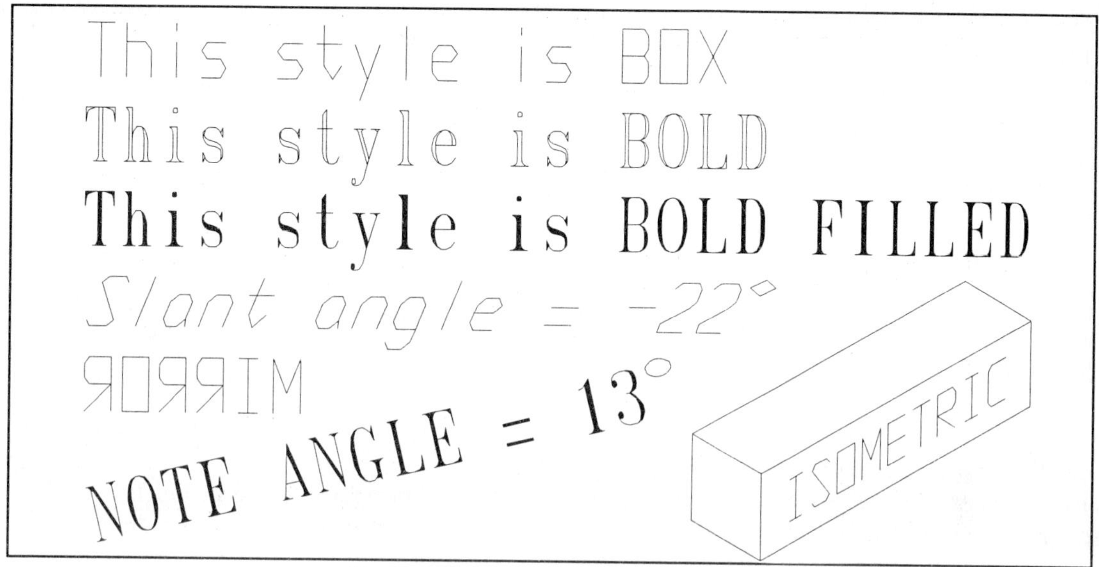

Figure L-2 Choices for text attributes

If text is too small to show clearly on the screen, Cadkey shows it as a line. The same text is often clearly readable in plots and printouts.

DIM FNT and **NOT FNT** (dimension font and note font) let you choose between two lettering styles, BOX and BOLD, shown in Figure L-2. The default is BOX. With either font, Cadkey asks you to make two choices:

Enter text slant angle =>

For vertical letters, press Return to accept the default angle of zero. For slanted letters, enter an angle between —31° and 31°. The traditional angle for slanted engineering lettering is -22°. (Don't enter the degree symbol, but do remember the minus sign. It's there because of Cadkey's convention of assigning negative angles to clockwise rotations.)

Fill font ?

Figure L-2 includes samples of filled and unfilled BOLD fonts. For BOX fonts, the two styles are the same; nevertheless, Cadkey keeps track of what you order. The difference shows up only if you change completed text from box to bold. If you chose filled box letters when you created the text, Cadkey will fill the bold text.

If you want bold lettering, it's often best to use box initially and change to bold when the drawing is complete. Bold text slows REDRAW time.

DIM PLC and **NOT PLC** (dimension placement and note placement) determine what point in a dimension, note, or label falls at the cursor when you place the text. For dimensions, this point is normally the center of the number, or, if there are tolerances, the center of the array of numbers. For notes and labels, it is normally the lower left corner of the first line.

But you can choose any of nine placement points. The left side of Figure L-3 shows these points for notes and labels. The center of the figure shows the placement point options for dimensions. For notes and labels, HORIZTL sets the placement point at the left end, the center, or the right end of the longest line of text; VERTICL, the bottom, center, or top of

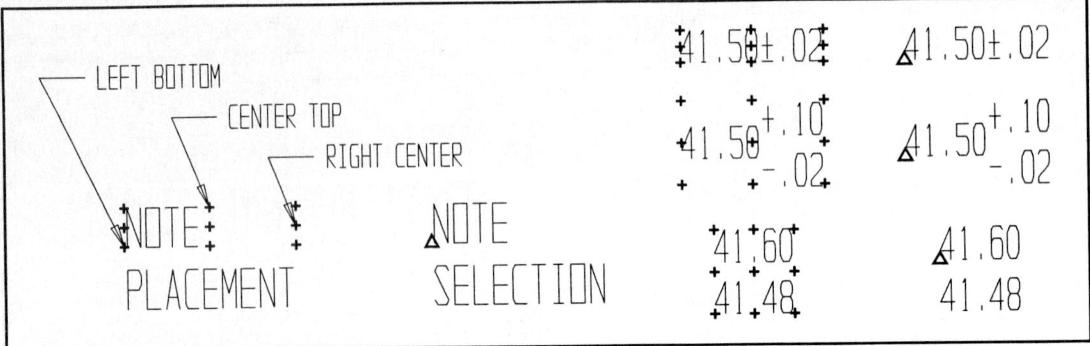

Figure L-3 Placement points (crosses) and selection points (triangles) for notes and dimensions

the first line. For dimensions, the placement points encompass the entire array of numbers, not just the first line.

Regardless of how you set the *placement* point for dimensions, notes, or labels, the *selection* point (for deletion, etc.) is the bottom-left corner of the first number in a dimension or the bottom-left corner of the first line of a note or label.

If you have trouble selecting text, it may be that the first line has leading spaces, or even that the first line is blank. Remember that spaces are characters too, and the bottom left corner of the first line can appear to be in the middle of nowhere.

NOT ANG (note angle) lets you write notes at any angle. Figure L-2 includes an example. This command does not affect labels, which Cadkey always writes horizontally. See DIMENSIONING STANDARDS for ways to vary the angle of the numbers in dimensions.

The ISOMETRIC example in Figure L-2 combines a note angle of 30° with a slant angle of —30°.

CHR ASP (character aspect ratio) controls the width-to-height ratio of letters and numbers (Figure L-4). You cannot set the ratio for notes and labels separately from that for dimensions. The default is 0.5. Traditional engineering lettering standards correspond to an aspect ratio more like 0.9. If this were not a dignified engineering handbook, it would show examples of the more entertaining values of aspect ratio, which can vary from 0.01 to 100.

Some Rules

When text is too small to read, Cadkey shows it on the screen as a line. Text that you cannot read on the screen is often legible in printouts.

In addition to letters, numbers, and punctuation marks, text can include the characters @#$%^&*()_-=+{}[]~/<>°±∅. You can enter the last three by holding down the Alt key

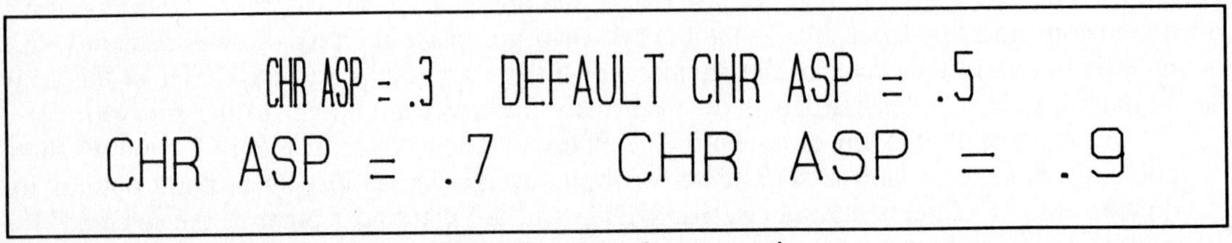

CHR ASP = .3 DEFAULT CHR ASP = .5

CHR ASP = .7 CHR ASP = .9

Fig 4. Samples of aspect ratio

while you enter, from the numeric keys on the right end of your keyboard, 248 for °, 241 for ±, and 174 and 175 for ∅. This last character is typed as two characters. Release the Alt key momentarily between 174 and 175. On the prompt line, ° and ± look like the characters you will see in the finished note, but ∅ looks like «». Another character is Alt-255. This is a *hard space*, a space that computers treat as an ordinary character rather than as a space. Cadkey automatically deletes trailing spaces, but it will leave them if the last one is a hard space.

Text shows only in the view in which you create it. A note in the front view does not show in the isometric.

CHANGE—Text Attributes

The CHANGE commands let you change the properties of existing text, using commands like those in the SET commands. You specify the new attributes you want, press F8 to signal that you are DONE, and tell Cadkey which entities to change. After you change these text entities, Cadkey returns you to the selection menu; thus you can, for example, use WINDOW to select a group of entities and then use SINGLE or any other position menu option to select a few more without having to reenter the changes you want.

You can change more than one attribute at a time. For example, you can, in one operation, change from BOX to BOLD letters, decrease letter height, and increase aspect ratio. You can select any combination of notes, labels, and dimensions, and in most cases the same changes will apply to all. For exceptions, see the notes that follow on the individual commands.

No matter what changes you make, the position of the lower left corner of the first character in the note, dimension, or label remains fixed. If you increase letter size in a dimension that is nicely centered, the larger letters will push it off-center to the right. For this reason, you often need to follow the TXT ATT (text attributes) commands with the TXT POS (text position) command.

FONT lets you select BOX or BOLD as the new lettering style.

HEIGHT resets the text height.

NOT ANG changes the angle at which notes are written. NOT ANG cannot change the text angle of labels or dimensions.

ASPECT resets the text aspect ratio.

MIRROR replaces a note with its mirror image. Before accepting this command, Cadkey asks whether you really want to do this. Labels and dimensions are unaffected.

SLANT sets the slant angle of the characters. Recall that slant angles are normally negative.

FILL specifies whether BOLD characters are to be filled (YES) or unfilled (NO).

DONE is the last option to select. It tells Cadkey that the changes you have specified are the only ones you want to make, and it lets you start selecting the entities to be changed.

There can be surprises in the changes that are in effect when you press DONE. Suppose you have just used TXT ATT—HEIGHT to change text height and used F10 to go back to the TXT ATT menu. Now, when you change some other text from BOX to BOLD, Cadkey changes its height also. The text height requested earlier is still in effect. F10 did not clear it.

F10 clears MIRROR and FILL, but none of the other TXT ATT commands. To start fresh, press F10 twice, reselect TXT ATT, and enter the changes you want to make.

CHANGE—Text Position

TXT POS lets you move text. When you select this option, Cadkey draws a rectangle surrounding the text. As you move the cursor, this rectangle moves with it to show the area the text will fill. Press the mouse button to select a new position. If you don't like the results, move the cursor and try again. When the position is right, press F10 to make it permanent. Then you can either select another entity to move or exit the TXT POS routine.

The position of the cursor relative to the rectangle that moves with it depends on the current NOT PLC or DIM PLC setting. The default setting for notes (BOTTOM, LEFT) puts the cursor at the lower left corner of the rectangle. The default for dimensions (CENTER, CENTER) puts it in the middle.

For dimensions with separate + and — tolerances, the rectangle is offset from the area the text fills. This offset usually means you have to use more trial and error in placing the text.

If you use TXT POS to move a dimension, the dimension-line arrows move with the text, but the points between which the dimension is measured stay the same. If you move a label, the leader moves with the text, but the point of the arrow remains fixed.

SNAP used with TXT POS is a good way to line up a chain of dimensions accurately.

UPDATE

UPDATE is another way to change text attributes. Suppose, for example, you start to dimension a drawing and decide that the numbers are too tall. With SET—DIM HT (or with DH in the STATUS WINDOW) you set Cadkey to use smaller numbers for future dimensions. You can then select DETAIL—UPDATE, pick the dimensions you have already placed, and press Return. All of the dimensions you pick are rewritten according to the current status of the SET commands. You can do the same thing with the CHANGE commands, but UPDATE is often more convenient.

UPDATE updates **DIM HT**, **NOT HT**, **DIM FNT**, and **NOT FNT**. It does not update **DIM PLC**, **NOT PLC**, **NOT ANG**, or **CHR ASP**.

In addition, you can update several properties of dimensions, such as tolerance magnitudes and formats, number of decimal places, and units. See UPDATE for a complete list. Be careful. You may update some things you would rather leave unchanged.

Levels

Cadkey's screen display is like a stack of transparent sheets, called levels. You can draw different parts of your drawing on different levels. Two properties are assigned to each level—whether it is the currently *active* level and whether it is *visible*. Because the active level is the one on which new construction takes place, only one level can be active at any one time. But you can make as many levels visible as you want. What you see on the computer screen and in plots and printouts are the entities on all the visible levels, but when you SAVE a drawing, you save all entities, regardless of whether they show on the screen.

When you draw a line, Cadkey puts it on whichever level is active. If you then REMOVE that level, Cadkey hides the entities on that level and the line disappears. If you later ADD that level, Cadkey makes it visible again and restores the line.

Why would you want to hide some of the entities on your drawing? One example is a floor plan that shows dimensions on level 4, plumbing on level 5, wiring on level 6, and construction lines or notes on level 7. By making some levels visible and hiding others, you can make a single drawing show several aspects of the floor plan. You can print one copy of the drawing for carpenters, another for plumbers, and still another for electricians. And no one but you needs to see level 7.

```
6 DISPLAY
  6 LEVELS
    1 ACTIVE*          ^L
    2 ADD
    3 REMOVE
    4 MOVE
      1 SELECT
      2 LEVEL
    5 LIST
      1 TURN ON
      2 TURN OFF
      3 TOGGLE
    6 MASK*          Alt-N
```

*The STATUS WINDOW lists these commands as ALEV and MLEV.

Problems with Hidden Levels

The term "active" can be misleading. In a broad sense, every level that is visible is active. If a level is visible, you can delete, trim, move, and otherwise operate on its entities, and its entities show in printouts. But in Cadkey, "active" has a limited meaning: the level reserved for current construction.

Making a level active usually makes it visible, but the active level can be hidden. If you get this combination accidentally, the results are puzzling: As you create new entities, Cadkey puts them on this hidden level, and you see nothing happening. Your first reaction may be that Cadkey has suddenly started to ignore all your commands. Until you sense what is going on, you are apt to create the same entity two or three times, setting the stage for other problems later on (See Deleted Lines Keep Coming Back in TROUBLESHOOTING).

By understanding how levels work, you take the mystery out of frustrating situations like this one. If a level has not been used before and you make it active, Cadkey automatically adds it to the list of visible levels. As a result, you tend to expect the active level to be visible. But if you have once hidden a level and later make it active, Cadkey remembers that you wanted it hidden and keeps it that way. If you want it visible, you must deliberately make it so.

The same problem can arise if you finish work on a level and then need to hide it. When you continue with other construction, it is all too easy to forget to switch the active level back to a visible one.

A similar problem can occur when you retrieve a PATTERN (see FILES). If parts of the pattern are directed to previously unused levels, those levels will be hidden. A common and disconcerting first reaction is that something went wrong with the pattern file.

The Commands

ACTIVE: The active level is the one being drawn on. Cadkey starts in level 1. Select any number from 1 to 255. (See the note that follows on level 256 if you want to venture into that level.) The level you select remains the active one until you select a new active level.

ADD lets you make additional levels visible. Separate the numbers with commas or dashes. 2,4–6,8 will make levels 2, 4 through 6, and 8 visible.

REMOVE hides the levels you select.

MOVE lets you move entities to a particular level. You can, for example, move all dimensions to level 3.

SELECT lets you pick the entities to be moved (see SELECTION MENU).

LEVEL moves everything on one level to a new level. Entities that do not show on the screen are included. Enter the level the entities are on; then the level to move them to.

When you move entities to a level not previously used, that level is initially hidden and the entities disappear. You might expect that you could make them visible again by making the new level active and therefore visible, but this does not work. The entities you moved remain hidden even though any new entities you created on that level would show. You need to use VISIBLE—ADD to restore the hidden entities.

You can prevent the problem if, before you use the MOVE–LEVEL command, you use ^L to make the new level active and therefore visible. This works even if you make it active for only an instant, switching to make some other level active before you execute the move command.

LIST displays an array of 256 levels, using reverse video to show which levels are visible. You can turn on any level (that is, you can make it visible) by selecting it with the cursor. To turn off a level, select either TURN OFF or TOGGLE from the menu; then select that level with the cursor.

You can change a number of levels at one time by *dragging* the cursor; that is, by selecting one number, holding the mouse button down while moving to another number, and releasing the mouse button. This action controls all levels included in the rectangle defined by the two points you select.

Exit LIST by pressing Return.

If you have used several levels in constructing a drawing, and if you are about as well organized as most of us, you may need to find out which entities wound up on which levels. Obviously, LIST can help, but consider another option: Use the ADD command to turn on all levels in the range you have been using. Select CONTROL—VERIFY—ATTRIB. Cadkey will tell you the level number of each entity you select. To move quickly from one entity to the next, press F10 rather than Return after you see the first field of data.

A better plan is to reserve a level, perhaps number 20, for a series of NOTES that record the levels you use and what is on each one.

MASK sets LEVEL MASKING (see SELECTION MENU), which limits the levels from which entities can be selected (for deletion, copying, etc.). For example, 3 restricts selections to entities on level 3, and —3 allows selections from all levels but 3. Enter 0 to remove level masking. You cannot mask on more than one level at a time. Your selection remains in effect until you change it.

Notes

Level 256 is a hidden level. When this level is active, the entities you create on it are invisible. To retrieve them, use MOVE–LEVEL to copy all entities from level 256 to some new level.

In CADKEY Light 4.0 these moves work as you would expect, but in CADKEY Light 1.5 level 256 has strange properties. When you move entities from it, they don't immediately reappear. Even though the new level is visible, entities transferred from level 256 are not. They remain hidden until you ADD the new level. (You can also make them appear by adding level 256. This does not make level 256 visible, but it removes the curse from the entities you have just moved and makes them visible.)

To send existing entities to level 256 in CADKEY Light 1.5, use MOVE—SELECT or MOVE—LEVEL. You will still be able to see the entities, and VERIFY—ATTRIB will tell you they are on level 0, which is not one of the levels Cadkey allows. If you then REMOVE level 256, the entities will disappear into level 256.

As noted earlier, entities on hidden levels are a permanent part of the database for the drawing. When you SAVE a file (see FILES), you save the hidden entities as well as the visible ones.

When you add entities to your drawing by using the MOVE/COPY/JOIN commands or by retrieving a PATTERN, these rules apply:

MOVE keeps entities on their original levels, regardless of the active level.

COPY and JOIN produce their copies on the active level. If you need to preserve the original level structure, you must copy entities one level at a time, changing the active level as you change the level being copied. LEVEL MASKING (see SELECTING ENTITIES) lets you select entities from just one level at a time.

PATTERNS may be retrieved on the active level, on the levels assigned to entities when the pattern was created, on a level whose number you key in, or on level numbers offset from the numbers assigned when the pattern was created. See FILES.

Line

The LINE commands provide a number of ways to create line entities.

ENDPTS draws a line connecting two points you select.

STRING draws a series of lines, starting each segment at the end of the preceding one. A special kind of string is a SKETCH line, described under POLYLINE.

PARALEL creates a line parallel to an existing line and equal to it in length.

THRU PT draws it through a specified point.

AT DIST draws it a specified distance from the existing line.

TAN/PRP offers six ways of constructing lines tangent to arcs, circles or points and/or perpendicular to lines, arcs, circles, or points. The complete list of rules, which you will find at the end of this section, is long. For most constructions you don't need this much detail, and, unless you run into trouble, one rule and two definitions will suffice:

When Cadkey has constructed a tangent or perpendicular, it is ready to construct another, starting with the entity you selected first. *Press F10 if you want to repeat the routine using a different first entity.*

A "perpendicular" to an arc or a circle is a radial line—one that if extended would pass through the center of curvature.

"Arc" means either an arc or a circle. (Think of a circle as a 360° arc.)

TAN PT draws a line tangent to an arc and through a point.

PRP PT draws a line perpendicular to a line or arc and through a point.

TAN TAN draws a line tangent to two arcs.

TAN PRP draws a line tangent to an arc and perpendicular to a line or arc.

PRP TAN does the same thing as TAN PRP, but you pick the entities in reverse order. You would use TAN PRP to draw several lines tangent to the same arc; PRP TAN, to draw several lines perpendicular to the same arc or line.

PRP PRP constructs a line perpendicular to two arcs or to a line and an arc. If you select two lines, it constructs a perpendicular to one of them (for details, see the more complete notes that follow).

HRZ-VRT draws a horizontal line, a vertical line, or both, through a selected point and extending to the edges of the screen.

ANGLE constructs a line at an angle to an existing line. The new line is as long as the reference line, and you specify the angle between the two. Positive angles rotate the line counterclockwise. CADKEY Light 1.5 starts the line at one end of the reference line–the end nearest your selection point. CADKEY Light 4.0 starts the new line wherever you want. Which end of the new line is the start depends on which end of the reference line the cursor was nearest when you selected it.

```
1 CREATE
  1 LINE
    1 ENDPTS
    2 STRING
    3 PARALEL
      1 THRU PT
      2 AT DIST
    4 TAN/PRP
      1 TAN PT
      2 PRP PT
      3 TAN TAN
      4 TAN PRP
      5 PRP TAN
      6 PRP PRP
    5 HRZ/VRT
      1 HORIZTL
      2 VERTICL
      3 BOTH
    6 ANGLE
    7 RECTANG
      1 CORNERS
      2 WID/HT
    8 N-GON
```

RECTANG offers two ways to create rectangles:

CORNERS lets you specify the positions of diagonally opposite corners. After you have selected the first point, a "rubber box" maintains a rectangle between that point and the cursor position, letting you see the rectangle before you complete its construction.

WID/HT determines the rectangle's dimensions by letting you type in its width and its height. You then specify the position of the lower left corner.

Cadkey gives you two other ways to create rectangles. The basic procedure is the same—you choose between the CORNERS and WID/HT options. CREATE—POLYLIN—RECTANG and CREATE—POLYGON—RECTANG create the rectangle as a single entity as opposed to the four entities produced by CREATE—LINE—RECTANG.

N-GON gives you a regular polygon of 3 to 100 sides. As with rectangles, you can also create regular polygons as POLYLINE or POLYGON entities. See POLYGON—REGULAR for details, or use the following brief instructions to construct a LINE polygon.

Rotation angle controls the slope of the bottom edge of the polygon. The CORNER/FLAT choice determines whether Cadkey measures the polygon radius to a vertex or to the center of a side. Respond NO to the question of grouping entities, or see GROUP for the advantages of responding YES.

CADKEY Light 1.5 constructs the polygon at the current depth, regardless of whether you are in 2D or 3D construction mode (see 2D/3D). In 3D mode, CADKEY Light 4.0 constructs it at the depth of the point you select for its center.

The TAN/PRP Commands

Nine rules govern these commands. Recall that the word *arc* as used here means either an arc or a circle.

1. A "perpendicular" to an arc is a radial line–one that if extended would pass through the center of curvature.
2. Cadkey lets you draw a "tangent" or "perpendicular" to a point. This is a line ending on the point. You can use one point, but not two, in this manner. For example, you can make TAN TAN give you the same results as TAN PT. This option is not spelled out in the command descriptions that follow.
3. Usually you can construct tangents or perpendiculars using positions on extensions of entities, but Cadkey does not always let you use the extension of an arc. If the arc falls short by a large angle, you may need to use a TRIM/EXTEND operation to extend it temporarily.
4. Many constructions have more than one solution. (You can draw four lines tangent to two circles.) To get the solution you want, select entities by placing the cursor close to where you expect tangents or perpendiculars to meet arcs or circles.
5. When Cadkey has constructed a tangent or perpendicular, it is ready to construct another, starting with the entity you selected first. *Press F10 if you want to repeat the routine using a different first entity.*
6. Some constructions imply a zero-length line (suppose you call for a line tangent to an arc and passing through a point entity that lies on that arc). For such constructions, tangents to arcs extend to the edges of the screen. Sometimes perpendiculars to arcs extend to the edges of the screen and sometimes they show as diameters. (The choice depends on the position of the point and the position of the cursor when you use it to select the arc.)
7. If Cadkey is in 3D mode and the entities you select do not lie in a plane parallel to the screen, perpendicular lines are perpendicular in the plane of the entities but in general do not look perpendicular on the screen. In 2D mode, perpendicular lines are perpendicular in the plane of the screen regardless of the orientation of the entities in space.
8. If Cadkey is in 3D mode and the entities you select do not lie in the same plane, you see **Invalid entity combination... press RETURN**.
9. The TAN/PRP commands refuse to construct lines perpendicular to POLYLINE and POLYGON segments unless Cadkey is in 2D construction mode (see 2D/3D).

TAN PT draws a line tangent to an arc and through a point.

PRP PT draws a line perpendicular to a line or arc and through a point.

TAN TAN draws a line tangent to two arcs. If you get a wrong answer–a line tangent to only one arc rather than to both, see DOUBLE–Application No. 1 under TRIMMING AND EXTENDING in Chapter 2. Or just try again, being more careful where you place the cursor when you select the arcs.

TAN PRP draws a line tangent to an arc and perpendicular to a line or arc.

PRP TAN does the same thing as TAN PRP. PRP TAN is the more convenient command if you want several perpendiculars to one entity–you select that entity only once. TAN PRP is more convenient if you want several tangents to one entity.

PRP PRP, with one exception, does the obvious between lines and arcs, constructing a line perpendicular to both entities.

The exception occurs when you select two lines. Cadkey draws the new line perpendicular to the first line you select, through the point where the two lines intersect. If they do not intersect, Cadkey draws the line through the point where they would intersect if one or both were extended. The new line extends to the edges of the screen.

Line Limit

```
7 CONTROL
  3 CONST
    4 L-LIMIT      Alt-L
      1 FUNCTN
```

In other versions of Cadkey, L-LIMIT gives you a choice between FUNCTION and SCREEN. This choice controls whether Cadkey draws certain lines beyond their normal limits, extending them to the edges of the screen. Because CADKEY Light does not offer the SCREEN option, the L-LIMIT command has been eliminated from CADKEY Light 4.0. It appears in CADKEY Light 1.5 but has no effect on construction there.

Line Type

CONTROL—ATTRIB—L-TYPE determines whether Cadkey will draw entities using (1) solid lines, (2) dashed lines, (3) centerlines, or (4) phantom lines. You can also press Alt-T or select L-TYPE in the STATUS WINDOW to invoke the line-type menu. See ATTRIB for details, including information on how to change line types of existing entities.

Line Width

CONTROL—ATTRIB—L-WIDTH lets you choose the line thickness Cadkey will use to draw lines, arcs, circles, and polylines. Pressing Alt-Y or selecting L-WID in the STATUS WINDOW are other ways to set line width. You can also change the line width of existing entities. See ATTRIB for details.

Masking

Suppose you want to DELETE all the POINTS on the screen. Or suppose you want to TRIM an arc that is so close to a series of lines that the arc is hard to select. Alt-M invokes **TYPE MASKING**, which lets Cadkey select only from the types of entities you specify. Under GEOM you may specify POINTS, LINES, etc.; under DETAIL, you may specify DIMENSIONS, CROSSHATCHING, etc. Or you can limit selections according to COLOR, LINE TYPE, LINE WIDTH, or PEN NUMBER. Alt-M invokes **LEVEL MASKING**, which lets Cadkey select entities from only one level or from all levels but one.

Your type masking selections are cleared when you initiate an operation, To make it work, you must start the operation first and then make your masking selections. Level masking stays in effect forever, so remember to clear it when you no longer need it.

See SELECTING ENTITIES for details.

Memory

7 CONTROL
5 STATUS

In CADKEY Light 1.5, **STATUS** shows the amount of free RAM (see DOS) in the computer and the amount of free space available on the disk that holds the Cadkey program. You see first the available RAM; then you press Return to see the how much disk space is available.

CADKEY Light 4.0 shows more detailed information, rounded to the nearest kilobyte, in a single table. This table lists the amount of free RAM and the amount of space in each of the directories set aside for overflow files.

If you plan to create a large drawing, it's a good idea, before you start, to check STATUS to be sure there is enough memory to accommodate your drawing.

Menu Options Window

The menu options window, near the top of the screen on the right, is a list of your options for selecting the next command. The numbers in this list refer to function keys—to select option 3 you press F3. See Chapter 1 for details and an illustration.

Mirror

The **MIRROR** commands—there are two of them—produce mirror images of patterns on the screen. X–FORM—MIRROR gives mirror images of geometrical constructions, including LINES, ARCS, and CROSSHATCHING, but leaves NOTES, LABELS, and DIMENSIONS untouched. See MOVE/COPY/JOIN for details.

DETAIL—CHANGE—TXT ATT—MIRROR replaces the text of an existing NOTE (but not that of a LABEL or DIMENSION) with its mirror image. See LETTERING for details and an illustration of the results.

MLEV

MLEV is a STATUS WINDOW entry that lets you limit the levels from which Cadkey can select entities. See Masking for a brief description or SELECTING ENTITIES for more detail.

Move/Copy/Join

```
4 X-FORM
   1 TRANS-R
      1 MOVE
      2 COPY
      3 JOIN
   2 TRANS-A
      1 MOVE
      2 COPY
      3 JOIN
   3 2D ROT
      1 MOVE
      2 COPY
      3 JOIN
   4 SCALE
      1 MOVE
      2 COPY
      3 JOIN
   5 MIRROR
      1 MOVE
      2 COPY
      3 JOIN
```

The X–FORM (transform) commands MOVE, COPY, and JOIN represent the most conspicuous difference between CADKEY Light 1.5 and CADKEY Light 4.0. The menu for Version 1.5 is on the left; that for Version 4.0, on the right. Three of the command names differ, and Cadkey terminates the commands differently, but the transformations the two versions make are the same.

Each option in the X—FORM menu lets you make the copies in any of three ways:

MOVE makes a copy and deletes the original.

COPY makes one or more copies and leaves the original.

JOIN makes one or more copies and leaves the original. It also adds lines joining points on the original to corresponding points on the copies. These lines connect point entities, the end points of lines and arcs, the ends and corners of polylines and polygons, and the 0° points of circles.

```
4 X-FORM
   1 DELTA
      1 MOVE
      2 COPY
      3 JOIN
   2 OLD-NEW
      1 MOVE
      2 COPY
      3 JOIN
   3 ROTATE
      1 MOVE
      2 COPY
      3 JOIN
   4 SCALE
      1 MOVE
      2 COPY
      3 JOIN
   5 MIRROR
      1 MOVE
      2 COPY
      3 JOIN
```

Trans-A or Old-New

Option 2 of the X-FORM menu is discussed first. TRANS-A, the CADKEY Light 1.5 name, stands for translate—absolute, which means that you specify the position of the copy in absolute terms. (Option 1, TRANS-R, stands for translate—relative, meaning that you specify the position of the copy relative to the position of the original; for example, you might ask for a copy one inch above the original.)

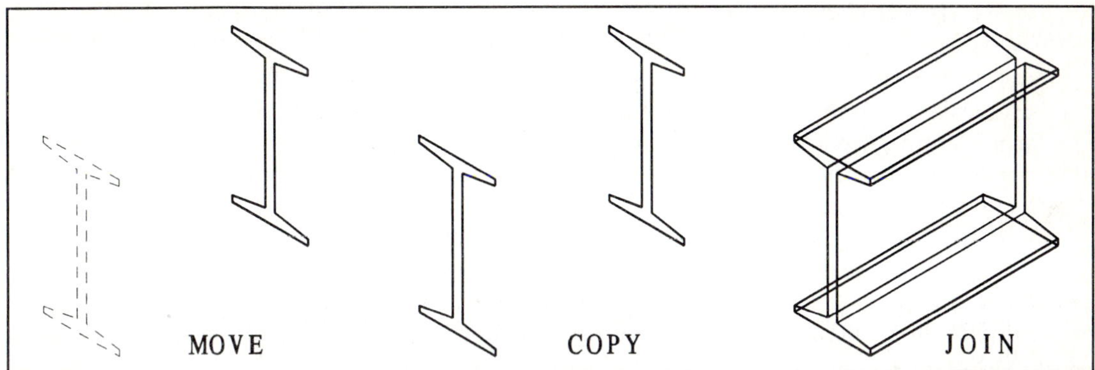

Figure M-1 MOVE, COPY, and JOIN examples

TRANS-A or OLD-NEW has you select the entities you want to move, copy, or join. It asks how many copies you want (MOVE skips this step); then it asks for a base position (the OLD position implied by the CADKEY Light 4.0 command name); finally it asks for a new base position. Cadkey puts the entities where this new base position implies.

Cadkey's response at this point depends on which version of CADKEY light you have. CADKEY Light 1.5 asks you for another base position and is ready to give you another copy at that position. CADKEY Light 4.0 backs out of the routine, taking you to the point where you select the entities you want to copy.

For MOVE, the CADKEY Light 1.5 procedure is the more convenient. If the new position is not quite right, you can immediately select another, and Cadkey shifts the entities accordingly. For COPY and JOIN, CADKEY Light 4.0 offers the advantage of safety. CADKEY Light 1.5 makes it too easy to put a copy where you don't want it. The notes that follow on PROBLEMS tell how this can happen and how CADKEY Light 4.0 prevents it.

Figure M-2 shows what happens when you ask for three copies. The V block in the upper left corner is the start of the drawing, and the triangle labeled a is the base position. If you select b for the new base position, you get the row of uniformly spaced copies along the top of the figure. If Cadkey puts the first copy one inch to the right of the original, the second is two inches to the right and the third is three inches to the right.

To get the vertical column of copies in CADKEY Light 1.5, you simply select another new base position at c. Selecting the base position at d gives a third set of copies.

Another way to get a row of three copies would be to ask for one copy and select three new base positions. Using SNAP would let you space the copies uniformly.

In CADKEY Light 4.0, adding the vertical column of copies is less convenient. You must reselect the entities to copy, specify three copies, select the old base position at a, and select the new base position at c.

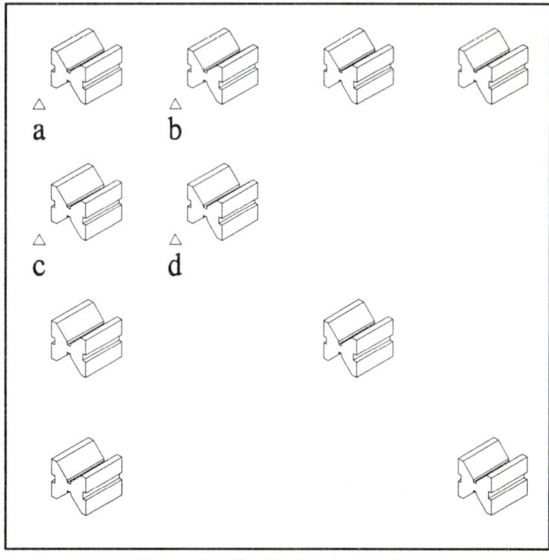

Figure M-2 Multiple copies

Trans-R or Delta

TRANS-R or DELTA differs from TRANS-A or OLD-NEW only in the way you specify the new base position. With TRANS-R or DELTA you specify not where the new position is, but how far it is from the old one. To do this, you key in values for delta x, delta y, and delta z; in other words, you specify the increments in x, y, and z that will take you to from the position of the original to the position of the copy.

If you use TRANS-R or DELTA, you need to know the difference between VIEW and WORLD coordinates (see COORDINATES or check the inside front cover). If Cadkey is in view coordinates, you position the copy by keying in dVX, dVY, and dVZ; that is, the changes in XV, YV, and ZV. In WORLD coordinates, you key in dX, dY, and dZ. (To key in a value of zero, just press Return.)

CADKEY Light 1.5 gives you an additional copy or series of copies every time you key in another set of delta values for a new base position. If you want multiple copies that are randomly spaced, you can ask Cadkey for one copy and key in a new position for each new copy. With COPY and JOIN, the values you key in determine how far the copy is from the original. With MOVE, the values you key in determine how far the copy is from the position you selected most recently.

CADKEY Light 4.0 makes repeated moves and randomly spaced copies more difficult, because you must reselect the entities each time you move or copy them.

2D Rot or Rotate

2D ROT or ROTATE rotates a set of entities about an axis perpendicular to the screen. You can use the MOVE option to change the angle of all or part of a drawing. If you ask for multiple copies, you get patterns like the one in Figure M-3, which shows the end view of an I-beam copied seven times. The rotation angle is 45°, and the small cross is the rotation origin. Recall that positive rotation angles are counterclockwise. If the original in Figure M-3 is at the top center position, the first copy is on its left.

Figure J-1 shows a three-dimensional pattern you can create with the JOIN option. It uses a 10° angle and 36 copies. The 36th copy coincides with the original, but you need it to create a complete set of joining lines.

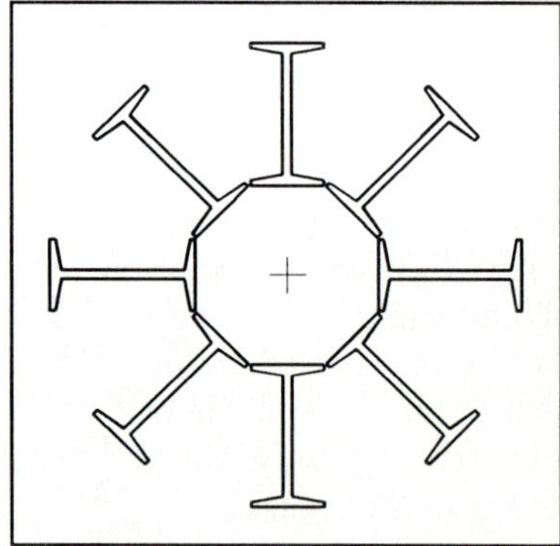

Figure M-3 ROTATE example

Scale

SCALE produces copies larger or smaller than the original. You specify the number of copies, a scaling origin, and a scale factor. Cadkey made the copy in Figure M-4 by putting every point on the copy 0.6 as far from the scaling origin (the small cross) as it is from the original, making the copy 60% as large as the original. A scale factor larger than 1 puts the copy farther from the scaling origin than is the original, making the copy larger.

Knowing the method Cadkey uses, you can calculate where the scaling origin should be to put the scaled copy where you want it; however, it is often easier to guess where the scaling origin should be and use TRANS-A—MOVE or OLD-NEW—MOVE to adjust the position of the copy.

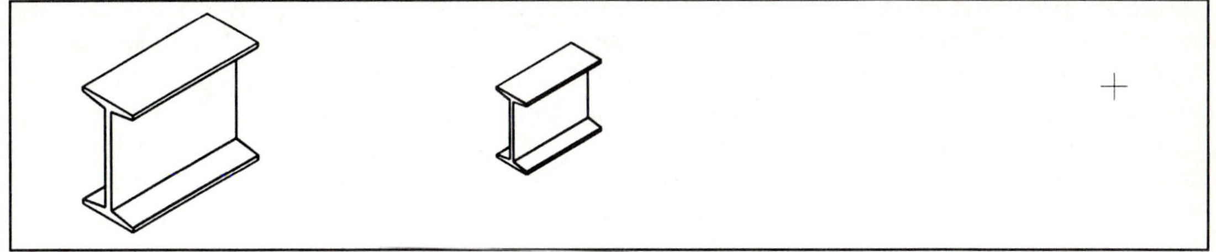

Figure M-4 SCALE example

If you ask for more than one copy, Cadkey applies your scale factor each time it goes from one copy to the next. This can make the scaling origin look like a vanishing point on a perspective drawing. Figure M-5 shows a V block and eight copies. The scale factor of .75 made each copy 3/4 as large as the copy preceding it. (For notes on how this drawing was made, see the subsection that follows on Applications)

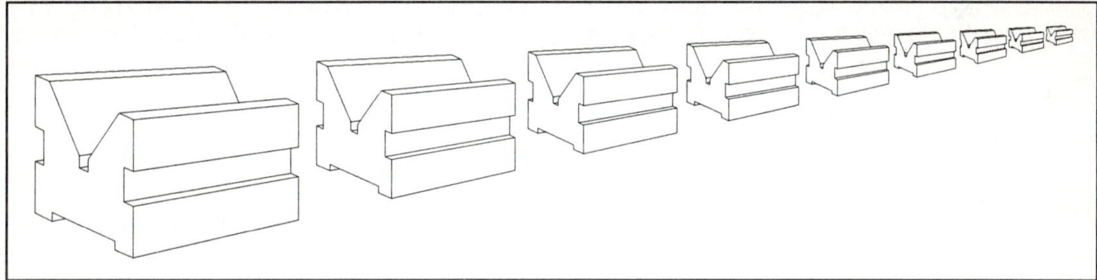

Figure M-5 Multiple copies produced by the SCALE command

Mirror

MIRROR makes a copy that is a mirror image of the original. You specify two points, and the line between them represents the edge view of the imaginary mirror. To be sure of the position of the reflecting plane, you can draw the line and use ENDENT to select its ends. If this line is the axis of symmetry of a symmetrical drawing, you can construct one half of the drawing and let MIRROR complete it.

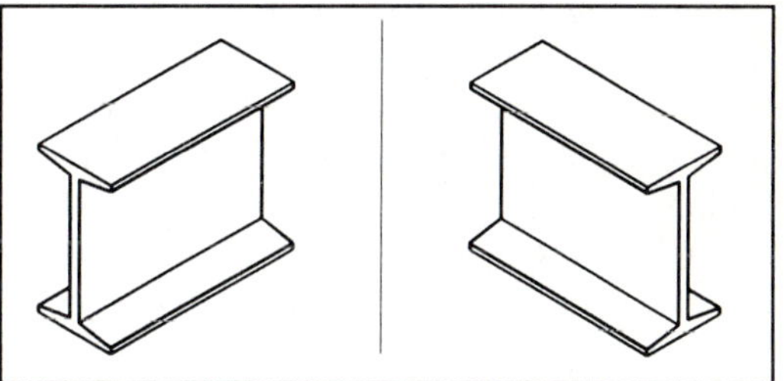

Figure M-6 MIRROR example

Applications

MIRROR can help you draw symmetrical objects quickly. To start the drawing of the V block in Figure M-7d, you need seven lines–the five heavy lines in Figure M-7a and the long horizontal and vertical lines that will act as mirroring planes. Start the drawing in VIEW 2. Use MIRROR–COPY twice, once across the vertical mirroring plane and again across the horizontal one. Use ENDENT to add the four lines that cross these mirroring lines. (Had you used MIRROR to duplicate these four lines, each would either be double or made up of two half-length segments.) Finally, delete the horizontal and vertical construction lines.

TRANS-R—JOIN or DELTA—JOIN provides the easiest way to extend a figure like this one into the third dimension. The following is a brief description of the method. If you want more detail, see the section on THREE-DIMENSIONAL CONSTRUCTION in Chapter 2. The second example in that section is like the procedure outlined here.

Switch to view 7 to obtain Figure M-7b.

Select COORD in the STATUS WINDOW to set VW/WLD coordinates to WLD. Use TRANS-R—JOIN or DELTA—JOIN to obtain the extrusion in Figure M-7c, setting dX = 0, dY = 3, and dZ = 0. (Your value for dY may be different, depending on the dimensions of your V block.) The resulting wire-frame drawing is three-dimensional and shows the V block correctly in all views.

To convert the wire-frame isometric view to the pictorial view in Figure M-7d, use ^Q to delete hidden lines and EDIT—TRM/EXT—FIRST to remove hidden parts of lines. If you happen to delete one too many of the join lines, you can restore it by using CREATE—LINE—PARALEL—THRU PT. Check the status window to be sure CONST is still set to 3D. Pick any other join line as the reference line, and with ENDENT pick a point that the missing join line should pass through. Trim or extend the line as necessary.

If you want to give the V block a perspective taper, as in Figure M-5, use SCALE—JOIN rather than the TRANS-R or DELTA command to extend the flat front surface view into the third dimension. The drawing that results is purely pictorial. Although the figure is three dimensional, its shape is not correct in three-dimensional space. The first V block in Figure M-5 was drawn with a scale factor of .85. The scaling origin used to construct this V block was also used as the scaling origin for making the eight copies.

Figure M-5 is not a true perspective drawing, although it resembles one. As the V blocks recede into the distance, the lines that slope upward and to the left should change slope to become more nearly horizontal.

Attributes of Copies

Copies and, if JOIN is used, the lines that connect copies to the original, have the same LINE TYPE (solid, dashed, etc.), COLOR, LINE THICKNESS, and PEN NUMBER as the original, even though Cadkey's current setting may call for newly created entities to be a different type. MOVE preserves the original LEVEL structure, but all new entities created by COPY and JOIN are created on Cadkey's current level, regardless of the level of the original entities.

POLYGONS and POLYLINES make copies that duplicate the originals, filled or unfilled. The lines that join them are ordinary lines, each a separate entity.

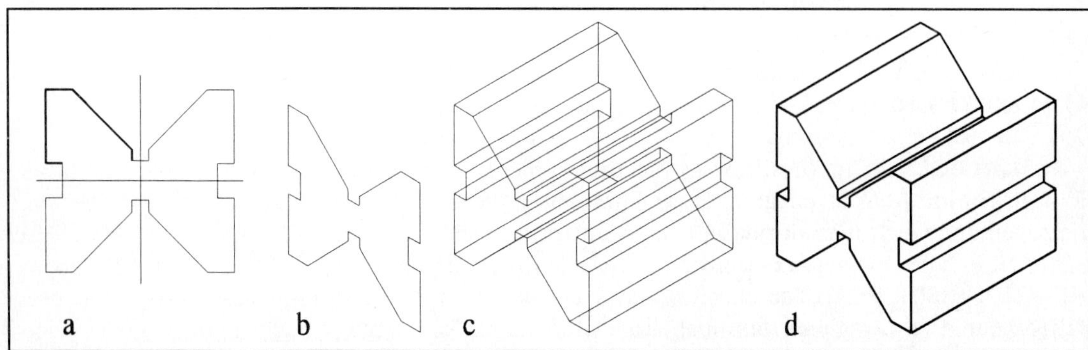

Figure M-7 Steps in creating a 3D drawing of a V block

Scale and Dimensions

SCALE changes the drawing as recorded in the DATABASE, permanently assigning new dimensions to its entities. But suppose you use SCALE to double the size of part of a dimensioned drawing. The size of the numbers doubles, the dimension lines move twice as far from the object, and the numbers stay the same. In other words, you get an exact copy, twice as large. If you then UPDATE the dimensions, the numbers change to reflect the new distances they cover, and the size of the numbers reverts to the size called for by the SET commands. The position of the numbers stays the same, twice as far from the object as before.

Rules Concerning Entity Types

MOVE and COPY work with all entity types. JOIN works with all of the GEOMETRICAL entities—LINES, POINTS, ARCS, CIRCLES, POLYLINES, and POLYGONS. JOIN makes copies of the DETAIL entities—DIMENSIONS, NOTES, LABELS, CROSSHATCHING, ARROWS, and WITNESS LINES—but does not join them.

In CADKEY Light 1.5, MIRROR and 2D ROT give trouble with some of the DETAIL entities. MIRROR does not work at all except for crosshatching. 2D ROT works well except with dimensions and labels. Figure M-8 shows what 2D ROT can do to a dimensioned drawing. The center drawing is the original. The figure on the left was rotated 90°; the one on the right, —45°. At —45°, Cadkey reclassifies horizontal and vertical dimensions as parallel dimensions (see DIMENSIONING), with bizarre results. Cadkey keeps the text in labels horizontal, and in the process leaves the leaders in awkward positions. Notes survive the rotation unscathed.

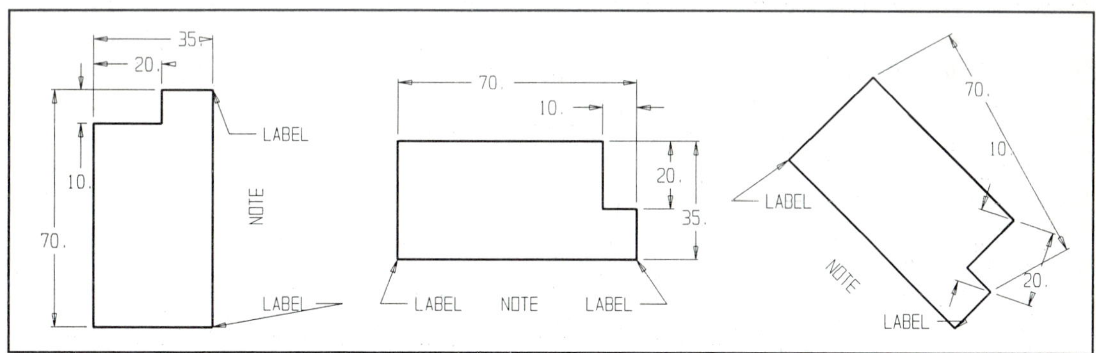

Figure M-8 2D ROT is not recommended for labels and dimensions

CADKEY Light 4.0 does better with DETAIL entities. MIRROR works with all of them, except that sometimes it shifts the text of dimensions to positions that are off center with respect to the arrows. Mirror reverses the text in notes to form a mirror image but leaves the text in dimensions and labels reading normally.

ROTATE in CADKEY Light 4.0 gives good results with dimensions, letting the text rotate with the rest of the drawing, but labels do not fare as well. As in CADKEY Light 1.5, the text in labels stubbornly stays horizontal.

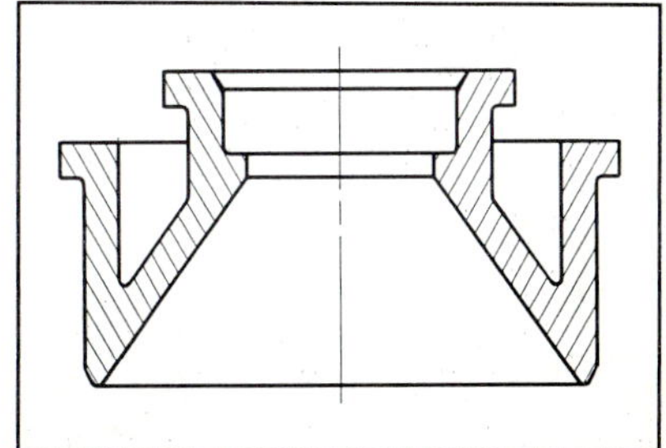

Figure M-9 An incorrect full section

Although both versions of CADKEY Light let you mirror crosshatching, you should resist the temptation to use this time-saving feature to put crosshatching in a symmetrical full section (Figure M-9). Letting the crosshatch lines slope differently in the two halves of the same piece of material is a serious violation of the rules of engineering graphics.

Other Rules

If the entities you are copying belong to a GROUP, you do not get a new subgroup. CADKEY Light 1.5 puts the copy in the same group and subgroup as the original. CADKEY Light 4.0 does not put the copied entities in any group. Use EDIT—GROUP—MAKE if you want to assign a new subgroup number to a copy made by either version of CADKEY Light. See GROUP for details.

If you use JOIN on grouped entities, the lines joining the copy to the original do not belong to any group.

Where two entities meet, you might expect the join lines generated by their ends to be double; however, Cadkey eliminates the duplicate lines.

Problems

Suppose you have just finished copying a large number of entities and now need to get rid of a few construction lines or other unwanted entities. You press ^Q and select the first entity. But instead of selecting the entity, Cadkey plasters another copy of the entities over your drawing.

This problem can easily occur with CADKEY Light 1.5. If you are lucky, the copy doesn't have too many entities and is not too intimately entwined with the parts of the drawing you want to save. If you are less fortunate, you may decide to start your drawing over rather than spend the next half hour deleting the unwanted copy one entity at a time. If you had the foresight to SAVE your drawing just before you started the copy command, you have no problem. You can load the drawing as it was before the copy command.

This scene typifies the kind of mistake that a moderately experienced user is apt to make. He finishes the copy routine but has not yet pressed Esc or F10 to exit it. Although ^Q usually interrupts whatever is going on, it does not interrupt the copy command at this point. He assumes ^Q is active when in fact Cadkey is waiting for him to select another base position to show where another copy goes. Either the prompt line or the history line would have warned him that ^Q wasn't functioning. The command line tells what to do next, and whenever an immediate mode command is active the history line shows an entry in reverse video. But a person who knows Cadkey well and who is pressed for time probably does not always stop to read everything on the screen.

CADKEY Light 4.0 avoids this problem by requiring more deliberate action for additional copies. For the same reason, most of the CADKEY Light 1.5 commands avoid the problem. But TRANS-A—COPY and TRANS-A—JOIN put you at risk.

Another problem is apt to hit the inexperienced Cadkey user. He tries to make a copy but nothing happens. Typically, he tries again. Still nothing.

This can happen when you are working with JOIN, trying, in the isometric view, to extend a flat drawing into a three-dimensional extrusion. Probably Cadkey is in VIEW coordinates and should be in WORLD coordinates (see COORDINATES). If you let dZ = 10 to create a vertical displacement, you can use the isometric view to watch your drawing expand into a pillar of complex shape. But if you carelessly let dZV = 10, the extrusion comes straight toward you.

The copy is there, but it doesn't show in the current view because it coincides with the original. In other views it shows but is wrong. See TROUBLESHOOTING for a possible way to recover from this problem.

Another problem can occur in CADKEY Light 1.5 but not in CADKEY Light 4.0. The default angle for 2D ROT is zero. If you carelessly accept this default, the rotation angle of zero makes all copies coincide. In CADKEY Light 4.0, the default angle for ROTATE is 30°. Carelessness may give you the wrong angle, but at least you can see that something is happening.

One form of insurance against such mishaps is to save your drawing before you use one of the MOVE/COPY/JOIN commands. Another is to use ^L to change the active LEVEL to one you have not used before. Any wrong entities you accidentally create will be on a separate level, and you can deal with them without disturbing other parts of your drawing.

N-gon

N-gon is the name Cadkey uses for two types of regular polygons. Cadkey reserves the more obvious term, polygon, for a particular type of entity. See POLYGON for construction methods and POLYGONS, POLYLINES, AND LINES COMPARED for an explanation of the terminology.

Note

A NOTE is text such as a title, your name, etc., that you place on a drawing. Each line of a note is limited to 128 characters (longer lines are truncated), and, unless you use the FILE option, each note is limited to 1024 characters or less. Notes show only in the view you use to create them.

If you see an error in a completed note, you can use DETAIL—CHANGE—EDIT TX to make corrections. (This option is not available for FILE-based notes.) See TEXT EDITOR for details.

3 DETAIL
- 2 NOTE
  - 1 KEY-IN
  - 2 DISK
  - 3 FILE
  - 4 DUMP NT

Basics—the KEY-IN Option

KEY–IN lets you type the note. Press Return to start a new line and press F6 (SAVE TEXT) to finish the note. To place the note on the drawing, put the cursor where you want to put the bottom left corner of the first line.

As you type the note, you see several choices (DEL LIN, JOIN LN, etc.) in the menu options window. For short notes, SAVE TX is the only option you are likely to need. The others can help you edit more complex notes. See TEXT EDITOR for more detail.

To correct typing errors, use the Backspace or Delete keys to delete wrong letters, and use the arrow keys to move through the text. The arrow keys move you up and down—from one line to the next—as well as side to side in one line.

Advanced Techniques

DISK lets you create a note with a word processor, store it as an ASCII file of 1024 characters or less, and import it into Cadkey. Cadkey asks you for a file name. If the file is in the default directory for note files (usually the NOT directory) you can omit the path designation but you must include the extension (see DOS if these terms are unfamiliar). Once you import the note into Cadkey, you can use the TEXT EDITOR to edit it as you would any note.

An ASCII file is a plain text file. Most word processors use special formatting characters to indicate bold text, italics, line centering, tab stops, etc.; but they can also, by stripping away these formatting characters, create ASCII files, sometimes called ASCII TEXT files or DOS TEXT files. Although you may prefer working with your favorite word processor, consider also Cadkey as a way to write ASCII files. See the discussion that follows on DUMP NT.

To test the DISK command, import BREAK.TXT, one of Cadkey's files. Import it as .\break.txt, where the period stands for the current directory, the one Cadkey is in. If you omit the .\ path designation, Cadkey looks for the note in Cadkey's default directory for notes.

FILE, like DISK, creates a note from an ASCII file, and you bring a file-based note into your drawing the same way that you bring in a disk-based note. There is no limit on the size of file-based notes, but the limit of 128 characters per line still applies. You cannot edit the note while running Cadkey. You must edit it in DOS.

The main difference between FILE and DISK is that Cadkey does not include the text of a disk-based note in its DATABASE. Cadkey records only the file name. Consequently, every time you load the drawing, Cadkey must find that extra file to get the contents of the note. If Cadkey cannot find the file, it will not load any of your drawing. You see the usual **Loading part file... please wait**; followed by **Cannot find file... press RETURN.**

DUMP NT creates an ASCII text file. If you have created a note that you would like to use in other drawings, DUMP NT provides an easy way to make it available.

Start with a note on your drawing that you created using the KEY-IN or DISK option, not the FILE option. When you select the note with the cursor, Cadkey asks for a file name. If you don't specify a path, Cadkey uses the DEFAULT directory for notes, normally the subdirectory NOT in the CADKEY directory (CADKEY Light 1.5) or the CKLIGHT directory (CADKEY Light 4.0) of the hard disk. If your file name doesn't include an extension, Cadkey adds the extension .NOT. For example,

File name you enter	File name Cadkey uses	Directory	Disk
NOTE.TXT	NOTE.TXT	Default	Default
NOTE	NOTE.NOT	Default	Default
A:\NOTE	NOTE.NOT	Root directory	A:
A:\ASSEMBLY\SCALE	SCALE.NOT	ASSEMBLY	A:

You can use either the DISK option or the FILE option to retrieve notes that DUMP NT has stored. You can edit DISK based notes using Cadkey's TEXT EDITOR, or you can exit Cadkey to go to DOS and use a word processor to edit the ASCII file.

Notes

To place a note, you normally put the cursor where you want the lower left corner of the first line of text. This corner is the default alignment point. To change the alignment point (for example, to make the center of the first line fall at the cursor position) use the NOT ALN command, described under LETTERING.

To SELECT a note (in order to DELETE it, MOVE it, EDIT the text, etc.), put the cursor at the bottom left corner of the first line of text. This *selection* point is fixed even though you used DETAIL—SET—TEXT—NOT PLC to change the *alignment* point for placing the note.

Until you press Esc or F10 to exit the NOTE routine, Cadkey lets you add copies of the same note wherever you place the cursor. If you don't like the position of the note, delete it, move the cursor, and try again. Or use DETAIL—CHANGE—TXT POS (see CHANGE) to move it.

You can control the height, shape, and font of letters and the angle at which the note is written. See LETTERING for details.

A related type of entity is a LABEL, which combines a note with an arrow.

Outline/Fill

POLYGONS and closed POLYLINES can appear in either of two forms: They can appear as OUTLINES, that is, as the ordinary line figures that you usually see in Cadkey drawings, or they can appear as FILLED areas; that is, as solid areas of color. See ATTRIBUTES.

Similar commands let you control whether BOLD letters are in outline form or filled form. See LETTERING.

Pan

6 DISPLAY	
2 PAN	Alt-P

PAN lets you move a drawing up, down, or sideways to reposition it on the screen. Cadkey draws a rectangle that shows the area the new view will include. Reselect its position as often as you need to get the right display, then press F10 to exit the routine.

Part and Pattern Files

PART is Cadkey's name for an entire drawing and also for the corresponding file stored on a computer disk. A PATTERN is a drawing that you can add to a part file. See FILES for details.

Pen

PEN number is a code number assigned to entities. It can specify which pen a plotter will use for each entity when it plots the drawing. (COLOR carries with it a similar code number, providing an alternate way to assign plotter pens.)

See ATTRIBUTES for details on assigning pen numbers and colors. See VERIFY to determine what numbers are assigned to entities already created.

Plane

PLANE is one of the options offered by the SELECTION MENU (see SELECTING ENTITIES). It lets you select all entities lying in a single plane in space. Define the plane by (1) selecting three points, (2) selecting a point and a line, (3) selecting two intersecting lines, (4) specifying a given depth in a given view, or (5) selecting an arc, circle, or line. Selecting an arc or circle gives the plane in which that entity lies. Selecting a line gives the plane passing through that line and perpendicular to the viewing plane.

Plot

PLOT sends the drawing to the plotter, which plots only the portion of your drawing that shows on the computer screen. Run the CONFIGURATION program (see Chapter 4) to specify the parameters that will make Cadkey compatible with your plotter.

```
7 CONTROL
  7 PLOT
    1 AUTO
      1 NO*
        1 PEN #
        2 COLOR
      2 YES*
        1 PEN #
        2 COLOR
    2 KEY IN
      1 PEN #
      2 COLOR
```

*The YES/NO response is to the prompt, "Do you wish to display the scale and offsets?"

When you call for a plot, Cadkey lets you assign certain parameters. These parameters are discussed first; a step-by-step description of the plot routine comes afterwards.

To plot a drawing, you must choose between **PEN #** and **COLOR**. These are code numbers assigned to the entities you create. Your choice determines whether PEN NUMBER or COLOR controls the pens your plotter selects. Suppose, you had created a line when Cadkey's settings were PEN # = 2 and COLOR = 4. If now you choose PEN # for plotting, the plotter draws that line with pen #2. If you choose COLOR, it uses pen #4.

COLOR also controls the color Cadkey uses to show these entities on color monitors. Pen number has no effect until it is time to make a plot.

Nothing requires that color #4, which is yellow on the screen, be the same color on the plot. Pen #4 could be a black pen that draws a wide line. At this point, color is simply a convenient code number. If your plotter has more than eight pens, COLOR, which offers fifteen choices, gives more flexibility than PEN #, which offers only eight.

The configuration program (see Chapter 4) can give the plotter's pen numbers something other than a one-to-one correspondence with Cadkey's color numbers. You can, for example, assign the plotter's #3 pen to colors 2 and 15. (You can do this remapping only with COLOR, not with PEN #.)

The AUTO—YES and KEY IN options let you also control the **plot scale** and the **x and y offsets**. Plot scale sets the drawing size, with a scale of 1 making a 1 mm distance show as 1 mm in the finished plot. A scale of 0.5 gives a plot that is half size. The x and y offsets shift the drawing on the paper, with positive values moving it to the right and up. These offsets are actual distances, not scaled distances: When the plot scale is 0.5, a 10 mm offset moves the drawing up 10 mm, not 5 mm. For most plotters, the default offsets are zero. Because these offsets are set by the configuration program (see Chapter 4), you would not ordinarily need to change them at this point. If they are properly set, Cadkey puts whatever is at the center of the computer screen at the center of the drawing area.

Plotting the Drawing

AUTO automatically scales the plot to make the drawing area correspond to what shows on the computer screen. If your drawing fills the screen, your plot fills the paper. If your screen shows a large blank area surrounding your drawing, so will your plot.

Auto asks, **Do you wish to display the scale and offsets ? (NO)**

NO takes you directly to the **PEN #/COLOR** choice described earlier. After you make that selection, the MENU OPTIONS WINDOW shows the selection menu, letting you choose which entities to include in the plot. Press Return to start the plot.

YES shows the **scale** and **offsets** Cadkey plans to use and gives you a chance to change them. The default scale lets the drawing fill the paper to the same extent that the drawing fills the computer screen. If Cadkey selects 0.587203 as the plot scale, you might want to change it to 0.5 to get a drawing that is accurately half size. If you see that the drawing will not be centered properly, you can reposition it by changing the x and y offsets, but it may be easier to use PAN (see ZOOM) to make these changes on the screen, where you can see the results. Finally, select a rotation angle, make the **PEN #/COLOR** choice, and press Return to start the plot.

KEY IN works the same way as AUTO—YES, except that the default drawing scale in CADKEY Light 1.5 is full size. For CADKEY Light 4.0, the default scale is the same as it would be with either AUTO option.

Desktop Publishing Applications

The PLOT command can be used to transfer images to desktop publishing programs such as Ventura Publisher, Aldus PageMaker, Mecca III Desktop Publishing systems, WordPerfect, and others. To prepare Cadkey to create the appropriate files, run option 3 in the CONFIGURATION program (see SET PLOTTER OPTIONS in Chapter 4). Select one of the Hewlett Packard HPGL plotters. Several steps after you make this choice, Cadkey asks whether to send plotter codes to a serial port, a parallel port, or a file. Specify a file name; and, if you want to direct the file to other than the main Cadkey directory, include a path in the file specification.

This one file name is used for all your HPGL files, and Cadkey does not warn you if you are about to overwrite an earlier file with the current one. One way to avoid overwriting files is to use one of the SYSTEM COMMANDS to go to DOS and rename the most recent HPGL file. (If you use this method, be sure that DOS actually executes the command as you intend—see SYSTEM COMMANDS.)

Provided your desktop publishing program accepts HPGL files, and many do, it can import the Cadkey plot file you have created.

Remember that an HPGL file is not a substitute for a PART file. When you create the HPGL file, also save your drawing as a part file.

Point

```
1 CREATE
   4 POINT
      1 POSITN
      2 ON ARC
      3 SEGMENT
         1 NUMBER
         2 DISTNCE
         3 ALONGC
```

A POINT is a particular kind of entity—a small cross you can create as a reference position for later construction. This definition is specific. Cadkey does not consider the endpoint of a line or the center of a circle to be a POINT.

POINT is also an option in the POSITION MENU, where selecting POINT causes Cadkey to snap to the nearest point entity.

The usual reason for creating point entities is to establish exact locations that will help you with later construction. When you no longer need these points, you can use DELETE—SELECT—ALL DSP—BY TYPE—GEOM—POINT—DONE to remove them. (If you use this sequence, use F2 rather than the mouse to select BY TYPE. Using the mouse risks accidentally selecting ALL instead of BY TYPE. See the CAUTION note in SELECTING ENTITIES.)

Cadkey offers over a dozen ways to put points where you want them:

POSITN offers all the usual choices (ENDENT, POINT, INTRSC, etc.) from the POSITION MENU. The second option, POINT, is more useful than it might seem: In 2D mode, it lets you duplicate, at a new depth, the position of a point entity already on the screen.

ON ARC puts points on an arc or a circle. Select the arc or circle, then enter the angular positions for the points, using Cadkey's ANGULAR CONVENTIONS (0° at 3 o'clock; 90° at 12). If you specify an angle that falls beyond the end of an arc, Cadkey puts the point on an extension of the arc. This is a 3D command (see 2D/3D). Cadkey places the points on the arc in space, regardless of whether the construction mode is 2D or 3D.

Cadkey measures angular positions as if you were looking at the arc or circle in the plane in which it was created. If you create a circle in the front view and place points on it while working in the isometric view, the points you place are the same as if you had stayed in the front view to place them. This property can cause an occasional surprise: If you create a circle in the right side view and use the left side view for placing points, you find Cadkey measuring angles clockwise from 9 o'clock rather than the usual counterclockwise from 3 o'clock.

The SEGMENT Options

SEGMENT places points on LINES, ARCS, CIRCLES, and POLYLINES, but not on POLYGONS. There are three ways of distributing the points, and all three follow these rules:

1. Positions are based on distances measured along the entity. For an arc, Cadkey measures distances along the curve of the arc rather than as straight-line distances. Regardless of whether the construction mode is 2D or 3D, these distances are distances in space. If you put equally spaced points on a circle that is not parallel to the display plane, the points will not look equally spaced on the current view.
2. For lines, arcs, and open polylines, Cadkey measures distances from either end. When you select one of these entities, place the cursor near the end you want to use as the reference point. For circles and closed polylines, where you place the cursor has no effect on how Cadkey measures distances. Cadkey measures along circles counterclockwise from the 0° point and measures along closed polylines backwards from the end point; in other words, if you construct a closed polyline in a counterclockwise direction, Cadkey measures distances clockwise from the end point. Trying to reverse this direction by changing the DATABASE SEARCH direction does not work.
3. Cadkey asks whether to group the points you place. Grouping can simplify deleting them when they have served their purpose. See GROUP for an explanation.
4. After you have selected the entity and the points have appeared, Cadkey asks you to select another entity to receive points distributed in the same way. Press F10 to specify a different point distribution for the next entity or Esc to exit the routine.

NUMBER divides the entity into a number of parts of equal length and places points at the ends of each part. An arc divided into four segments thus gets five points—one at each end and three at the division points. (The arc is "divided" only in the sense that Cadkey calculates the point locations. The arc remains a single entity.)

DISTANCE puts a point at the end of an entity and puts additional points at fixed distance along the entity. If you specify a distance of 0.1", Cadkey fills the entity with points spaced 0.1".

ALONGC places a single point the specified distance from the end of the entity.

Polygon — Regular

1 CREATE
  1 LINE
    8 N-GON
  5 POLYLIN
    3 N-GON
  8 POLYGON
    1 CTR+RAD
    2 CTR+SID

Cadkey offers three ways to create regular polygons: A LINE N-GON consists of N line entities. A POLYGON is a single entity with N segments. A POLYLINE N-GON is also just a single entity. These three polygons can look the same, and the three construction methods are similar.

The discussion that follows is mainly on construction details, but it also includes comparisons of these three entity types. If you want more detail than this on how to choose between them, see POLYGONS, POLYLINES, AND LINES COMPARED.

Regardless of whether the command you are using is LINE—N-GON, POLYLIN—N-GON, or the CTR+RAD option of POLYGON, Cadkey's first four prompts ask for the same information:

Number of sides: The upper limits are:
100 for a LINE—N-GON
8 for a POLYGON
1500 for an unfilled POLYLIN—N-GON
50 for a POLYLIN—N-GON if you intend to fill it later.

Rotation angle: 0° makes the bottom side horizontal. Positive angles rotate the polygon counterclockwise.

Option for specifying radius: You may specify the size of the polygon by the radius of the circumscribed circle or the radius of the inscribed circle. Choose between CORNER, the distance from the center of the polygon to a vertex, and FLAT, the distance from the center to the middle of one side.

Radius: Enter the desired value.

The remaining steps depend on which type of polygon you are constructing.

POLYGON—CTR+RAD requires an extra step: Cadkey asks whether the polygon should be an OUTLINE or a FILLED figure. If you select OUTLINE, Cadkey will, at the end of the next step, give you a line drawing of the polygon. If you select FILLED, Cadkey generates a matrix of 256 colors and asks you to use the cursor to select one. Cadkey will draw the polygon as a solid area of color.

Indicate center: For a POLYLINE or POLYGON, Cadkey draws the figure when you indicate its center.

LINE requires one more step. Cadkey asks, **Group entities ? (NO)**. Pressing Return accepts NO, the default choice. YES prompts you for a group name (eight characters or less). Grouping can simplify later operations by letting you select an entire line polygon or group of line polygons rather than having to select the sides individually. See GROUP for details.

CREATE—POLYGON—CTR+SID is an alternate way to create a polygon. This command lets you specify the size of a regular polygon by the length of one side rather than by a radius. Otherwise, the procedure is like the one just described.

If you chose not to fill a POLYGON when you created it but want to fill it now, or if you want to fill a closed POLYLINE, use CONTROL—ATTRIB—OUT/FIL—FILLED. Pick a color from the matrix of choices Cadkey displays; then select the entities you want filled. See ATTRIBUTES for a fuller description.

In 3D mode, CADKEY Light 4.0 constructs all regular polygons parallel to the display plane and at the depth you specify for the center. CADKEY Light 1.5 constructs POLYLINE N-GONS this way, but it puts LINE N-GONS and regular polygons in the POLYGON family at the current depth, as though Cadkey were always in 2D mode (see 2D/3D).

POLYGON—the Entity

```
1 CREATE
   8 POLYGON
      1 CTR+RAD
      2 CTR+SID
      3 RECTANG
         1 CORNERS
         2 WID/HT
      4 STRING
```

A POLYGON is a closed entity of three to eight straight segments. Because it is a single entity, you can select the entire figure in a single step. You can fill any POLYGON (that is, show it as a solid area of color) either at the time you create it or at a later time. See ATTRIBUTES for information on filling POLYGONS.

Most of what can be said about POLYGONS you can find elsewhere in this handbook; therefore what follows is just an outline of what the POLYGON commands do. See POLYGONS, POLYLINES, AND LINES COMPARED if you wonder which entity type to use.

CTR+RAD creates regular polygons similar to those you can create as POLYLINES or LINES. See POLYGON—REGULAR for details.

CTR+SID creates regular polygons by specifying the length of one side rather than by specifying the polygon radius. POLYLINES and LINES do not offer you this option. Again, see POLYGON—REGULAR for details.

RECTANG—CORNERS creates rectangles by letting you specify the positions of diagonally opposite corners. See RECTANGLE.

RECTANG—WID/HT creates rectangles having the width and height you specify. Position the rectangle by specifying its lower left corner. See RECTANGLE.

STRING lets you construct polygons with up to eight sides and of any shape. See STRING for details.

POLYGONS, Polylines, and LINES Compared

If you want to create a regular polygon, a string (a series of lines joined end-to-end), or a rectangle, you can create it as a POLYGON, a POLYLINE, or as four LINES. If you construct rectangles using standard single-thickness lines, you have no way, by just looking at the computer screen, to tell one type from another.

In two ways, POLYGONS and polylines resemble one another and differ from LINE figures. (1) POLYGON and POLYLINE create a rectangle, for example, as a single entity; LINE creates it as a set of four entities—the four lines that comprise its sides. (2) A POLYGON or a closed polyline can be **filled**—shown as a solid block of color rather than as an outline.

Polylines and POLYGONS consist only of straight lines connected end-to-end. You cannot include arcs. Polylines can be either closed or open ended and can consist of many lines. POLYGONS can only be closed (the last line must end where the first line starts), and they can have no more than eight sides.

You may have sensed problems in nomenclature and in use of upper-case letters. Cadkey, needing short terms in its menu, gives POLYGON a meaning narrower than the conventional one. In Cadkey, a POLYGON is a closed, single-entity configuration, constructed under the POLYGON option of the CREATE menu. A regular polygon that is a polyline or a string of LINES is an N-GON. In this handbook, "POLYGON" conforms to Cadkey's definition, and "polygon" has the more general dictionary meaning. Similarly, "LINE" means a figure created using one of the CREATE—LINE commands, and "line" has the broader generic meaning. (In other parts of the handbook, when confusion is unlikely "line" can have either meaning.)

The topics that follow show the differences between the three types of figures and the properties you may want to consider as you decide which to use. For details on construction methods for specific figures, see RECTANGLE, POLYGON—REGULAR, and STRING.

Number of Entities

Because they are single entities, POLYGONS and polylines are often easier to handle than LINES. To MOVE, DELETE, or CROSSHATCH a rectangle, you select one entity, not four. (GROUP lets you do this with a LINE rectangle, but less conveniently.)

If you accidentally delete a polyline or POLYGON, ^U (undelete) restores it, but ^U restores only one element of a LINE figure, even if you have combined its entities to form a group.

Trimming, Extending, and Breaking

A disadvantage of single-entity figures is reduced flexibility. You can cut a notch in one side of a LINE figure, and you can use FILLET to round its corners, but you must take POLYGONS as they are. You can move them around and change them in size, but to change their shapes, you must delete and reconstruct them, using LINE entities if necessary.

Polylines can be unpredictable, but they are more cooperative than POLYGONS. You cannot use the extend part of the TRIM/EXTEND commands on internal segments of polylines, but you can trim them anywhere, and you can extend the end segments of open polylines. TRM/EXT operations work best when the entities involved actually intersect. If they do not intersect, you usually get what you want, but sometimes you get unexpected results.

You cannot use FILLET—CHAMFER with POLYGONS or polylines. FILLET—ARC works with both POLYGONS and polylines, but only in NO TRIM mode and only when Cadkey is in 2D construction mode (see 2D/3D). After you add arcs to a polyline, you can trim the polyline to them, but the number of steps makes the process inconvenient, and in adding the arcs you lose the advantage of a string that is a single entity.

EDIT—BREAK—DOUBLE (see BREAK) divides a closed polyline into three parts rather than the usual two. The third break is where you closed a STRING when you constructed it, or at the right or left end of the bottom side of a polyline N-GON or rectangle.

Number of Sides

POLYGONS can have only 3 to 8 sides. Polylines can have more: If you use POLYLINE–N-GON to construct a regular polygon, you can create one with as many as 1500 sides, but you cannot fill a closed polyline, regular or not, if it has more than 50 sides. With LINE–N-GON, you can construct a regular polygon with 150 sides.

Wide Lines

Polylines have an advantage over LINES and POLYGONS when you use wider-than-normal lines (see ATTRIBUTES). POLYGONS are not even in the running here. They give you only one line width—the minimum.

The segments of wide LINE entities have sharply defined ends that leave notches where lines meet at corners. Figure P-1 shows the notches that LINES have and how polylines fill them in. Figure P-1 also shows how the three kinds of figures respond to the FILL command (the topic that follows). The POLYGONS have different shapes than the other figures—a reminder that POLYGON is quite limited on number of sides.

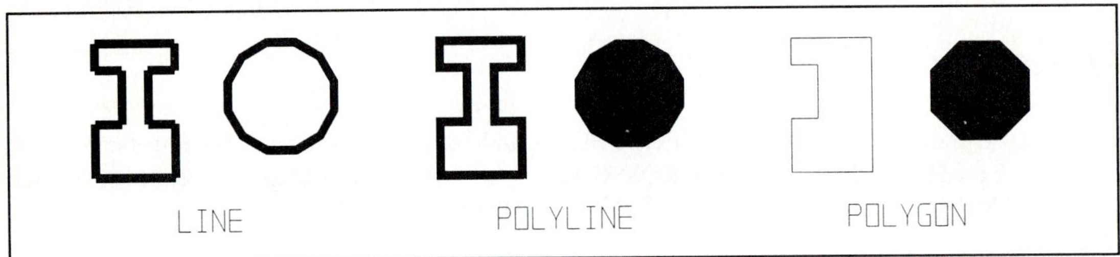

Fig. P-1 Response of figures to L-WIDTH and FILL commands

[Because you cannot include arcs in polylines, you cannot always use polylines to avoid notches at corners. Sometimes, when you have a thick arc meeting a thick LINE at an angle, you have a corner that could stand improvement. A trick helps: Use FILLET ARCS to round the corners, using the line width you used in the lines and using a small radius (for some reason, .01" works better than .001"). The image on the screen may show rough corners, but the printout looks fine.]

Filled Areas

You can FILL both POLYGONS and closed polylines; that is, you can show them as solid areas of color rather than as outlines. See ATTRIBUTES for details. You cannot fill LINE figures.

You can fill POLYGONS as you create them, or you can create them in outline form and use CONTROL—ATTRIB—OUT/FIL—FILLED to fill them later. With polylines, you don't have this choice. Cadkey creates them only in outline form, but you can use CONTROL—ATTRIB—OUT/FIL—FILLED to fill completed outlines. You can also reverse the process for either entity type. CONTROL—ATTRIB—OUT/FIL—OUTLINE converts a filled figure to an outline. This process is useful if you need to do some editing and find a solid block of color obscuring part of your drawing.

Entity Types and the Position Menu

When a POLYGON or polyline is complete, ENDENT and CENTER work as you would expect, snapping the cursor to the end or the middle of any segment you select. But if the point you want to snap to lies on a segment of the same entity you are constructing, Cadkey won't let you use it. If, for example, you want to close a polyline string, you cannot use ENDENT to do it. Cadkey gives you a way around this particular problem—you press Return to bring the end of a polyline string to the start point. But ending a segment of a string at an intermediate corner is harder. See STRING for one example of this problem.

ENDENT snaps to the ends of polyline and POLYGON segments, just as if these entities were made up of strings of LINE entities.

CENTER snaps to the center of the segment you select.

INTRSC is less cooperative. If two segments of a single polyline or POLYGON cross one another or meet at a corner, you would expect INTRSC to find their intersection, but Cadkey does not recognize an entity as intersecting itself. When segments of two different entities meet or cross, INTRSC works smoothly. But INTRSC becomes unreliable when you try to find a *potential* intersection (a point beyond the end of one or both segments—the point where the segments would meet if they were longer). Although potential intersections work with LINES, they do not work when the intersection lies on an extension of a POLYGON segment.

For a potential intersection with a polyline segment, Cadkey looks first not for the intersection you want, but for an actual intersection by another segment of the same polyline. If none exists, it usually finds the intersection you are looking for; but sometimes it finds instead a potential intersection using a different segment of the same polyline.

ALONGL cannot be used with POLYGONS or polylines. Cadkey gives you an **Entity not found** error message if you try. Instead, for polylines you can use CREATE–POINT–SEGMENT–ALONGC option to place a POINT and then snap to that point (see the next paragaph).

The position menu for POINTS includes three options for distributing points along entities: SEGMENT—NUMBER, SEGMENT—DISTNCE, and SEGMENT—ALONGC. None of these work with POLYGONS. They work with LINE entities, but you can use them on only one segment of a string at a time. With polylines, they give excellent results. Strictly speaking, these are not position menu options, but you can use them as such by putting a point entity at the position you want and snapping to that point. See POINT for more detail.

SEGMENT—NUMBER divides the entire length of a polyline into a number of equal-length segments and puts a point at the end of each segment. If you specify ten segments, you get eleven points—one at each end and nine between segments. On a closed polyline, one point is double.

SEGMENT—DISTNCE fills the polyline with points spaced the distance you specify. Select the entity near the end you want to use as a starting point. If you select a point beyond the first bend, Cadkey may start the points at the wrong end, even though you may be much closer to the end you want than you are to the other.

SEGMENT—ALONGC (along curve) places a single point a specified distance from the end of the polyline. Select the entity near the end you want to measure from.

Polyline

```
1 CREATE
  5 POLYLIN
    1 STRING
    2 RECTANG
      1 CORNERS
      2 WID/HT
    3 N-GON
    4 SKETCH
```

A POLYLINE is a single entity made up of a series of straight lines joined end to end. The polyline may be open or closed. "Closed" means that the last line ends where the first one starts. Except for SKETCH lines, the types of figures POLYLINE can create can also be created in two other ways. See POLYGONS, POLYLINES, AND LINES COMPARED for ways to decide which alternative best meets your needs.

Polylines offer several advantages: (1) Because a polyline is a single entity, you can handle a complex geometrical figure as a single unit. (2) You can fill a closed polyline to produce a solid area of color. (3) If a polyline figure consists of thick lines, Cadkey draws its corners more smoothly than it would draw them for a string of LINE entities. Figure P-1 in the preceding section illustrates the second and third points.

After you have completed a closed polyline, you can FILL it using CONTROL—ATTRIB—OUT/FIL—FILLED. Select the color you want from the palette that appears and select the entities you want to fill. CONTROL—ATTRIB—OUT/FIL—OUTLINE lets you reverse the process, converting a filled block to outline form. At the same time it lets you select the color of the outline. See ATTRIBUTES for details.

STRING creates a series of straight lines, with each new line starting at the end of the preceding one. Press Return to end the string. Cadkey asks whether to close the entity. If you select YES, Cadkey adds one more line connecting the last point to the start of the string.

Pressing F10 deletes the last point, leaving a rubber band between the cursor and the next-to-the-last point. You then have three options. You can continue the construction by reselecting the last point. You can press Return, which leads to the YES/NO choice on whether to close the polygon. Or you can press F10 a second time to end the construction at that next-to-the-last point. With this third option, Cadkey senses that you may be unhappy with more than the last line and gives you a choice of whether to delete the polyline or leave it on the screen. See STRING for more detail.

RECTANG lets you construct a rectangle by (1) indicating diagonally opposite corners or (2) specifying its width, its height, and the position of its lower left corner. See RECTANGLE.

N-GON is Cadkey's name for a regular polygon. See POLYGON—REGULAR for details, or just follow the prompts.

SKETCH, as the name implies, produces a polyline of random shape. Press the mouse button and hold it down while moving the mouse. Cadkey uses a series of short straight lines to record the path of the mouse on the screen. The left side of Figure P-2 shows one application

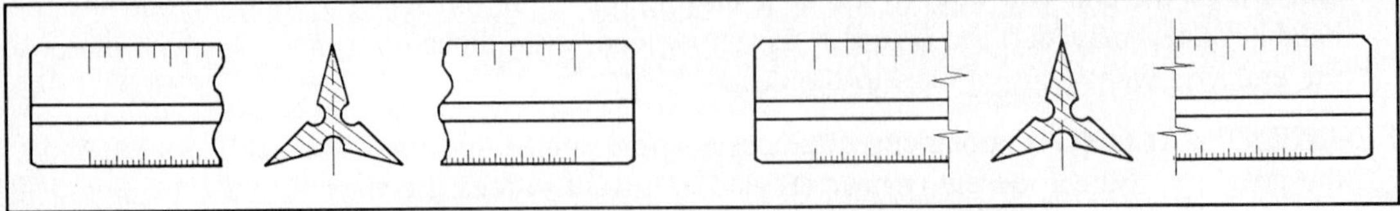

Figure P-2 Two methods of creating break lines

of such a line. Two short break lines make room for a revolved section and also let the drawing of a civil engineer's scale fit in a small space.

You can interrupt the generation of the sketch line at any time by releasing the mouse button. If you move the cursor and hold down the button again, Cadkey connects your last point with the new position and lets you continue as before. This last feature is not obvious—Cadkey does not generate a rubber band to show that the sketch line will continue.

You finish a sketch line almost the same way that you finish a polyline chain. When you press either Return or F10, Cadkey ends the line and asks whether to save it (first attempts are often less than perfect). YES makes the line permanent; NO gives you a chance to try again.

Discussion of Sketch Lines

Because you draw sketch lines freehand, it is hard to get them looking just right. The following is a discussion of some of the problems you can expect, together with some ways to get around them.

Cadkey's CONFIGURATION file (see Chapter 4) sets a minimum length for sketch-line segments. If CADKEY Light 1.5 is configured for inches, the default setting of 0.5" gives sketch lines that are much too coarse for this particular application. CADKEY Light 4.0, with a default minimum length of 0.1", works better.

If your copy of CADKEY Light 1.5 is configured for millimeters, its default setting of 0.5 gives a minimum segment length that is 0.5 mm rather than 0.5", even though the configuration file lists the setting as an inch dimension. This 0.5 mm length is about right for this problem. With CADKEY Light 4.0 configured for millimeters, its 0.1" default setting translates to 0.1 mm, giving you sketch lines with too many segments. (The resolution of your mouse may affect this minimum, giving longer segments than Cadkey calls for.)

Solutions to the half-inch problem illustrate the nature of your options. The most basic approach would be to use the configuration program to change this default length to 0.05" The prompt to look for is **Enter the minimum increment for sketching**. Find it hidden under **Set graphics options** and **Select graphics device**.

But it may be easier to accept the half-inch setting. Use Alt-A to set the drawing scale to 0.5. Draw two oversize sketch lines from the top of the screen to the bottom. Don't try to connect them to anything. If your viewport is about six inches high, you have room for a little over 20 segments, about as many as you need to make each line look right.

Putting the lines in the right place requires a little fussing. With CREATE—LINE—HRZ/VRT—HORIZTL—ENDENT, draw a temporary horizontal line through the top endpoint of whichever sketch line has the lower top end. Draw another through the bottom end of whichever line extends down the least. Use EDIT—TRM/EXT—DOUBLE (see TRM/EXT) to trim the sketch lines to these horizontal lines, making them the same height. Use CONTROL—VERIFY—DIST—2 ENTS (see VERIFY), to measure the distance between the horizontal lines and thus find the height of the sketch lines. Use X-FORM—SCALE—MOVE—SINGLE (see MOVE/COPY/JOIN) to reduce the lines to the right height. The scaling origin Cadkey asks for can be anywhere. Make the scale factor the line height you need divided by the height you just measured. Enter it as a fraction such as 1.125/15.374565, letting Cadkey do the arithmetic.

The lines are now the right shape and size. Use X-FORM—TRANS-A—MOVE—SINGLE with CADKEY Light 1.5 or X-FORM—NEW/OLD—MOVE—SINGLE with CADKEY Light 4.0 to move them, one at a time, to the right places. Use one end of the sketch line for the base position (put the cursor beyond the end of the line to keep ENDENT from accidentally selecting the end of an internal segment), and use a point on your drawing for the new base position.

If you expect to need short break lines again, you might want to scale these two lines to heights of 1" and save them as a PATTERN (see FILES). They would then be ready to be imported, scaled to any length and drawn at any angle, the next time you need them.

After reading the preceding discussion, you may decide to substitute the break lines shown in the right half of Figure P-2. This type of line is meant for long breaks and is the one to use if the break line extends halfway across the drawing, but it is not out of place here. Draw it as a polyline string. Use SNAP to keep the main line vertical, press PgDn a couple of times to keep the snap distances short enough, and please draw the zigzags with segments that are close to horizontal, not ones with slopes near 45°.

Position Menu

1 CURSOR
2 POINT
3 ENDENT
4 CENTER
5 INTRSC
6 ALONGL
7 POLAR
8 DELTA
9 KEY-IN

The position menu appears when you are to specify locations, as when you tell Cadkey where to put the endpoints of a line you are creating. All options except one—CURSOR with SNAP turned off—allow precise positioning without requiring you to place the cursor carefully. ENDENT can select the end of a line when the cursor is almost half an inch away from the line and closer to the center of the line than to its end. The effect is similar to SNAP, which pulls the cursor to the nearest point on a rectangular grid.

You can change options in the middle of a construction; for example, you can select the start of a line with ENDENT and the end with INTRSC. An asterisk in the position menu shows which selection method is active.

Depending on the CONFIGURATION file setup, Cadkey may mark your selection with an x. If this selection was not what you intended, press F10 to cancel it and try again.

CURSOR selects the point at the cursor. (See SNAP for a way to make this selection method precise.)

POINT selects the POINT entity nearest the cursor. This point must be one made using the CREATE—POINT command. Cadkey's definition of a point does *not* include endpoints of lines, points on the visible grid or the snap grid, or other well defined locations that we normally think of as points.

ENDENT selects the nearest end of an entity. It selects the end point of a line, polyline segment, POLYGON segment, or arc, or the 0° point (the 3 o'clock position) of a circle.

CENTER selects the midpoint of a line, the midpoint of a segment of a polyline or POLYGON, the center of a circle, or the center of curvature of an arc. When you select an arc or circle to specify its center, put the cursor on the arc, not at the center.

INTRSC selects the intersection of two entities. If the entities do not meet, the chosen point lies where they would intersect if they were extended.

ALONGL selects a position on a line, a given distance from its endpoint. Select the line near the end from which you want to measure the distance. A prompt appears, showing total line length. Key in the desired distance. Negative distances place the point beyond the end of the line. CREATE—POINT—SEGMENT—ALONGC (see POINT) gives you a way to locate similar positions on arcs, circles, or polylines.

POLAR locates a point using polar coordinates. It places only one point and does not draw a line from the polar origin to that point. Select an origin by any method except POLAR or DELTA; then enter values of distance and angle from that temporary origin. Angles are measured from the horizontal, with 0° at 3 o'clock and 90° at 12 o'clock.

DELTA is like POLAR except that it asks you for the x, y, and z displacements from the temporary origin. (See also the notes under KEY-IN.)

KEY-IN specifies points by their cartesian coordinates. If you just press Return instead of keying in a value, Cadkey enters the default value of 0.

Cadkey uses two coordinate systems. You can tell which is in use by whether the first prompt asks for a value for X (a WORLD coordinate) or for XV (a VIEW coordinate). To change, press F10 to remove the prompt and ^V to switch systems.

View coordinates are the more obvious system: XV is to the right, YV is up, and ZV is perpendicular to the screen, with positive values toward you. World coordinates are fixed with respect to the object in space and look different in different VIEWS. See COORDINATES for an explanation, or see the inside front cover of this book for illustrations of the world coordinate system in Cadkey's eight standard views.

Related Information

If you need greater detail on the position menu options, you can find it in the tutorial exercises in Chapter 2. The section titled POSITION MENU is obviously appropriate, but see also the section on THREE-DIMENSIONAL CONSTRUCTION.

See the notes under CURSOR. They cover some of the finer points of the selection process, such as why it can be a poor idea to position the cursor accurately.

POLYGONS and POLYLINES may give you trouble when you try to apply some of the position menu options. ENDENT and CENTER generally treat polygon and polyline segments the way they would treat individual line entities. INTRSC works with actual intersections but is unreliable for potential intersections. ALONGL does not recognize polygons or polylines. For details, see, under POLYGONS, POLYLINES, AND LINES COMPARED, the notes titled Entity Types and the Position Menu.

Another way to indicate position is to put a POINT entity at the location you want and then snap to that point. This method gives you additional options, in many cases letting you select positions that would otherwise be difficult to specify. See POINT.

Three-Dimensional Construction

If you are constructing in three dimensions, you need additional information on how the position menu options work; if not, you can, for the moment, safely ignore the following.

The rules depend on whether the construction mode is set to 2D or 3D (See 2D/3D and DEPTH). The purpose of the 3D setting is to let you work with a partially constructed drawing, selecting positions that coincide in space with locations on the object. 2D mode, in spite of the name, also lets you draw in three dimensions, with the third dimension controlled by the value currently selected for DEPTH.

ENDENT illustrates how these two modes work. In 2D mode, ENDENT selects a point that in the current view appears to coincide with the end of an entity, but that may be closer to you or farther from you than the endpoint you selected. In 3D mode, ENDENT selects positions that coincide in space with the endpoint. With two exceptions, the other position menu options work similarly. The exceptions are:

1. The point selected by CURSOR is always at the current depth.
2. Coordinates that you KEY-IN *usually* override the depth setting, regardless of the 2D/3D mode. See 2D/3D for more detail.

With the construction mode set to 3D, INTRSC requires not only that the entities intersect on the computer screen; they must also intersect in space. If you get an **Intersection not found** error message when you pick lines that seem to intersect, the lines are probably at different depths.

Suppose a line is 4" long in space but, because of its angle, projects as 2" long in the plane of the screen. To select the center of the line with ALONGL, you would key in 1" if the construction mode were set to 2D; 2" if it were set to 3D.

In 2D mode, the origin used by DELTA is at the working depth; in 3D mode, at the depth of the selected point.

This discussion is not meant to be comprehensive. See 2D/3D for more information.

Print

7 CONTROL
6 PRINT

PRINT sends the drawing to the printer, which prints what you see on the computer screen. If the screen shows only a small area of the drawing, you get a blown-up printout of that region.

Typically, the copy Cadkey prints is roughly to the scale shown on the screen (the number after S: in the STATUS WINDOW), but the exact scale depends on how the monitor screen size compares to the printing area. For example, a SCALE setting (see ZOOM) of .858, a number determined by trial and error, gives printouts that are accurately full size with my computer.

The quality of a printed copy depends partly on the capabilities of the printer. It also depends on whether Cadkey's CONFIGURATION program is set for low, medium, or high resolution. It is not limited by the quality of the image on the computer screen.

Printing does not start immediately. The initial delay and further delays after printing starts represent the time needed to convert the mathematical specifications of lines, arcs, etc. to a pattern of dots.

Recall

```
2 EDIT
   3 RECALL
      1 LAST      ^U
      2 LEVEL
      3 ALL
         1 ALL
         2 BY TYPE
         3 EX TYPE
```

LAST recalls (undeletes) the last entity deleted. If a GROUP was deleted, LAST recalls only one entity of that group.

LEVEL restores all entities deleted from the specified level.

ALL can recall all deleted entities. BY TYPE and EX TYPE (see TYPE MASKING, described under SELECTING ENTITIES) allow more selective restoration, by, for example, recalling only arcs and circles. You can also make this command selective by pressing Alt-N to invoke LEVEL MASKING (see SELECTING ENTITIES). Level masking limits selections either to one level or to all levels but one. If you use level masking, remember to reset it to zero (no masking) when you are finished. Otherwise it remains in effect indefinitely.

Limitations

Groups that are deleted are recalled as just a series of entities; in other words, they lose their identities as groups.

RECALL does not restore parts of entities that have been removed by TRM/EXT. (But usually the EXTEND part of the TRM/EXT command can restore such parts.)

When you SAVE a drawing, Cadkey removes all records of deleted entities. When you reload the drawing, you replace the current version with a version that contains only those entities that have survived all of your editing. Entities on hidden LEVELS are still there, but entities you have deleted are not. RECALL—ALL can bring back only those entities deleted since the last LOAD command. As will be noted shortly, you can use this fact to advantage.

Techniques

The problem with RECALL—ALL is that recalling all deleted entities usually recalls too many unwanted ones. In a heavily edited drawing, it may be easier to reconstruct the entities you want back than to clean up the clutter produced by RECALL—ALL. There are several ways to reduce the pain:

1. SAVE your drawing (see FILES) before trying RECALL—ALL. This gives you the option of restoring your drawing to what it was before the recall operation.
2. As already noted, the MASKING options built into the RECALL command can limit the types of entities you recall.
3. Before you get into trouble, make it a habit to SAVE and LOAD your drawing occasionally. When you save a drawing, Cadkey removes all records of deleted entities. When you reload the drawing, you replace the current version with the fresh, uncluttered one. RECALL—ALL can bring back only those entities deleted since the last LOAD command, and these are the ones you are most likely to want to recall. As a side benefit, getting rid of these unnecessary records often speeds Cadkey's response to your commands. Under FILES, see Cleaning up a Part File.

4. If you know ahead of time that the entities you are deleting are some you might want back, you can, instead of actually deleting them, use DISPLAY—LEVELS—MOVE (see LEVEL) to hide them on an unused level. This gets the entities conveniently out of the way but makes it easy to recall them or to permanently delete them later.
5. If it is important that you recall some entities, and if you know they will bring back a lot of unwanted entities with them, you can use a more elaborate procedure involving LEVELS. In the most complex case, you have been working on several levels and need to recall entities that were on several levels.

   With DISPLAY—LEVELS—MOVE—LEVEL, empty the levels you have been using. These are the levels on which the recalled entities will reappear, and the MOVE operation keeps the entities currently on the screen from being mixed with those you recall. You might move all entities from level 1 to level 11; all those from level 2 to level 12, etc.

   Now use RECALL. You may want to recall one level at a time. Find the entities you want, and use DISPLAY—LEVELS—MOVE—SELECT to move them up ten levels. With DELETE—LEVEL, get rid of the remaining entities on the level you recalled.

Rectangle

```
1 CREATE
  1 LINE
    7 RECTANG
      1 CORNERS
      2 WID/HT
  5 POLYLIN
    2 RECTANG
      1 CORNERS
      2 WID/HT
  8 POLYGON
    3 RECTANG
      1 CORNERS
        1 OUTLINE
        2 FILLED
      2 WID/HT
        1 OUTLINE
        2 FILLED
```

Cadkey creates three types of rectangles. CREATE—LINE—RECTANG creates a rectangle consisting of four line entities. CREATE—POLYLIN—RECTANG creates a rectangle in which the four sides are a single entity. CREATE—POLYGON—RECTANG also creates a rectangle that is a single entity.

POLYGON and POLYLINE rectangles can be filled; that is, you can draw them as solid areas in the color you specify. You can, if you wish, fill POLYGONS when you create them, or you can, in a separate operation, fill either POLYGONS or POLYLINES after you create them.

You can easily modify LINE rectangles. For example, you can cut notches in their sides and round their corners. You can modify POLYLINE rectangles, but with more difficulty. The MOVE/COPY/JOIN commands can change the size and orientation of POLYGON rectangles, but nothing can change their shapes. See POLYGONS, POLYLINES, AND LINES COMPARED for more detailed discussions of these three entity types.

Except for the OUTLINE/FILLED choice for POLYGONS, construction methods are the same for all three types of rectangles:

CORNERS lets you specify the positions of diagonally opposite corners. After you have selected the first corner position, a "rubber box" maintains a rectangle between that point and the cursor position, letting you see the rectangle before you complete its construction.

WID/HT determines the rectangle's dimensions by letting you enter its width and its height. You then specify the position of the lower left corner.

OUTLINE creates rectangles in the normal manner, showing each as four straight lines. For POLYGONS, these are always thin lines. The LINE WIDTH command can give LINE and POLYLINE rectangles thicker sides, but you can create POLYGONS only with the thinnest line width.

FILLED invokes a palette of 256 colors. Use the cursor to select the color you want and the rectangles you create will be solid areas of that color. It is often a good idea to create rectangles in unfilled form and use CONTROL—ATTRIB—OUT/FIL—FILLED to fill them later. Filled areas can obscure parts of the drawing, hampering further construction.

In the CORNERS mode, Cadkey creates the three types of rectangles at the current depth, regardless of the 2D/3D mode setting. The WID/HT mode sometimes responds to the 2D/3D setting and sometimes does not. See 2D/3D for details, or play it safe and always set DEPTH to the value you want for the rectangle. (That way you don't have to remember detailed rules.)

Redraw

```
6  DISPLAY
   1  REDRAW      ^R
```

Some computer programs call the REDRAW operation "refreshing" the screen. Many of Cadkey's operations leave behind some clutter, and work is easier if you periodically eliminate this clutter by using **^R** to redraw the display. (Redraw is not the only way to do this. When you change VIEWS or use one of the ZOOM commands, Cadkey redraws the screen.)

There are less obvious reasons for using redraw. When you DELETE an entity, you see blank spots where it crosses other entities, and redraw fills in these empty patches. The most pronounced effect occurs when two lines coincide and you delete one of them. Both temporarily disappear. It's not until you redraw the screen that you see that the other remains. See TROUBLESHOOTING for a discussion of some of the problems related to this phenomenon.

Rotation

There are many ways in which Cadkey either rotates entities or puts them at specific angles. For details, see the topics referred to in the paragraphs that follow.

One of the MOVE/COPY/JOIN options—2D ROT in CADKEY Light 1.5 or ROTATE in CADKEY Light 4.0—lets you rotate one or more entities around a center of rotation that you specify. You can either rotate the entities or leave them where they are and make one or more copies in rotated positions. See MOVE/COPY/JOIN.

The text of NOTES is usually horizontal, but DETAIL—SET—TEXT—NOT ANG (see LETTERING) lets you write notes at other angles. DETAIL—CHANGE—NOT ANG (see CHANGE) lets you change the angle of notes you have already written.

The letters used in NOTES, LABELS, and DIMENSIONS can be slanted, as in italics. DETAIL—SET—TEXT—NOT FNT and —DIM FNT (see LETTERING) let you choose between BOX and BOLD fonts and then specify the slant angle of the lettering. DETAIL—CHANGE—

NOT ANG and –DIM ANG (see CHANGE) lets you slant the letters in completed notes, labels, and dimensions.

CREATE–LINE–ANGLE (see LINE) lets you create a line at a given angle to an existing line.

There are several ways to change the angle at which you see a three-dimensional drawing. See VIEW.

POLAR (see POSITION MENU) gives you control over angular positions by letting you specify displacements in polar coordinates.

FILES–PATTERN–RETRIEV (see FILES) lets you import one drawing into another (for example, you can import a resistor symbol into a circuit diagram). When you retrieve a pattern, you specify its size and angle.

Part of the process of creating a regular polygon (see POLYGON–REGULAR) is to specify the angle the base makes with the horizontal.

Several of the methods for constructing ARCS use the start and end angles as a way of specifying arc length.

You can place POINTS at specific angular positions on arcs and circles.

See ANGULAR CONVENTIONS for information on how Cadkey measures angles and angular positions.

Save

```
5  FILES
   1  PART
      1  SAVE        ^F
      2  LOAD
      3  LST/LOAD
   2  PATTERN
      1  CREATE
      2  RETRIEV
      3  LST/RTRV
```

SAVE records a drawing on a disk. The most obvious reason to save a file is that you don't want to lose your drawing when you turn off the computer at the end of a work session. But you should also save periodically in case mother nature, the power company, or your computer unexpectedly ends your work session for you. See FILES for details on saving your drawings.

In addition to the basic SAVE routine, two others let you save files: (1) When you LOAD (retrieve) a file or use LST/LOAD to load it, the new file replaces everything currently in memory. To avoid loss of your present drawing, Cadkey asks whether you want to save your current part first. If you do, select YES and follow the normal SAVE procedure. (2) When you EXIT Cadkey, it asks whether to save the part drawing before terminating. Again, select YES to start the SAVE routine.

CREATE is for a PATTERN file what SAVE is for a PART file. However, saving a pattern is a more complex procedure because you first specify what parts of your drawing you want to include. See FILES for details.

Scale

The term **scale** applies to several of Cadkey's functions:

ZOOM—SCALE lets you change the size of the image on the screen by keying in a new value for the scale of the drawing. See ZOOM for details on this command and on related commands for changing image size.

MOVE/COPY/JOIN—SCALE lets you change the sizes of selected entities. This scale command is more basic than ZOOM—SCALE in that it not only changes how large the entities appear on the screen; it also changes their dimensions as recorded in Cadkey's database. See MOVE/COPY/JOIN for details.

DETAIL—SET—UNITS lets you create a drawing using metric units but scale dimension values to make them show in inches. See UNITS for ways to dimension a drawing in a different set of units than those you use for construction.

See DIMENSIONS AND THE TEXT EDITOR for a way to dimension distances that cannot be shown to scale.

FILES—PATTERN—RETRIEV lets you scale patterns that you insert into your drawings. Patterns are typically subassemblies that you draw once to avoid having to redraw them every time you need them. See FILES.

See PLOT and PRINT for ways to control the scale of plots and printouts.

See LETTERING for ways to scale the size of NOTES, LABELS, and DIMENSIONS. You can preset both the height and the width-to-height ratio of letters. You can also change letter height and shape in completed notes, labels, and dimensions.

Sectioning

A sectioned drawing is one that uses a cutaway view to show what an object looks like on the inside. See CROSSHATCHING for notes on creating the section lines used in this type of drawing.

Selecting Entities

You select an entity if you want to DELETE it, MOVE it, or otherwise operate on it. Often you will select several entities for one operation. For example, to move part of a drawing you need to tell Cadkey which entities to move.

To select an entity, move the cursor within 1/2" of it and press either the mouse button or the space bar. Cadkey picks the closest entity and either highlights it or marks it with a small triangle. If the mark falls on the wrong entity, showing that Cadkey misunderstood your intention, press F10. Cadkey cancels the selection and, depending on how the CONFIGURATION file is set, may confirm the cancellation with the symbol #. After the cancellation, continue the selection procedure.

Placing the Cursor

Cadkey first searches an area called the selection trap and selects the first entity it finds there. The selection trap is a circular area two tenths of an inch in diameter, centered on the cursor. If Cadkey finds nothing in this area, it searches an area one inch in diameter and picks the entity nearest the center of the cursor. As the drawing gets more complex, the search takes longer.

You can speed the search by placing the cursor inside the selection trap—within one tenth of an inch of your target. But if there is more than one entity this close, you can have a problem. Within this small area, Cadkey picks the first entity it finds, not necessarily the closest one. Ideally, you should move the cursor within a tenth of an inch of the entity you want but keep it farther than this from other entities. If this is difficult, Cadkey gives you other ways to cope with selection problems. See the subsection that follows on Problems with Crowded Drawings.

To select a **CIRCLE**, place the cursor on its circumference, not at its center. To select **DIMENSIONS**, **NOTES**, and **LABELS**, place the cursor at the lower left corner of the first line of characters. (See LETTERING for an illustration showing this selection point.) For **CROSSHATCHING**, place the cursor anywhere on the first or last crosshatch line. If you have trouble, use a WINDOW (see ZOOM) to enlarge the corner where this first line appears. If you still have trouble, see CROSSHATCHING.

Problems with Crowded Drawings

When entities are closely spaced, it is hard to keep Cadkey from picking the wrong ones. Four techniques can help. Each of these ways offers a second advantage: By giving Cadkey fewer entities to check, these techniques make the selection process faster.

1. Alt-W creates a WINDOW (see ZOOM), letting you select an area of the drawing and expand it to fill the screen. This makes closely spaced entities easier to select. Alt-B returns you to the previous view.
2. Alt-M calls the TYPE MASKING menu, described later, which lets you specify the type of entity you want to select. If you specify ARC/CIR, Cadkey selects the nearest arc or circle even if other entities may be closer.
3. Alt-N calls the LEVEL MASKING routine, also described later, which limits selections either to a specified LEVEL or to all levels but one.
4. Alt-R changes the direction in which Cadkey conducts its DATABASE SEARCH. DB in the STATUS WINDOW shows this direction. If two entities are directly under the cursor and DB is set to FWD, Cadkey will pick the entity you created first. To get Cadkey to pick the other one, switch the setting to DB:BACK. For details, see Selection Trap and Selection Techniques in the section titled CURSOR.

The Selection Menu

The SELECTION MENU offers several ways to select entities, and most options let you select several of them at a time. You cannot invoke this menu directly, but it appears when you execute routines such as CROSSHATCH, MOVE, DELETE, and PATTERN.

```
1 SINGLE
2 CHAIN
3 WINDOW
4 GROUP
  1 SELECT
  2 BY NAME
5 PLANE
  1 3 PTS
  2 PT/LINE
  3 2 LINES
  4 VW/DPTH
    1 VALUE
    2 POSITN
  5 ENTITY
6 ALL DSP
  1 ALL
  2 BY TYPE        Alt-M
    [Masking menu]*
  3 EX TYPE
    [Masking menu]*
```

*See the discussion that follows on Basic Type Masking.

SINGLE lets you use the cursor to select one *or more* entities. ("SINGLE" means you select them one at a time). If you accidentally select the wrong entity, press F10 once to cancel your most recent selection. Pressing it twice cancels all selections.

If the entity you select is part of a GROUP, Cadkey lets you choose whether to select the single entity, the subgroup, or the entire group. See the notes on GROUP that follow.

CHAIN selects a string of entities connected end to end; for example, the boundary of an area to be crosshatched. Select the first entity; then indicate a point—its position is not critical—that shows Cadkey which direction to go in following the chain. Select a terminating entity (the last link), or press Return to select the entire chain.

The chain ends when Cadkey encounters a break, when two entities in the chain touch but not at their endpoints, or when an entity in the chain lies entirely off the screen. A break occurs if Cadkey is in 3D construction mode (see 2D/3D) and the entities do not connect in three-dimensional space. If a chain forms a closed loop, and if you did not specify a terminating entity, the chain does not necessarily end when it meets the start point. If Cadkey finds a side branch there, it follows it to continue the chain.

If the chain branches, as it often does in complex drawings, CHAIN may not follow the path you want. Depending on Cadkey's CONFIGURATION, you may see marks that let you monitor the route the chain takes. Cadkey asks whether its selection is OK, letting you reject it if it is not. Cadkey also asks whether the selection is complete. NO shifts you to the SINGLE mode, letting you add entities to those that CHAIN has selected.

WINDOW asks you to draw a rectangular window by selecting diagonally opposite corners. Cadkey then selects all entities *completely* enclosed by that window. If you want to include a DIMENSION in a window, be sure to enclose the arrows and witness lines as well as the number.

A different WINDOW command, initiated by Alt-W and described under ZOOM, starts another way to select a group of entities. As before, you define the window by specifying diagonally opposite corners. Cadkey expands the window to the limits of the screen. You then use ALL DSP, described below, to select *all* entities that show in whole or in part.

Note the differences in results: The first window command lets you use any rectangular window, and it selects only those entities it completely encloses. The window used in the Alt-W—ALL DSP routine conforms to the shape of the computer screen, and every entity that shows is selected, even if you can see only a small part.

GROUP selects all entities in a group or subgroup, regardless of whether all its entities show on the screen. (Entities are grouped so they may be handled as a unit rather than individually. An example of a group is a collection of 35 entities that form the side view of a bolt. In a drawing with ten of the bolts, each bolt would be a subgroup and the ten subgroups would comprise the group. See GROUP for notes on entity grouping.)

SELECT selects a *subgroup* when you select one of its entities.

BY NAME selects an entire *group* when you key in its name.

SUGGESTION: Consider using SINGLE (or ^Q) to select grouped entities. It is safer and more flexible than GROUP—SELECT or GROUP—BY NAME, and it performs similar functions. GROUP is faster—it has fewer steps and executes the command immediately. But SINGLE is more forgiving. If you use GROUP—SELECT or GROUP—BY NAME to move or delete and happen to select the wrong group or subgroup, Cadkey moves or deletes it immediately. But DELETE—SINGLE responds with **Entity belongs to a group - Choose selection option (GROUP)**. The inset shows the choices that appear in the menu options window.

1 GROUP
2 SUBGRP
3 ENTITY

Watch Cadkey's response to your selection to confirm that the group you selected is the one you wanted to select. Then, after you press F1 to choose GROUP or F2 to choose SUBGROUP, check the prompt line to see how many entities you selected. **Select entity #251** shows that Cadkey has made 250 selections. If you have ten subgroups, each with 25 entities, you know that the entire group, not just a subgroup, was selected. If this is not what you intended, press Esc or press F10 twice to cancel all selections.

PLANE selects all entities lying in a plane in space. There are several ways to specify the plane:

3 PTS lets you select three points. Check CONST in the STATUS WINDOW for the current setting of the construction mode. 2D gives you a plane at the current DEPTH. 3D, which is probably what you want, lets you select a plane passing through specific points on the object (see 2D/3D).

PT/LINE constructs a plane through a point and a line.

2 LINES constructs a plane through two lines that intersect or that would intersect if extended. For parallel lines, this command won't work. Instead, use ENDENT with either 3 PTS or PT/LINE.

VW/DPTH lets you specify a VIEW parallel to the plane you want. You can specify the DEPTH in that view or select a point on your drawing and pass the plane through that point. To save the time it would take to draw the new view, Cadkey stays in the current one.

ENTITY selects the plane passing through the line, arc, or circle you select. If you select a line, the plane is the one passing through the line and perpendicular to the screen.

ALL DSP can select every entity displayed on the screen, including those that extend beyond the screen limits and thus show only partly. You can use WINDOW and PAN (see ZOOM) to control how many entities the screen shows.

ALL selects everything on the screen. (The next two options also operate on the entire screen, but the MASKING MENU makes them more selective.)

BY TYPE and **EX TYPE** use the MASKING MENU, described in the next subsection, to limit selections to certain types of entities. This is a handy command when you have used a number of POINT entities as construction aids and are finished with them. Select BY TYPE–GEOM–POINT–DONE, and Cadkey can select only the points.

CAUTION: Have you ever selected an item from the menu options window and had the mouse, when you press the button, move ever so slightly and select the option next to the one you want? Here, that could be a disaster. If you accidentally select ALL instead of BY TYPE, Cadkey starts deleting everything on the screen, and neither Esc nor F10 can interrupt the process. *Use the F2 function key, not the mouse, to select BY TYPE.*

Basic Type Masking

The **MASKING MENU** appears when you select BY TYPE or EX TYPE from the SELECTION MENU. But you can also invoke the BY TYPE option by pressing Alt-M. If, in a COPY operation (see MOVE/COPY/JOIN), you want to copy only ARCS AND CIRCLES, you can press Alt-M, select GEOM–ARC/CIR–DONE, and use a WINDOW to select the entities you want to copy. Cadkey will ignore all entities in that window except arcs and circles.

Don't let the term *masking* confuse you. Cadkey's masking functions might better be described as windows, because they specify which entities Cadkey has access to, not which ones are blocked. But *window* has other meanings in Cadkey.

For reasons explained in the subsection that follows on Problems with Type Masking, this works only if you start the copy operation before you press Alt-M. If you press Alt-M first, Cadkey selects *all* entities enclosed by the window.

BY TYPE lets Cadkey select only the entity types you specify. If, for example, you select GEOM, press F1 (POINT), press F3 (ARC/-CIR), and finally press F8 (to say you are DONE), Cadkey can select points, arcs, and circles but will ignore lines, notes, and other entity types. This makes it easier, for example, to select an arc in a region covered by closely spaced lines.

1 GEOM
- 1 POINT
- 2 LINE
- 3 ARC/CIR
- 5 POLYGON
- 6 POLYLIN
- 8 DONE

2 DETAIL
- 1 REG DIM
- 2 LABEL
- 3 NOTE
- 4 WIT/ARR
- 5 X-HATCH
- 7 GEN DIM*
- 8 DONE

3 COLOR
4 L-TYPE
5 L-WIDTH
6 PEN #
7 DONE

*GEN DIM is an entity type not available in CADKEY Light.

Cadkey records your selections at the bottom of the screen. If you select an option by mistake, select it again to remove it from the list.

EX TYPE puts the types you specify off limits. Pressing F3 under EX TYPE—GEOM is equivalent to pressing F1, F2, F5, and F6 under BY TYPE—GEOM.

Masking for Combinations of Types

To select options from more than one part of the masking menu, don't press **F8 (DONE)** until you really are. Press **Return** to exit each part of the menu and shift to the next part. The prompt line does not remind you that you can use this option.

If you select several options in only one category, the mask gives Cadkey access to all those options. For example, if you select red and green, Cadkey can select any entity of either color. If you select from more than one part of the masking menu, the entity selected must simultaneously satisfy more than one set of criteria. For example, if you pick CIRCLE, LINE, L-WIDTH = 3, L-WIDTH = 5, PEN # = 2, and PEN # = 3, an entity, to be selected, must be a line or a circle, and must have a width of 3 or 5, and must have a pen number of 2 or 3. (If you have studied logic-circuit theory, the concepts of *and* and *or* as applied here will be familiar to you.)

Problems with Type Masking

Type masking can give you problems if you don't understand that it stays in effect for *one* operation. Suppose you press ^Q to delete some POINT entities, using type masking to avoid selecting lines and arcs that pass through the points. You select the points without difficulty, but find after you delete them that you missed a couple. When you press ^Q again to delete them, you find that Cadkey can select whatever is nearest the cursor unless you reinvoke type masking. Starting the operation has cleared type masking.

Often, each new *part* of an operation clears type masking. In the CREATE menu, for example, if you use ENDENT to draw a line between the ends of two arcs, and if you mask on ARC/CIR, Cadkey can select only an arc or circle for the start point; but, unless you mask on ARC/CIR again, Cadkey can select any entity for the end point. Selecting the first point cleared type masking.

If you have trouble getting type masking to work, the reason is probably that you called the masking menu before you were into the application that needed it. An example illustrates the right and wrong procedures: Suppose you press ^Q to DELETE a series of entities. Pressing Alt-M and then selecting GEOM—ARC/CIR limits the deletions to arcs and circles. But if you reverse the order, pressing Alt-M first and ^Q second, type masking won't work. ^Q, because it starts a new operation, clears your masking menu selection.

If Cadkey ignores or fails to act on one of your selections, it probably means you made an inappropriate selection. Suppose, for example, that you are using DETAIL—CHANGE—TXT ATT—NOT ANG to change a text attribute—the angle at which some NOTES are written. Suppose also that you try to mask on POINT or LINE. Clearly, for this command, these are meaningless choices. Cadkey gives you no error message. It simply fails to record your entry on the prompt line. Cadkey responds differently if you try to mask on REG DIM or LABEL. Although these choices seem more reasonable, they are also inappropriate—the note angle command can't rotate anything but notes. Cadkey records these entries as if they were legitimate but ignores them when it executes the NOT ANG command.

Level Masking

Either MLEV in the STATUS WINDOW or ^N can set level masking, which limits the LEVELS from which Cadkey can select entities. The status window shows the setting: 3 means Cadkey can select only from level 3. —3 means Cadkey can select from any level but 3. 0 means Cadkey can select from any level.

Level masking, unlike type masking, stays in effect until you reset it.

Hidden Entities

With two exceptions, if an entity doesn't show on the screen, Cadkey cannot select it. These exceptions occur when you select a GROUP or select everything on a given LEVEL. If you use other selection methods, you can hide entities to keep them from being selected. Three ways are to (1) use PAN to move them off the screen, (2) hide the level they are on with DISPLAY—LEVELS—VISIBLE—REMOVE (see LEVELS), or (3) move them to a hidden level with DISPLAY—LEVELS—MOVE (see LEVELS).

Set

The SET commands take care of a large number of formatting choices such as lettering style, whether dimensions show tolerances, and whether dimension-line arrows point in or out. What follows is a brief summary of these commands. You will find more detail under the topics to which they apply.

```
3 DETAIL
  9 SET
    1 ARROWS*     ^A
    2 WIT / LDR*  ^B
    3 DIM REP
    4 TEXT
    5 TOLER
    6 STANDRD
    7 UNITS
    8 -
    9 VER DIM
```

*The STATUS WINDOW gives access to these commands.

ARROWS controls dimension-line arrows. The normal position is between witness lines, but you can put them outside when distances are short and dimensions become crowded. See DIMENSIONING.

WIT/LDR lets you omit one or both of the witness lines or one or both of the arrows that Cadkey normally supplies as parts of the dimensions it creates. It also gives you the option of making the dimension line solid, with the dimension written above or to the left of the dimension line. See ARROWS/WITNESS LINES—CONTROL.

DIM REP determines whether Cadkey shows dimensions as decimals, as fractions, or as feet and fractional inches. This command also lets you set precision. It controls the number of decimal places shown and whether fractional-inch measurements are given to the nearest 1/2", the nearest 1/4", etc. See DIMENSIONING STANDARDS.

TEXT controls letter heights, fonts, aspect ratio, the base positions used to place text on the drawing, and the angle at which NOTES are written. See LETTERING.

TOLER sets tolerance values and the form tolerances take. See TOLERANCES.

STANDRD controls three bookkeeping aspects of dimensions and their tolerances. You can show or omit leading or trailing zeros. You can choose whether to use dimensions in the form Cadkey provides or to edit the text of dimensions as you create them. You can change the base position that Cadkey uses when it places a dimension on your drawing. See DIMENSIONING STANDARDS.

UNITS lets you dimension in inches, millimeters, feet, centimeters, yards, meters, or units of your choice. (This choice does not affect the system of units Cadkey uses for construction.) See UNITS.

VER DIM turns the **Accept dimension?** prompt on and off. With it off, Cadkey accepts all dimensions as you create them. The usual ON setting gives you a chance to modify dimensions after a first look at them.

VER DIM also determines whether you accept LABELS automatically or Cadkey gives you an **Accept label?** choice. DIMENSIONING STANDARDS covers this command (but gives little additional detail).

Related Commands

CONTROL—ATTRIB, like SET, offers several ways to control the nature of the entities Cadkey creates. These options set color, line type, line thickness, pen number, and whether closed POLYLINE and POLYGON figures such as rectangles show as outlines or as solid areas of color. See ATTRIBUTES.

The SET commands establish, before you create entities, what those entities will be like. DETAIL—CHANGE and DETAIL—UPDATE let you change the properties of entities you have already created. See CHANGE and UPDATE.

Shell

SHELL is a standard computer term for a feature that lets you leave the program you are running, go to DOS (perhaps to delete, rename, or copy a file), and return to the program you were running at exactly the point where you left off. CONTROL—SYSCMD—SHELL is such a feature, but Cadkey also offers three other versions of this feature under CONTROL—SYSCMD. See SYSTEM COMMANDS.

Before you use one of these commands, save your file (see FILES). There is some risk that your computer will lock up and you will need to reboot it.

Single

SINGLE is the first option of the selection menu. This menu appears when Cadkey needs to know which parts of a drawing you want to include in an operation. The word *single* means not that you are limited to selecting one entity, but that you are to select the entities singly. See SELECTING ENTITIES for details on this and other selection menu options.

Size

Several sets of commands affect sizes. The ZOOM commands make the drawing appear larger or smaller on the screen but do not change the sizes of entities as recorded in Cadkey's DATABASE. MOVE/COPY/JOIN–SCALE is a way to make individual entities or groups of entities larger or smaller. See SCALE for a longer list of the commands in this category.

Sketch

CREATE–POLYLIN–SKETCH lets you generate an irregular line as a series of short straight segments. While holding down the mouse button, you move the mouse to trace out the path you want the line to follow. The result is, conveniently, a single entity. See POLYLINE for details.

See STRING for another way to generate this type of configuration in a more methodical manner.

Snap

An invisible snap grid, which may or may not coincide with the visible grid (see GRID), establishes a rectangular array of points. With SNAP on, the cursor does not move smoothly across the screen, but is constantly pulled to the nearest grid point. The grid spacing is initially 1/2" or 10 mm, depending on Cadkey's CONFIGURATION, but you can repeatedly double this increment or cut it in half by pressing the PgUp and PgDn keys. If distances on your drawing are integral multiples of the snap-grid spacing, snap gives you an easy way to position entities precisely.

The scale of the drawing affects snap distances. If the snap distance is 1/2" and your drawing shows half size on the screen, the jump distance on the screen will be 1/4".

```
6 DISPLAY
  7 GRID/SNAP
    5 SNAP OPT
      1 ON*     ^X
      2 OFF*    ^X
    6 SNAP INC
    7 SNAP ALN
    8 SNAP=GRD
```

*The STATUS WINDOW lets you toggle between SNAP:ON and SNAP:OFF.

SNAP OPT lets you turn snap ON or OFF.

SNAP INC sets the snap increments—the spacings between points of the snap grid–to the values you key in. You control the vertical and horizontal spacings separately. You don't need to have snap on to be able to set these increments.

SNAP ALN shifts the snap grid to make one of its points coincide with any point you specify. You can, for example, align the snap grid with a corner of the part you are drawing.

SNAP=GRD sets the spacing and position of the snap grid to make it coincide with the visible grid. (GRID=SNP gives the reverse process of fitting the visible grid to the snap grid.)

Solutions to Problems

If SNAP seems not to be working or gives strange results, consider three possibilities:

If the PgUp and PgDn keys have no effect on snap distance, you may be using the numeric keypad on the right side of the keyboard with the Num Lock switch ON. With this setting, the PgUp key enters 9; the PgDn key, 3. Cadkey ignores both inputs.

If turning snap on and off seems to make no difference, you may have pressed PgDn often enough to make the snap distance very small. Try pressing PgUp a few times. Or use DISPLAY–GRD/SNAP–SNAP INC to see what the snap increment is. A number like 0.015625 tells you that you should make it bigger.

If the snap distance gets very large, you would expect that one step could make the cursor skip completely across the screen, so that you could lose the cursor completely. To prevent this, Cadkey disables snap, and the symptoms are the same as when the snap distance is very small. As in the preceding problem, check the snap increment to see what is going on.

Related Commands

You can make Cadkey snap to points on your drawing as well as to points on the snap grid. See INDICATING POSITION for notes on ENDENT, POINT, CENTER, and INTRSC.

Status

Selecting CONTROL–STATUS shows the amount of free RAM (random access memory—see DOS) in the computer. In CADKEY Light 1.5 you press Return to see a second line of data showing the amount of free memory in the disk Cadkey uses for overflow files. CADKEY Light 4.0 shows all the data in one table.

When possible, Cadkey stores the DATABASE for your drawing in RAM. When your drawing gets too large to store this way, Cadkey puts part of it on a disk. (At this point you may notice that Cadkey becomes slow in selecting entities.) If the disk–the backup storage–also fills up, Cadkey is suddenly unable to respond to any command, and there is no way that you can save the drawing you have on the screen. If you are working on a complex drawing, you should monitor STATUS occasionally to be sure this does not happen to you.

Status Window

The Status Window starts about halfway down on the left side of the screen. This window shows the first part of the data in the left column of Table S-1, giving you information about Cadkey's current configuration.

The Status Window entries do not all show at once, but are divided into two or more pages. How many entries you can see at one time depends on your monitor. A CGA monitor–a bit primitive for Cadkey–shows only two entries at a time, an EGA monitor shows ten, and a VGA monitor gets everything on two pages by showing twelve at a time. To see the next page of data, select --more-- (at the bottom of each page). Continuing to select --more-- returns you to the first page.

Any parameter you can see in the Status Window you can also change. For example, if you move the cursor to SNAP and press the mouse button, you toggle the setting between SNAP:ON and SNAP:OFF. (If you have a CGA monitor, you can cycle through all twelve pages to see the entries, but using the cursor to change the entries works only with the first six pages of commands.)

There is a second way to initiate many of the options shown in the status window—you can use IMMEDIATE-MODE COMMANDS. The key combinations in the last column of this table show which commands you can execute in this way.

Table S-1 shows reminders only, not explanations of each command. Refer to the topics in UPPER CASE letters for more information.

Some operations include steps that you cannot interrupt by either an immediate mode command or a trip to the status window. When this happens, try again at a different point in the operation. Suppose, for example, that while you are typing the text of a NOTE you remember that you should have changed the letter height. When you try to select --more-- to get to NH in the STATUS WINDOW, Cadkey doesn't respond. Even if NH were already showing you would not be able to get the cursor to select it. But as soon as you finish keying in the note and are ready to indicate its position, you can make all the changes you want, and the changes will apply to the current note.

VIEW=1	1 = top VIEW. See also inside front cover	Alt–V
ALEV=1	Active LEVEL.	^L
MLEV=0	Masking level. See SELECTING ENTITIES.	Alt–N
COLOR=1	1 = green. See ATTRIBUTES.	Alt–X
CONST:3D*	Construction mode. See 2D/3D.	^W
COORD:VW*	COORDINATE system: VW = view; WLD = world.	^V
D=0.000000	DEPTH, the coordinate perpendicular to the screen.	^D
S=1.000000	SCALE of the drawing. See ZOOM.	Alt–S
GRID:OFF	GRID is a rectangular array of dots.	^G
SNAP:OFF*	ON lets the cursor move only to points on the SNAP grid.	^X
L-TYPE=1	LINE TYPE can be solid, dashed, centerline, or phantom.	Alt–T
L-WID=1	LINE WIDTH	Alt–Y
PEN=1	Pen number used for plotting. See ATTRIBUTES.	Alt–Z
DB:FWD*	Cadkey reads its DATABASE forward	Alt–R
NH=0.300000	Lettering height for notes and labels**	
DH=0.300000	Lettering height for dimensions**	
AS=0.500000	Character aspect ratio for all lettering**	
RT=0.000000	(Rotate Text) Text angle for notes**	
NF=1	Text font for notes and labels**	
DF=1	Text font for dimensions**	
WIT:BOTH	Both WITNESS lines of dimensions are drawn.	^B
ARR:IN*	ARROWS for dimensioning are placed inside witness lines.	^A
LDR:BOTH	Both LEADERS of dimensions are drawn.	

*Selecting these entries does not invoke a menu—it simply toggles the function between its two possible states.
**See LETTERING for explanations of these commands.

Table S-1 Contents of the status window

String

1 CREATE
1 LINE
2 STRING
5 POLYLIN
1 STRING
8 POLYGON
4 STRING
1 OUTLINE
2 FILLED
3 DETAIL
4 ARR/WIT
1 ARROWS
2 STRING
2 WITNESS
2 STRING

Each of the five STRING commands creates a series of straight lines, with each new line starting at the endpoint of the preceding one. Strings made up of LINES, ARROWS, or WITNESS LINES need little explanation. For these entity types, the only difference between a string and a series of individually created entities is that the string command saves you the trouble of selecting the start point of each new segment—Cadkey simply uses your most recent endpoint selection. POLYLINES and POLYGONS offer more fundamental differences.

Choice of Entity Type

If you can think of a use for a string of arrows, the ARROWS option is the obvious choice. If you want entities that show only in the view you use to create them or entities that POSITION MENU options such as ENDENT will ignore, use the WITNESS option (see ARROWS/WITNESS LINES—CONSTRUCTION). Otherwise, your choice of entity types for lines is between the three types normally used for geometric construction—LINES, POLYLINES, and POLYGONS.

Each polyline or POLYGON string, although it has multiple segments, is a single entity. This is a convenience if you want to handle a string as a unit. It can be a nuisance if you need to modify the shape of a string. Most changes to polyline strings require you to BREAK the string, thereby sacrificing the advantage of a string that is a single entitiy. POLYGONS are more stubborn: You cannot change their shapes in any way.

One advantage of a POLYGON is that you can FILL it, that is, make it show as a solid area of color (see ATTRIBUTES). You can fill it when you create it or at a later time. In other respects, it is more limited than other entity types. You cannot edit it, give it thicker lines, give it more than eight sides, or make it open ended.

You can also fill a closed polyline. Although you cannot fill it when you create it, you can do so later in a separate operation. When you need thicker-than-normal lines, polylines have a unique advantage: The corners of polyline strings are filled in; whereas a string of thick LINES, because of the squared-off ends of its segments, shows small notches at corners.

See POLYGONS, POLYLINES, AND LINES COMPARED and ARROWS/WITNESS LINES—CONSTRUCTION for fuller detail.

Construction Details

If your string is a POLYGON, the first thing to do is to tell Cadkey whether you want it in OUTLINE or FILLED form. To fill it, follow the prompts (or see ATTRIBUTES for details.)

For any of the five kinds of strings, you start the string by selecting the start point of the first segment. From then on, you select only the endpoints of the segments.

Pressing F10 gives results that depend on the entity type. For LINES, ARROWS, or WITNESS LINES, F10 cuts the last rubber band, ending the string.

To end a POLYGON or polyline string, press Return. If the string is a polyline, Cadkey asks whether to close it. If you select YES, Cadkey adds one final line from the point you selected last to the start of the string. If the string is a POLYGON, Cadkey gives you no choice, automatically closing the string with this last line.

There are three reasons you might press F10 while constructing a polyline or POLYGON. (1) F10 cancels the last point you selected. The rubber band jumps from the last point to the next-to-the-last point, leaving you free to select a new location. (2) Pressing F10 twice is a quick way to cancel the entire figure. Cadkey asks, **Save current entity ? (YES)**. Select NO and the string disappears. YES ends the construction at the next-to-the-last point. A polyline is finished at this point, but for a POLYGON, Cadkey adds one last segment to close it. (3) Habit is strong, and if you are used to working with LINE strings, you may press F10 to end the string. If so, you have the annoyance of finding that the string did not end and that you have to reselect the last point. One might argue that this minor accident shouldn't happen. The prompt line reminds you, **RETURN to exit**; however, many experienced users tend to ignore the prompt line because they "know" what to do next.

A Problem with ENDENT

The steps in creating a particular STRING (Figure S-1) illustrate a problem you may encounter in POLYGON and polyline construction. These steps also offer another reminder of POLYGON properties.

Suppose you start construction at the end of the handle of the Dipper. Things proceed exactly as though you were creating a LINE string. Your final step is to use ENDENT to bring the end of the last line of the bowl to the base of the handle. But ENDENT doesn't work. Cadkey gives you an **Entity not found** error message.

This problem doesn't occur with a complete POLYGON or polyline. After you finish the construction, ENDENT and other POSITION MENU options work as you would expect, snapping to the end of any segment you select, but while the entity is under construction, Cadkey won't recognize any reference points on it. In Figure S-1, the last line ends where it should only because POINT entities marked the star positions and Cadkey was snapping to these points.

Using POLYGON is not the way to draw this figure. It gives the extra line shown in the lower figure. Recall the rules for POLYGONS: They may have eight sides at most and they must be closed. Finishing the last line of the bowl gives the seventh line. Cadkey, knowing there is only one line left, and knowing where it must end, draws it in without asking permission.

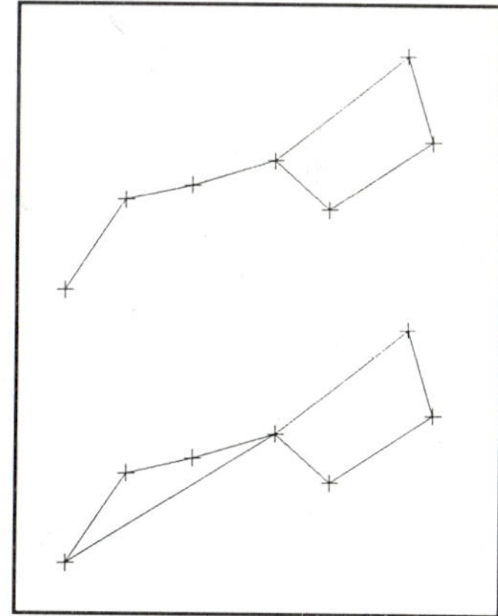

Figure S-1 Big Dipper

System Commands

The system commands return you temporarily to DOS, letting you execute commands you could not otherwise run from within Cadkey. SAVE your file first. Complex operations can tamper with the computer's memory and crash the system. The result is that you must reboot the computer and lose whatever is in active memory. (If you wonder what "DOS" and "reboot" mean, you probably aren't ready for the system commands. These terms apply not to Cadkey but to computer use in general. Refer to DOS in this chapter, ask your instructor, get a book, or just ignore this topic and get back to learning Cadkey.)

Don't use the system commands to load memory-resident programs. They would use memory that has been released only temporarily and would give trouble after you returned to Cadkey.

```
7 CONTROL
  8 SYSCMD
    1 NONE
    2 TEXT
    3 GRAPHIC
    4 SHELL
```

SHELL is discussed first because the procedure is most straightforward. SHELL takes you to DOS and reminds you to type EXIT to return to Cadkey. Type any command or series of commands: Copy some files, delete a file to free up memory on a disk, or change a file name. But if your computer has just the standard 640 k of RAM, you are limited in what you can do. Cadkey, still running in the background, ties up enough memory that many programs are too big to fit in the memory that remains. If Cadkey immediately redraws the Cadkey display, it means there is not enough free memory to handle the shell routine.

Typing EXIT is DOS's standard way of getting out of a DOS shell and back to the original program. You will find Cadkey exactly as you left it, ready for your next command.

NONE is a fast-in-fast-out variation of SHELL, useful for simple DOS operations such as renaming or copying a file. Your drawing remains on the screen. The prompt line, your only contact with DOS, is brief. Cadkey tells you, **Executing system command...** and returns you to Cadkey after a single DOS command.

The brevity of this message can be a problem. Suppose you ask DOS to rename a file, but you make a typing error when you enter the file name. You don't see the DOS error message telling you the file does not exist. All you see is the perfunctory **Executing system command...**, making you think the file was actually renamed. If you ask for a directory, DOS takes the time to create one; but you see no sign of it on the screen. (If you wonder whether it's really there, enter DIR A:>PRN. Your printer will print the A: directory.)

Although NONE can run simple programs, it's risky. If you try FORMAT A:, you must remember to press Return to start the process—the message reminding you to do so will not appear. And DOS is quite likely to format the disk but lock up the keyboard so you have to reboot the computer. SHELL is kinder. On some systems it lets you format a disk with no problems, but that is no guarantee it will always do so.

TEXT, like SHELL, shows the normal DOS display, but after it executes one DOS command it prompts you to **press RETURN to continue**. Pressing any key returns you to Cadkey.

GRAPHIC is more abrupt than TEXT. Like TEXT, it shows the DOS commands. But the DOS response, for example, 1 File(s) copied, shows on the screen for only a few milliseconds before you are returned to Cadkey. With the Dir command, GRAPHIC creates the directory and immediately returns you to Cadkey, letting you see only what you can read on the fly. (Dir A: ¦more works better.)

Unless you use these commands a lot and get to know what they can and cannot do, stick to SHELL. If it can't execute a command or run a program, you get a message that tells you so. NONE, TEXT, and GRAPHIC are more likely to tackle a command too big to handle and crash the system.

Text Editor

EDIT TX invokes the **on-line text editor**, a simple word processor for editing NOTES, LABELS, and DIMENSIONS. Whenever you type in text, the menu of the text editor appears. Most of the time you will ignore it, but if you need to change the wording of a note or correct more than simple typing errors, it's there to help. The text editor can also change existing text. Use the menu to call the text editor; then select the note, label, or dimension you want to edit.

The text editor uses two sets of keys—those common to most other word processors, such as the arrow keys, and the function keys, which invoke commands unique to Cadkey.

```
3 DETAIL
   7 CHANGE
      3 EDIT TX
         1 DEL LN
         2 JOIN LN
         3 INSERT
         4 APPEND
         5 DEL END
         6 SAVE TX
         7 ABORT
```

Conventional Editing Keys

Most of the conventional editing keys move the **cursor**, a marker that shows where you are in the text. If you have used word processors, these key functions will be familiar to you.

The four ARROW KEYS move the cursor right or left one character at a time, and, if there is more than one line of text, move it up or down one line at a time. Unlike full-featured word processors, Cadkey displays only one line of text at a time. This line appears at the bottom of the screen, following the **Edit text:** prompt.

Home moves the cursor to the beginning of the current line.

End moves the cursor to the end of the current line.

Backspace deletes the character to the left of the cursor.

Del deletes the character at the cursor.

Insert (the Ins key, not F3) toggles between INSERT and OVERWRITE modes. At the upper left corner of the screen, **INSERT** or **OVERWRT** appears in reverse video to show which mode you are in. You see the main difference when you make corrections in the middle of an existing line of text. As you type, INSERT mode inserts the new characters, pushing the rest of the line to the right to make room. OVERWRITE mode types over existing characters, replacing them with new ones. The default mode, and usually the more useful of the two, is the insert mode.

Enter (or Return) in insert mode: (Notes on **overwrite** mode appear later in a separate subsection.) Pressing Return once starts a new line. If some text follows the cursor, Cadkey starts the new line with the character at the cursor. Although you might expect the cursor to stay with the same character and reappear at the beginning of the new line, Cadkey places it at the end.

If you press Return twice when the cursor is at the end of a line, you don't create a second new line or even a first. Instead, you save the note and terminate the editing session.

Although Return gives you an easy way to save a note, it's better to develop the habit of pressing F6 (SAVE TX). If you absent-mindedly use Return when the cursor is not at the end of a line, you break the current line at the cursor.

Function Keys

These notes apply to INSERT mode. For all of the function key commands but one, DEL END, it makes no difference where the cursor is.

DEL LIN deletes the current line and moves to the line above it.

JOIN LN joins the current line with the one that follows it. The cursor moves to the end of the combined line.

INSERT inserts a blank line above the current one and moves to the blank one.

APPEND inserts a blank line below the current one and moves to the blank one. (You can do the same thing by pressing Return when the cursor is at the end of a line.)

DEL END deletes all characters between the cursor and the end of the line, including the character at the cursor.

SAVE TX ends the editing session and saves the text. If you are editing an existing note, label, or dimension, Cadkey replaces the version on the screen with your edited one. If you are creating a new entity, Cadkey asks you where to place the text.

ABORT ends the editing session. If you are editing an existing note, label, or dimension, Cadkey leaves the original unchanged. If you are writing new text, Cadkey deletes it and returns to the NOTE menu. F10 and Esc also end the session this way, with Esc taking you back to the main menu.

Overwrite Mode

OVERWRT is best suited for occasional use within one line of text. Most commands are the same in the two modes, but Return and two function-key commands are different. Unless you use the text editor a lot, you may find it easier to stick to insert mode and not have to remember separate rules for overwrite mode.

Return does not start a new line. If another line of text follows the one you are on, Return moves the cursor to the end of that next line. If nothing follows the line you are editing, Return moves the cursor to the end of the current line.

If the cursor is at the end of a line and you press Return twice, the first time moves the cursor down one line (or, if you are on the last line, does nothing). The second time deletes whatever line the cursor is on at the time and ends the editing session by saving the text.

INSERT or APPEND moves the cursor to the end of the next line, or, if there is no next line, to the end of the current line.

Rules and Comments

The text editor limits you to 128 characters per line and 1024 characters total. Additional characters are dropped.

File-based notes (see NOTE) can have over 1024 characters; but, because they are stored in separate files rather than in Cadkey's database, you cannot edit them from within Cadkey.

When you replace an existing note, label, or dimension with an edited version, Cadkey puts the first character of the text where the first character was before. If the text was nicely centered to begin with and if editing made the lines of text longer, the text will be off center to the right. In the same way, adding more lines can throw the text off center vertically. DETAIL—CHANGE—TXT POS provides an easy way to correct these problems. See DIMENSIONS AND THE TEXT EDITOR for examples.

Special Characters

Alt-key combinations can produce special characters—the degree symbol °, ±, the diameter symbol ∅, and a hard space. Hold the Alt key down while you enter three digits from the numeric keypad. (The row of numbers along the top of the keyboard don't work.) The degree symbol is Alt-248; the ± sign, Alt-241. The diameter symbol has two parts. The first half is Alt-174; the second half, Alt-175. Briefly release the Alt key after entering the first three numbers. A hard space, Alt-255, is a space that Cadkey treats the same way it would treat a letter of the alphabet. Cadkey usually strips away spaces at the ends of lines of text, but will not do so if the final space is Alt-255.

Tolerances

Tolerances tell how much a dimension is allowed to vary. For example, 1.25 ± .01 says that the part the machinist makes, to be acceptable, must measure between 1.24" and 1.26".

Three sets of commands affect tolerances.

The SET—TOLER commands determine whether dimensions show tolerances, how large the tolerances are, and what form they take. These choices stay in effect until you again use the SET commands to assign new ones.

CHANGE and UPDATE give you two ways to change tolerances in dimensions you have already created. CHANGE asks you to specify the changes you want to make. UPDATE looks at the choices you have made in the SET commands to see what tolerance values to use and what format to use to show them.

The SET Commands

Cadkey lets you treat tolerances in three basic ways (Figure T-1). You can omit them, you can use +/— tolerances to show how much a dimension can deviate from its design value, or you can use limit dimensions to show the maximum and minimum values a dimension can have. Because the formats for ANGULAR and LINEAR tolerances are the same, all of the examples that follow use linear dimensions to illustrate both types.

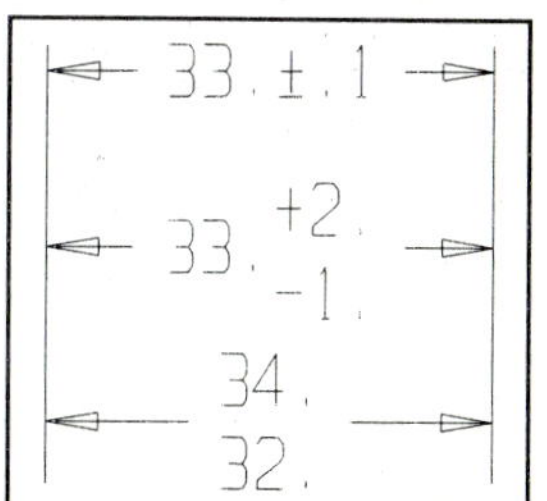

Figure T-1 Tolerance options

NONE, Cadkey's default, shows dimensions as simple numbers without tolerances.

+/— tolerances are shown in the first two dimensions of Figure T-1. (The third example in Figure T-1 shows LIMIT dimensions.) The first dimension has symmetrical tolerances; the second, tolerances that allow the dimension to be oversize by 2 mm but undersize by only 1 mm.

POS TOL and **NEG TOL** set the magnitudes of these tolerances. In the first and third examples in Figure T-1, the POSITIVE TOLERANCE is 1 and the NEGATIVE TOLERANCE is —1. (If you forget to enter the minus sign, Cadkey reminds you.) The second dimension has tolerances of +2 and —1.

DBL UP offers a YES/NO choice on whether to double up tolerances when the positive and negative tolerances have equal absolute values. (If the values are unequal, doubling up is impossible.) YES writes the tolerances as one number. NO writes them separately. Figure T-2 shows both styles.

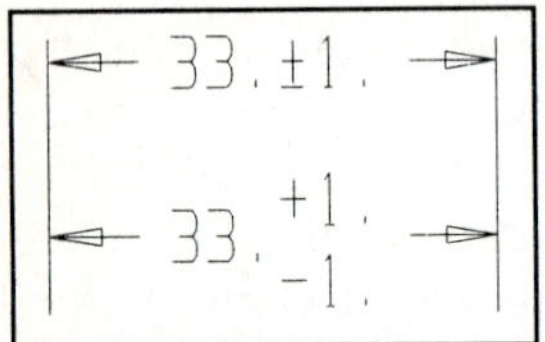

Figure T-2 Double-up options

0 REP lets you choose between the patterns in Figure T-3. When the positive tolerance or the negative tolerance is zero, YES drops the plus or minus sign and the decimal point from the zero tolerance. If SET (see DIMENSIONING STANDARDS) calls for tolerances to two decimal places, a zero tolerance could show as +.00, +0.00, or 0, depending on the settings for repressing signs, for leading zeros, and for trailing zeros.

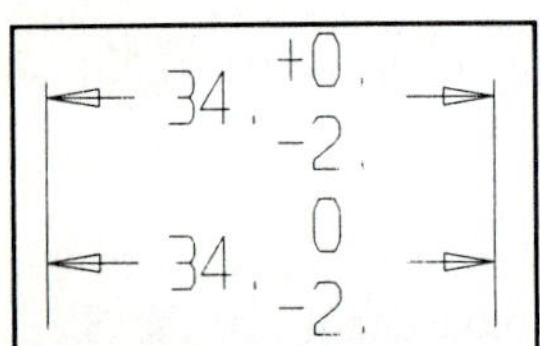

Fig. T-3 Repression of sign with zero tolerance

LIMIT tolerances, shown in the third example in Figure T-1, give the smallest and largest values allowed for the dimension. Cadkey calculates these limits from the design value and the plus and minus tolerances you assign. In this example, the limits of 33 and 31 correspond to a dimension of 32 ± 1.

Like the +/— command, the LIMIT command lets you set values for POS TOL and NEG TOL. When you assign tolerances, it doesn't matter whether you do so while in the +/— part of the menu or in the LIMIT part. The tolerances you assign continue to apply to all dimensions, whatever their form.

- 3 DETAIL
  - 7 CHANGE
    - 3 EDIT TX
    - 8 TOLER
      - 1 VALUES
        - 1 POS TOL
        - 2 NEG TOL
        - 3 BOTH
      - 2 TYPE
        - 1 NONE
        - 2 +/—
        - 3 LIMIT
  - 8 UPDATE
  - 9 SET
    - 5 TOLER
      - 1 ANGULAR *
      - 2 LINEAR
        - 1 NONE
        - 2 +/—
          - 1 POS TOL
          - 2 NEG TOL
          - 3 0 REP
          - 4 DBL UP
        - 3 LIMIT
          - 1 POS TOL
          - 2 NEG TOL

*All the options for linear tolerances are available also for angular tolerances.

The CHANGE Commands

EDIT TX, which lets you make changes in completed NOTES, LABELS, and DIMENSIONS, gives you a way to add tolerances to dimensions that have none or to change the values of existing tolerances. When different dimensions get different tolerances, the procedure that is usually easiest is to create all the dimensions with the same tolerances and then use EDIT TX to change them. The alternative–going through DETAIL—CHANGE—TOLER—VALUES for each change–can be tedious. See TEXT EDITOR for more details on how Cadkey edits text.

For fractional inch dimensions, for dimensions in feet and inches, or (in CADKEY Light 4.0) for angular dimensions in degrees, minutes, and seconds, Cadkey does not provide tolerances. If you want to assign tolerances to such dimensions, using the text editor is the only way you can do it.

Select the dimension you wish to edit. If a tolerance exists and you want to change it, use the Backspace or Delete keys to remove characters; then add the numbers you want. If no tolerance exists, simply type it in. To type the ± symbol, hold down the Alt key, type 241 using the keypad on the right side of the keyboard, and then release the Alt key. To type in the ° symbol, use the same process with Alt-248. Press F6 (SAVE TX) when you finish editing the dimension. The revised dimension appears on the screen.

Limitations: After you have edited a dimension, the command that changes its form from +/— to LIMIT still works; but the other CHANGE—TOLER commands do not.

Dimensions that you carefully put in just the right places may have their positions thrown off by editing. Use DETAIL—CHANGE—TXT POS to reposition them. See DIMENSIONS AND THE TEXT EDITOR for more details on coping techniques.

TOLER is another way to change tolerances of existing dimensions. After you enter the change you want, select the dimension or dimensions you want to change. Cadkey does not let you change tolerance values and tolerance type in one operation. To change both, you must execute the TOLER command twice.

VALUES lets you enter new values for the tolerances. Select **POS TOL** if you want to change only the positive tolerance; **NEG TOL** to change only the negative one; **BOTH** to change both.

TYPE lets you change the type of tolerance to **NONE**, +/—, or **LIMIT**.

The UPDATE Command

UPDATE can be an alternative to the CHANGE command. In one step, it changes tolerances, along with several other parameters that affect dimensions, to the parameters currently called for by the SET commands. Typically, UPDATE requires more preparation than does CHANGE, but it gives you control over more variables and it takes care of all the desired changes at once. When you execute the UPDATE command and select the dimensions you want to change, the dimensions are rewritten according to the current SET parameters for:

Lettering style (height, font, slant, and fill—see LETTERING)
Value representation (decimal, fraction, etc.—see DIMENSIONING STANDARDS)
Precision (see DIMENSIONING STANDARDS)
Dimension scale (see UNITS)
Leading and trailing zeros (see DIMENSIONING STANDARDS)
Tolerance mode (none, +/—, or limit)
Tolerance values
Doubling up of +/— tolerances
Whether to display zero tolerance without sign

Not changed are:

Lettering aspect ratio
Arrows and witness lines (both, first, second, none, solid)
Arrows in/out

All of these changes leave the lower-left corner of the first number where it was before the UPDATE operation. If added text or larger lettering makes repositioning necessary, use DETAIL—CHANGE—TXT POS.

Trim/Extend

2 EDIT
1 TRM/EXT
1 FIRST
2 BOTH
3 DOUBLE
4 DIVIDE
5 MODAL

The TRIM/EXTEND commands are used to change the lengths of existing entities. In the simplest case, two entities cross, and one of them is trimmed by cutting away the part extending past the intersection.

If the entities do not meet, their geometry must be such that they would intersect if one or both were extended. If the entity to be trimmed extends past the potential intersection, it is trimmed at that point. If it is too short to reach the potential intersection, it is extended until it does. In what follows, the word *trim* means either the trimming or the extending process.

Two notes on Cadkey's prompts: (1) The **trimming entity** is the one that forms the *boundary* where trimming occurs. (2) Despite what you may infer when Cadkey asks you to **Select entity to TRIM**, in all but the DIVIDE command you select the entity by placing the cursor on the portion you wish to *keep*, not on the part to be trimmed away.

Cadkey trims LINES, ARCS, CIRCLES, and POLYLINES, but not POLYGONS.

FIRST trims one entity. Select first the entity to trim; next, the trimming entity—the boundary line.

BOTH trims two entities where they intersect.

DOUBLE uses two trimming entities to cut off both ends of a line, arc, or open polyline. It is the only TRM/EXT command that can cut away part of a circle or a closed polyline.

DIVIDE uses two trimming entities, cutting a piece out of the middle of a line, arc, or open polyline. When trimming arcs, be careful to put your selection point on the part of the arc you want to *remove*.

MODAL trims or extends a number of lines, arcs, or polylines, making all end at a single trimming entity.

Rules for POLYGONS and Polylines

You cannot trim a POLYGON. Its shape is fixed.

You can use a POLYGON, a closed polyline, or an internal segment of an open polyline as a trimming entity—a boundary line—if the intersection or the potential intersection lies on the trimming entity. Results are not always predictable. When you extend an entity to meet a POLYGON or polyline, and when that entity, if extended, would cross the POLYGON or polyline in more than one place, Cadkey may not extend the entity to the intersection you want.

The free end of an open polyline behaves the same way that you would expect a line or arc to behave. Cadkey lets you use an imaginary extension of the free end in either of two ways.

You can extend the first or last segment of an open polyline to a potential intersection. You can also use an extension of the first or last segment as a boundary for trimming other entities.

You can trim an open polyline at any point. If you use DIVIDE, the result is two polylines. A closed polyline, like a circle, responds only to DOUBLE.

Notes

A common source of frustration is a segment that returns after you thought you had trimmed it away. You cut away half of a line; then, when you REDRAW the screen, the line is suddenly full length again. You try to trim it again, and this time the trim command doesn't work. See TROUBLESHOOTING for an explanation and a solution.

If you accidentally cut away something you wanted to keep, one of the TRM/EXT commands usually offers the easiest way restore the deleted portion. (RECALL is not an option. It brings back deleted entities, but not trimmed portions of entities.)

With DOUBLE and DIVIDE, it doesn't matter where you put the selection point on a LINE you want to trim, but be careful with selection points on arcs and circles. Arcs, particularly, have a way of trimming themselves in ways other than the one you want. Usually you can use TRM/EXT—FIRST to coax the arc back to where you want it.

It is difficult to make DOUBLE work improperly, but you can get unexpected results if you ask DIVIDE to remove segments from entities too short to extend from one trimming entity to the other.

An arc or a circle used as a trimming entity can in general trim another entity in either of two places. With an arc as a trimming entity, it's easy to forget that the second point can be on an extension of the arc. Place your selection points near where you want trimming to occur.

Troubleshooting

Most of the problems you are apt to have with Cadkey involve specific commands and are noted in the topics that cover those commands. If, for example, you have trouble getting crosshatching to work, look under CROSSHATCHING for guidance. But a few problems occur often or seem to have more mysterious origins. These are discussed in the notes that follow.

Deleted Lines Keep Coming Back

A fairly straightforward problem occurs when you delete a line and think it is gone; and then, later, when you do something that redraws the screen (you might press ^A for AUTOSCALE, press ^R for REDRAW, or switch to a new VIEW), the now-forgotten line suddenly reappears.

To understand what happened, you first need to know two properties of the Cadkey display. (1) If two lines coincide in a view, you usually see no clue that the line is double. (2) When Cadkey deletes an entity, it blanks out everything in the space the entity occupied. You see this effect whenever you delete an entity that crosses other entities. Deleting the entity creates gaps wherever it crossed those that remain. Deleting several entities can give your entire drawing a moth-eaten look. Pressing ^R to REDRAW the screen cleans up the drawing by restoring the missing patches.

If two lines coincide, deleting one makes both disappear completely. One is gone; the other is waiting for REDRAW (or something similar) to restore it. When it pops up again, delete it and you will be rid of it. Maybe.

It's not unusual, particularly when Cadkey is new to you, to have *several* coinciding lines. The notes that follow on Nothing Happens tell some of the ways this situation arises. If a line you are trying to delete comes back more than once, press ^Q again to delete it, and this time select the same line over and over. (It helps to use Alt-W to create a small WINDOW around the line, making it less likely that you will select some other entity instead.) If ten lines remain, Cadkey will let you select the composite line ten times. On the eleventh attempt, Cadkey will either jump to some nearby entity or it will tell you **Entity not found... press RETURN to continue**. If it selects the nearby entity, press F10 to cancel the selection; then press Return to execute the deletion. If you get the error message, press Return twice: once to clear the error message, once to complete the deletion process.

If you trim a line, and the part trimmed away comes back, you have the same problem (two or more lines that coincide) in a form that makes the problem more puzzling. The initial TRIM operation cuts away the end of one line, temporarily blanking the same end of the other. But the undesired end returns as soon as you redraw the view. The instinctive response is to use the trim command again. This time nothing happens. Because Cadkey keeps picking the same line to trim (see DATABASE SEARCH for the reason), the line it selects is already trimmed, and the untrimmed line is unaffected.

DELETE the untrimmed line. Select it by putting the cursor on the end you tried to trim away. The line you want to keep is safe–it no longer extends into this area. REDRAW to check your result, and use ^U (see UNDELETE) if you inadvertently delete a line you need to keep. If the trimmed end comes back again, you have more than one duplicate line to remove. Use ^Q and select the line repeatedly, as described earlier.

Nothing Happens

Usually the true situation is that nothing seems to happen. When an operation produces no visible results, the natural instinct is to repeat it, usually creating later problems by generating those troublesome double lines described earlier. In several situations, Cadkey can appear to be doing nothing when it is actually responding to all commands.

Using more than one LEVEL can trigger two problems. If you used level masking and forgot to turn it off, Cadkey will refuse to select entities on other levels. If your work with levels has left the active level hidden, Cadkey will nevertheless draw on it, but will appear to be doing nothing. The lines you create will be hidden until you think to make the level visible.

Switching to a new VIEW often yields a blank screen. The entities are beyond the edge of the screen, and Alt-A retrieves them.

When COPY gives no visible result, the copy may fall offscreen or it may coincide with the original. In the first case, Alt-A reveals the copy. In the second case, check the coordinate system. Failure to distinguish between VIEW and WORLD coordinates (see COORDINATES) is a common source of trouble, putting the copy in a different position than the one you intended. Switching to another VIEW (try view 7) is usually the best way to confirm that a copy was made. The next subsection on JOIN Gives the Wrong Result is an example of how to delete a copy that falls in the wrong place.

Sometimes nothing happens because Cadkey is not ready for more input. Searching the DATABASE to find which entity you selected takes time. While Cadkey is searching, the prompt that tells you to do something—something you already did—remains on the screen, but the cursor won't move. This temporary lockup is normal when the drawing is large. Try to be patient.

JOIN Gives the Wrong Result

The last subsection tells how using the wrong coordinate system can give you an incorrect copy. This could happen, for example, when you create a wire-frame drawing of a gear (Figure 2-45 in Chapter 2). If you use the wrong set of coordinates for the JOIN operation, and if you don't save your drawing before that operation, you have 296 entities to delete.

In view 2, the front view, the wire-frame drawing should look like Figure T-4a. If you used VIEW instead of WORLD coordinates when you constructed it, it looks like Figure T-4b. The bottom horizontal line contains all the entities in the original two-dimensional drawing of the gear. The top horizontal line contains a copy of these entities, which are all displaced sideways from the positions they should have. The lines in between are, of course, the join lines. The next thing to do is to get rid of all the entities except the original set along the bottom line.

Use Alt-A, if necessary, to get all the drawing on the screen; then use Alt-P to PAN the drawing (see ZOOM) to put the bottom line off the edge of the screen. The screen should now show the bottom of the drawing clipped off, as in Figure T-4c.

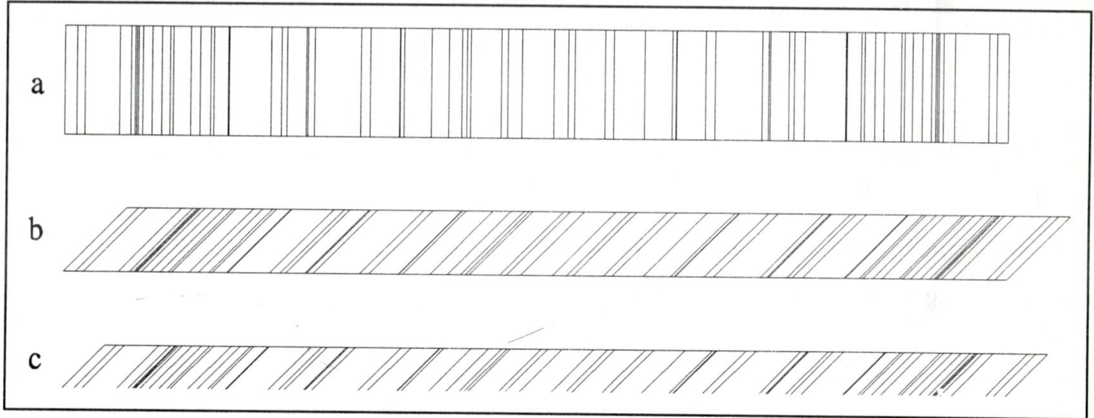

Figure T-4 Correcting a JOIN operation

DELETE—SELECT—ALL DSP—ALL deletes all entities that show on the screen, even though only parts of the join lines show. This operation therefore deletes all entities in the top line and all of the join lines, leaving the bottom line, containing the original view of the gear, undisturbed. You can return to view 7, where all the trouble started, and try again.

Drawing is in Wrong View

Switching to view 7 and seeing the wrong orientation can be your first clue that you carelessly started a drawing in view 1 when you should have started it in view 2. To salvage your drawing, switch to view 5, the side view. Use X-FORM—2D ROT—MOVE if you have CADKEY Light 1.5, or use X-FORM—ROTATE—MOVE if you have CADKEY Light 4.0 (see MOVE/COPY/JOIN). KEY-IN 0, 0, 0 as the rotation origin and 90 as the rotation angle. The drawing that was in view 1 is now in view 2.

The Cosmic-Ray Effect

Occasionally on a single computer, and a little more often on computer networks, a Cadkey command will fail to work or will start giving strange results. The effect is as though something—static electricity, perhaps—has temporarily disrupted a small part of the computer's memory, creating a problem that cannot be explained. Sometimes, if you exit a routine with Esc or F10 and then get back into it, the trouble disappears. Other times the only cure seems to be to save the drawing (see FILES), exit Cadkey, reload Cadkey, and reload the drawing.

Sluggishness

If Cadkey starts taking ten times as long as before to select an entity, your drawing has probably become complex enough that the DATABASE no longer fits in RAM (see DOS), and Cadkey has directed some of it to overflow files. If these files are on a hard disk or, worse yet, on a floppy disk, it takes an appreciable time to access them.

If you have deleted a large number of entities, the records of these deleted entities remain, cluttering up the database. Notes on Cleaning up a Part File (see FILES) tell how to get rid of these old records. This cleanup may eliminate the overflow files.

If your computer has enough RAM, consider setting up a RAM disk and using the CONFIGURATION program (see Chapter 4) to direct your overflow files there. Cadkey can access files on RAM disks quite rapidly.

If the suggestions in the last two paragraphs are not ones you can apply, the improvements you can expect to achieve easily are probably less than spectacular. Reversing the DATABASE SEARCH direction with Alt-R can speed selection if you are working mostly with entites you have created recently. Using LEVELS or a WINDOW to reduce the number of entities on the screen may help. But ultimately you may have to choose between expensive additions to your computer and developing the habit of patience.

See also ERROR MESSAGES.

Tutor

TUTOR presents a series of lessons in which Cadkey guides you through the construction and dimensioning of a three-dimensional part. These lessons expose you to many of Cadkey's commands and give you useful tips on efficient ways to construct drawings.

TUTOR is not automatically installed when you install Cadkey. If you get an error message when you try to use TUTOR, exit Cadkey, find the disk labeled Tutor Disk, switch to the drive you put that disk in, enter INSTALL, and follow the prompts.

When you start a new lesson, check it off in the list on the right so you can continue without repeating or skipping a lesson.

TUTOR has you construct the Finger Guide in Figure T-5. The final drawing includes a border Figure T-5 does not show.

- 5 FILES
  - 9 TUTOR
    - 1 WELCOME
    - 2 2D BASE
    - 3 2D EDITS
    - 4 XFORMS
    - 5 PLANE
    - 6 3D CONST
    - 7 LINEAR
    - 8 LAYOUT
    - 9 QUIT

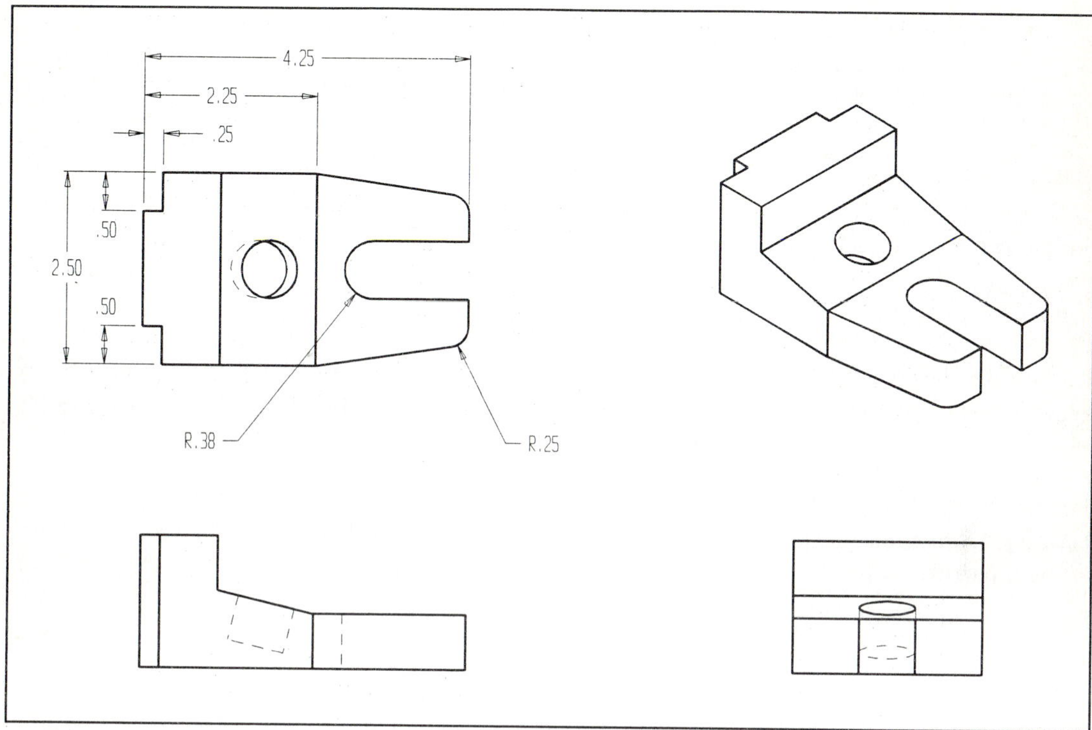

Figure T-5 Drawing of the Finger Guide used for the TUTOR exercises (Courtesy Cadkey, Inc.)

You can do the tutorial with a monochrome monitor, but a color monitor is strongly recommended. The tutorial makes extensive use of color to tell you what is happening and what you should do next. Text on a gray background presents general information, usually telling you what the next step will accomplish. Text on a blue background tells you the specific steps to take to carry out the next step. Text on a red background, which appears when you make a mistake, tells you what you should have done and lets you try again.

Lines in the drawing are also color coded. Dashed yellow lines are entites you are to create. Solid green lines are completed lines in the drawing. Dashed red lines are entities or parts of entities you are to delete. White lines are entites you are to select. It is when Cadkey uses these white lines that a color monitor is important. With a monochrome monitor, you may have to guess which line to select, wait for Cadkey to rebuke you for picking the wrong one, and repeatedly try to select the right one.

At the end of any step, you can press Esc to select from the choices you see in the inset. CONTINUE lets you continue with the tutorial and is the selection to make if you press Esc accidentally. REPEAT takes you back over the steps you took to get to the present place in the tutorial. QUIT lets you exit the tutorial. If you select QUIT, you choose between SAVE, which leaves the drawing on the screen, and DELETE, which deletes it. If you pick SAVE, you can use Cadkey, free of the restraints imposed by the tutorial, to work independently on the drawing, as you would work with any drawing you had created. Feel free to experiment. Any damage you might do to the drawing on the screen has no effect on the drawing Cadkey uses to start the next step of the tutorial.

1 CONTINUE
2 REPEAT
3 QUIT
  1 SAVE
  2 DELETE

The TUTOR menu offers eight options:

WELCOME gives you brief summaries of the seven lessons and shows the drawings you are to create. It then points out the elements of the Cadkey screen display. It outlines the procedure to be used in the tutorial lessons.

2D BASE uses basic two-dimensional modeling options to start the drawing of the base of the part.

2D EDITS lets you edit the basic structure to complete the drawing of the base.

X-FORMS uses the JOIN command to extend the drawing of the base into the third dimension.

PLANE adds a new view to Cadkey's list of eight standard views, creates a line in this view, and uses that line to create an angled plane between the front and back sections of the finger guide.

3D CONST adds a circle and transforms it to form a pocket in the center of the finger guide, completing the construction of the three-dimensional model.

LINEAR adds linear dimensions and makes a pattern file of the dimensioned drawing.

LAYOUT creates a layout drawing from four pattern files. Cadkey has you save this drawing as a part file.

EXIT lets you leave the TUTOR program.

How well TUTOR runs depends on your equipment. If you have an old monochrome monitor and an 8088-based computer, you may find the prompts hard to read and progress painfully slow. With more up-to-date equipment the tutorial should go smoothly.

2D Rotate

2D ROT is a CADKEY Light 1.5 command (the equivalent CADKEY Light 4.0 command is ROTATE) that lets you rotate one or more entities around an axis normal to the screen, either putting the original entities in the rotated position or leaving them where they were and making one or more copies in the rotated position. See MOVE/COPY/JOIN.

2D/3D

2D and 3D are construction modes used to create three-dimensional drawings. 2D mode lets uses DEPTH to create the third dimewnsion. 3D mode lets you attach new construction to specific points in space on a partially completed three-dimensional drawing.

If this topic is new to you, the best way to get a feel for it is to go through the tutorial on THREE-DIMENSIONAL CONSTRUCTION in Chapter 2. If you don't do this, at least read the short note on DEPTH here in Chapter 3.

```
7 CONTROL
  3 CONST
    3 2D/3D
      1 2D*     ^W
      2 3D*     ^W
```

*The STATUS WINDOW lets you toggle between CONST:2D and CONST:3D.

Position Menu

If you know how ENDENT works in three-dimensional construction, you will find the other position-menu commands easy to understand. Most of them work the same way as ENDENT, snapping to specific positions on your partially completed drawing (see POSITION MENU). In 2D mode, the positions they specify coincide in the current view with points on the drawing, but they are at the current depth and do not necessarily coincide in space. In 3D mode, these positions coincide in space with points on the drawing.

Figures T-6 and T-7 show Cadkey's four-viewport display (see VIEWPORTS). DISPLAY—VWPORTS—AUTO SET lets you see four views at one time. The arrangement of views is standard for mechanical drawings: The front view is on the lower left, with the top view above it and the right-side view on its right. The upper right view is the isometric.

Both of these figures started with a horizontal rectangle. The top views (in the upper left quarter of Figures T-6 and T-7) show the true shape of the rectangles. The front and side views (in the bottom half of each figure) show them on edge, as just horizontal lines. In Figure T-6, the rectangle is the lower line of each pair. The isometric views (upper right) show more pictorial views, looking down at an angle on the rectangles.

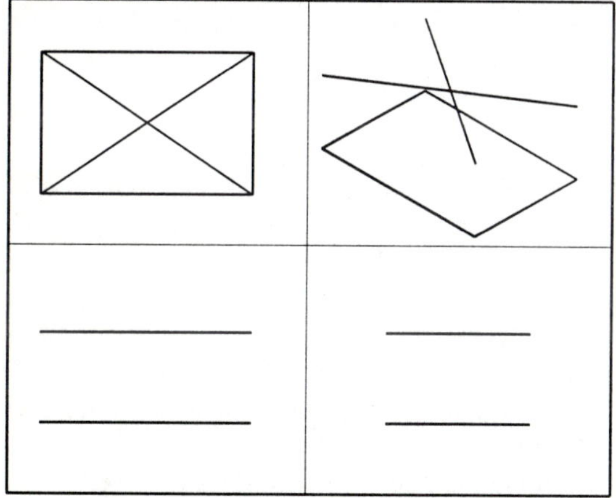

Figure T-6 Diagonals added in 2D mode

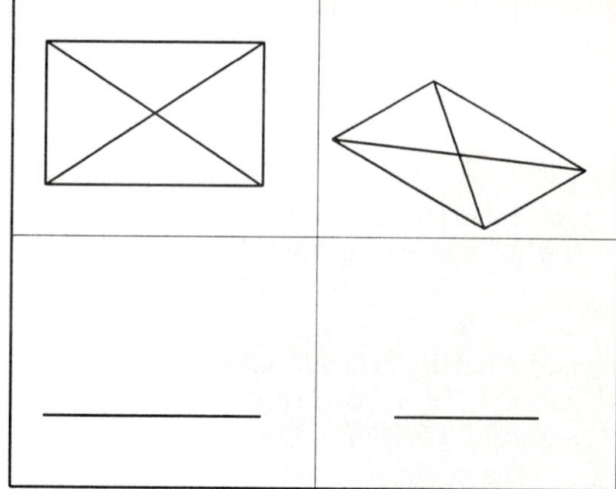

Figure T-7 Diagonals added in 3D mode

Figures T-6 and T-7 show what happens when you use ENDENT to add two diagonals to the top view. DEPTH is set to put the diagonals about an inch above the rectangle. In the top view, the results are the same regardless of the mode. ENDENT puts the ends of the diagonals precisely on the corners of the rectangle. In 2D mode, the depth setting puts these lines above the rectangle. In 3D mode, ENDENT overrides the depth setting, creating diagonals that truly connect the corners.

Seven of the POSITION MENU options work the way ENDENT does. In 2D mode, the points they select are at the current depth; in 3D mode, they coincide in all three dimensions with points on the drawing. The seven commands governed by the 2D/3D setting are:

POINT	**ALONGL**
ENDENT	**POLAR**
CENTER	**DELTA**
INTRSC	

The two remaining position menu options are CURSOR and KEY-IN.

CURSOR is a 2D function. Points selected by CURSOR are at the current depth, as though Cadkey were always in 2D mode.

KEY-IN often works as a 3D function. For many operations, the coordinates you key in override the depth setting, giving you the depth you key in even when Cadkey is in 2D mode. But see the next subsection for a warning.

At this point, you should be able to start drawing in three dimensions. Because the details in the rest of this section are not likely to affect your first attempts at three-dimensional construction, you may want to stop and apply what you have learned. Practicing these basic skills will make it easier, when you return to this section for more specific information, to understand the detailed set of rules that govern all of Cadkey's commands.

Position Menu Technicalities

POLAR and **DELTA** require you to select a temporary origin and then specify a displacement from that origin. You select the origin using CURSOR, POINT, ENDENT, CENTER, INTRSC, or ALONGL, and the depth of this origin depends on the 2D/3D setting just as the depth of any point would. Then, regardless of the 2D/3D setting, POLAR puts the final point at the same depth as the origin and DELTA locates the final point using the x, y, and z displacements you key in.

KEY-IN can trick you. When you key in the endpoints of a line using 2D mode, the coordinates you enter take precedence over the current DEPTH setting, and it is easy to start thinking of key-in as a 3D function, always overriding the depth setting. But key-in is inconsistent. In 2D mode, you get the DELTA origin at the depth you key in, but the POLAR origin appears at the current depth. If, in 2D mode, you construct a rectangle using the WID-HT option, a POLYLINE rectangle appears at the depth you key in for the lower left corner; a LINE rectangle, at the current depth. For a POLYGON rectangle, the rule depends on whether you are using CADKEY Light 1.5 or CADKEY Light 4.0.

The commands most likely to catch you by surprise are the CTR+RAD and CTR+DIA options for cerating arcs and circles, when you find you have created an arc or circle at the current depth rather than at the depth you keyed in.

Because the rules for key-in in 2D mode follow no easily remembered pattern, the long list of details is not spelled out here. Instead, you are encouraged to switch to 3D mode when you need to depend on key-in for depth. The alternative–using key-in to get 3D results while you are in 2D mode–is not good practice, and some of the habits you would develop are habits you would have to break when you switch from one Cadkey version to another.

For the most part, when you are working with the various ways to indicate position, you see nothing in Cadkey's immediate response to remind you of whether you are in 2D or 3D mode. Only INTRSC and ALONGL give occasional clues:

INTRSC in 3D mode requires the entities you select to intersect in space. If they intersect on the screen but are at different depths, you see an error message.

ALONGL responds differently in the two modes when the line you select is not parallel to the display plane. Consider a line four inches long that, because it makes a 60° angle with the display plane, projects on the screen as a two-inch line. In 2D mode, Cadkey prompts **Enter distance (2.000000)** = >, where 2.000000 is the projected length—the length that shows on the screen. If you enter 1, Cadkey picks a point that appears to be at the center of the line but which, because it is at the current depth, may or may not lie on the line in space. In 3D mode, the prompt becomes **Enter distance (4.000000)** = >, where 4.000000 is the length of the line in space. Entering 1 gives you a point on the line, one-fourth of the way from the end of the line.

CREATE Commands that Work as Expected

In 3D mode, you would expect to create enties using the depths of whatever points you select. In 2D mode, you would expect Cadkey to ignore the third dimension of these points and create entities at the current depth. Most of the time this is what happens. For example, if you draw a circle through three points at different depths, 3D mode gives a circle that passes through the points in space and that looks like an ellipse in the current view. In 2D mode, a circle through the same three points looks like a circle, as though the three points were all at the same depth.

But as you think about it, the idea of what you should expect gets more complicated. The parameters you ask for in some constructions do not lead to a unique three-dimensional solution. For example, LINE—RECTANG—CORNERS defines a rectangle by the positions of diagonally opposite corners. In 3D mode, Cadkey could draw an infinite number of rectangles between these corners. Rather than pick an arbitrary solution, Cadkey proceeds as if in 2D mode and constructs the rectangle at the current depth.

Sometimes it is more logical for Cadkey to follow 2D/3D techniques for only part of the construction. The CTR+EDG option defines a circle by its center and a point on its circumference. In three dimensions, these two points permit an infinite number of solutions. Cadkey follows your 2D/3D choice when it fixes the center point, but it ignores the depth of the point you pick for the edge and draws the circle in a plane parallel to the display plane and at the depth of the center.

Thus, commands that operate predictably follow these rules:

1. In 2D mode, Cadkey creates the entities in a plane parallel to the display plane and at the current depth.
2. In 3D mode, if the points you specify imply one and only one solution, Cadkey constructs that solution in three dimensional space.
3. In 3D mode, if the construction uses a single reference point (the center of a circle or polygon, or the corner of a rectangle drawn with the WID-HT option), Cadkey draws the figure in a plane parallel to the display plane and passing through the reference point.
4. In 3D mode, if the points you specify could lead to an infinite number of solutions, Cadkey proceeds as if in 2D mode.

2D/3D Commands

The following CREATE commands respond totally to the 2D/3D mode setting. In 2D mode they create entities at the current depth; in 3D mode they create entities through the positions in space that you specify.

LINE—ENDPTS
—PARALEL—THRU P
—TAN/PRP
LINE, POLYGON, or POLYLIN—STRING
ARC or CIRCLE—3 PTS
—TANGENT
ARC—ROUND
FILLET—ARC
POINT—POSITN

In 3D mode, the three TANGENT commands (LINE—, ARC—, and CIRCLE—) and the related FILLET—ARC command require that the reference entities lie in a single plane. In 3D mode, the LINE—TAN/PRP—PRP commands give lines that are perpendicular in space but do not necessarily look perpendicular in the current view. In 2D mode, parallel and perpendicular lines look parallel and perpendicular in the current view but are at the current depth and are not necessarily parallel and perpendicular in space.

When an ARC, CIRCLE, or FILLET—ARC command creates an arc or a circle in a plane that is not parallel to some already-defined view, Cadkey adds the plane of that entity to the list of available views. For example, if you create a circle that is not parallel to an existing view, Cadkey creates a plane through that circle. You get your first clue that this has happened when you change views and see the prompt **Enter view number or choose menu option (1–9) =>** instead of the usual **Enter view number or choose menu option (1–8) =>**.

Commands with a 2D/3D Start Point

Several commands follow the 2D/3D setting in selecting a starting point (for example, the center of a circle or the corner of a rectangle) and then create all entities at the depth of that starting point:

LINE—HRZ/VRT	
—RECTANG—WID/HT	
—N-GON	**(CADKEY Light 4.0)**
ARC or CIRCLE—CTR+RAD	
—CTR+DIA	
—CTR+EDG	
POLYLIN—N-GON	
POLYGON—RECTANG—WID-HT	**(CADKEY Light 4.0)**
—CTR+RAD	**(CADKEY Light 4.0)**
—CTR+SID	**(CADKEY Light 4.0)**

2D Commands

These 2D commands would lead to ambiguous results in 3D mode; therefore they construct at the current depth even when Cadkey is in 3D mode:

LINE—PARALEL—AT DIST
ARC—BEG+END
CIRCLE—TWO-PTS
LINE, POLYGON, or POLYLIN—RECTANG—CORNERS
POLYLIN—SKETCH

3D CREATE Commands

These commands function as though Cadkey were always in 3D mode:

POINT—ON ARC
—SEGMENT—NUMBER, —DISTNCE, or —ALONGC
FILLET—CHAMFER

POINT—ON ARC and POINT—SEGMENT always construct entities as though Cadkey were in 3D mode because, for these commands, this mode almost always gives the more useful results. Because reasons for making FILLET—CHAMFER a 3D command are harder to concoct, you will find this command also included in the Unpredictable list.

The angular positions of POINTS on arcs (here, the term includes circles) are measured in the plane in which the arc was created. The distances that POINT—SEGMENT uses are measured along the entity in space, not along its projection in the current view.

FILLET—CHAMFER gives an error message if the entities to be connected are not coplanar.

Unpredictable CREATE Commands

Most commands in the unpredictable category are there because they fail to follow the patterns that other commands seem to set. LINE—ANGLE is there because there is no set of similar commands to make clear what you ought to expect.

The following table tells whether each command responds as a 2D or 3D command when you use ENDENT or a similar option to set the position of an entity.

COMMAND		RESPONSE
LINE—N-GON	**(CADKEY Light 1.5)**	**2D**
—ANGLE		
POLYLINE—RECTANG—WID-HT		**2D**
POLYGON—RECTANG—WID-HT	**(CADKEY Light 1.5)**	**2D**
—CTR+RAD	**(CADKEY Light 1.5)**	**2D**
—CTR+SID	**(CADKEY Light 1.5)**	**2D**
FILLET—CHAMFER		**3D**

As you can see by what is *not* in this list, CADKEY Light 4.0 offers fewer surprises than CADKEY Light 1.5.

In some cases, you may find it easier to put Cadkey in a safe construction mode and at a safe depth than to try to remember which command does what. For example, because **FILLET—ARC** is a 2D/3D command and **FILLET—CHAMFER** is a 3D command, you may choose to think of both, not just FILLET—CHAMFER, as being in the unpredictable category.

LINE—ANGLE creates a line at an angle to a reference line. In all cases, Cadkey sets the angle not in space, but between the *projections* of the lines in the display plane. CADKEY Light 1.5 starts the new line at one end of the reference line and draws it parallel to the display plane. In 2D mode, the line is at the current depth; in 3D mode, it is at the depth of the start point.

In CADKEY Light 4.0, the new line can start at any point you select. 2D mode puts the entire line at the current depth. In 3D mode, the line starts at the depth of the point you select and makes the same angle with the display plane as does the reference line. For example, assume a reference line with one end at a depth of 0 and the other at a depth of 1. In 3D mode, you select the reference line near the end that has a depth of 1; then you select, for the start of the new line, a point with a depth of 4. The new line will start at a depth of 4 and end at a depth of 3. (The resulting geometry resembles what the ROTATE command (see MOVE/COPY/JOIN) would give you. If the reference line projects as one inch long on the screen and if you set 90° as the angle between the lines, they will appear to be perpendicular in the current view but will make an angle of 60° in space.)

Commands for Manipulating Entities

Several commands respond in a straightforward way to the 2D/3D setting, using the three-dimensional coordinates of reference points you select:

MOVE/COPY/JOIN—TRANS-A (CADKEY Light 1.5)
—OLD-NEW (CADKEY Light 4.0)
—SCALE
VIEW—NEW—3 PTS
PATTERN

For MOVE/COPY/JOIN—TRANS-A, MOVE/COPY/JOIN—OLD-NEW, and PATTERN, you select a base position and then indicate a new base position. The operations shift entities by the difference between these two base positions. If you use a base position at depth = 0 when you create a pattern and a base position at depth = 2 when you retrieve it, an entity originally at depth = 5 will have a depth of 7 in the copy.

For MOVE/COPY/JOIN—SCALE, a scale of 60% works in three dimensions to put the copy 60% as far from the scaling origin as the original is.

For VIEW—NEW—3 PTS, the new view will have a line of sight normal to the plane through the three points. (Don't select these points in 2D mode without changing depth, or the new line of sight view will be the same as the current one. The views will differ only in that the new one will in general be rotated and have the origin of its coordinate axes shifted.)

Several commands give results independent of the 2D/3D setting:

TRM/EXT and **BREAK** always operate in 2D mode. They trim and break entities at apparent intersections in the current view.

MOVE/COPY/JOIN—2D ROT (CADKEY Light 1.5), **MOVE/COPY/JOIN—ROTATE** (CADKEY Light 4.0), and **MOVE/COPY/JOIN—MIRROR** make transformations in two dimensions, but they are 3D operations in the sense that the depths of entities in the original are preserved in the copies.

MOVE/COPY/JOIN—TRANS-R (CADKEY Light 1.5) and **MOVE/COPY/JOIN—DELTA** (CADKEY Light 4.0) place entities according to x, y, and z displacements you key in. This shift in position is independent of the 2D/3D mode.

^D, which sets DEPTH, is a 3D function. If you use the POSITN option in 2D mode, and if you use ENDENT to select the end of an entity, Cadkey changes the depth to the depth of that end. The VALUE and OFFSET options also operate in 3D mode.

Undelete

```
2 EDIT
  3 RECALL
    1 LAST   ^U
```

EDIT—RECALL—LAST recalls the entity most recently deleted. Other operations can intervene. If, for example, you have trouble with a TRIM/EXTEND command and suspect the cause is a double line, you can DELETE the line and then REDRAW the screen to make sure you have not deleted something you wanted to keep. If you find that you should not have deleted the line, you can use ^U to restore it.

Units

```
3 DETAIL
  7 CHANGE
    9 DIM SCL
  8 UPDATE
  9 SET
    7 UNITS
      1 INCH
      2 MM
      3 FEET
      4 CM
      5 YARD
      6 METER
      7 USER
```

Cadkey comes from the factory configured for inches, but you can configure it to work in inches, millimeters, feet, centimeters, yards, or meters, with everything, including letter heights, measured in the same units. Although you need to use the CONFIGURATION program, directly or indirectly, to alter this basic setup, the commands described here give you a way to change one aspect of Cadkey's operation: the units for dimensioning.

The **SET—UNITS** command, like all the SET commands, affects future operations and remains in effect until you change it. With Cadkey configured for inches, choosing MM multiplies dimension values by 25.4; thus Cadkey dimensions a one-inch distance as 25.4. But UNITS does not affect construction. You still construct a 25.4 mm square as 1" x 1".

With Cadkey configured for millimeters and UNITS set to INCH, the opposite conversion occurs. If you construct something 25.4 units long, Cadkey dimensions it as 1.00.

The UNITS command does not scale tolerance values. If, with UNITS set to INCH, Cadkey would dimension a distance as 1.00 ± .01, then, with UNITS set to MM, it would dimension the same distance as 25.40 ± .01.

INCH, MM, FEET, CM, YARD, and METER simply multiply dimensions by whatever factor will convert them from the units Cadkey is using for construction to the units you want for dimensions. And USER lets you assign your own conversion factor. If Cadkey is configured to construct in inches and you want to dimension in millimeters, you would normally select MM, but selecting USER and assigning a value of 25.4 would give the same result.

CHANGE–DIM SCL does the same thing as UNITS, but it affects existing dimensions rather than dimensions not yet created. You specify a dimension scale factor and then select the dimensions to be scaled. A scale factor of 25.4 converts a dimension of 1.00 ± .01 to 25.40 ± .01. But note that the scale factor always applies to the original dimension. To convert the 25.40 dimension back to inches, use a scale factor of 1, not 1/25.4.

UPDATE gives you another way to change existing dimensions. First, use SET—UNITS to select the units you want to convert to; then use DETAIL—UPDATE. When you select the dimensions you want to change, Cadkey modifies them to conform to what the SET commands call for. You accomplish the same thing with DIM SCL, but UPDATE also responds to other SET commands such as the ones that set lettering height or font. Sometimes this property of update is useful; sometimes it causes you to make more changes than you want. See UPDATE.

Alternative Methods

If your drawings are sometimes in metric units and sometimes in English, the most obvious way to make things work smoothly is to set up two CONFIGURATION files. Exit Cadkey. If the current configuration file is set for inches, enter **copy config.dat config.eng**. This command (see DOS) makes a second copy of the configuration file, giving it a new name. Then type CONFIG to change Cadkey's configuration (see Chapter 4). Select **Set program options** and select **millimeters**. (To keep other aspects of Cadkey's configuration unchanged, press Return in response to all the other questions the configuration program asks you.) After you exit CONFIG, enter **copy config.dat config.met**.

To run Cadkey in metric units, enter **copy config.met config.dat** before you start Cadkey. To run it in English units, enter **copy config.eng config dat**. These copy commands overwrite the config.dat file with whichever configuration file you need for the units you want to use.

An extension of this method gives you additional flexibility. With Cadkey configured for inches, start Cadkey and immediately SAVE the blank screen display as **English**. Exit Cadkey and configure it for millimeters. Restart Cadkey and again save the blank screen display, this time as **metric**.

These two files are all it takes to switch Cadkey back and forth between English and metric modes. Suppose you start Cadkey when CONFIG.DAT is set for inches. Cadkey is then ready to operate in inches. But if you load the **metric** file, you find that letter heights, drawing scale, snap distance, and other parameters have the values they would have had if you were to load Cadkey with CONFIG.DAT set for millimeters. Cadkey is ready not only to dimension in millimeters, but also to construct in millimeters.

If you are not familiar with batch files, you may want to find a book on DOS that describes them. A batch file can copy the correct configuration file, load the video driver (see page 1), start Cadkey, and finally, after you exit Cadkey, remove the video driver from memory.

SCALE provides a quick alternative to these methods. If Cadkey is configured for inches and you want to draw in millimeters, you can set SCALE to .04 (1/25.4 if you want to be fussy). This scale reduces the drawing to make a one-inch distance one millimeter long on the screen. Cadkey will then think it is working in inches even though it is effectively in millimeters. Reset note height and dimension height (see LETTERING) to about 8 so letters will be large enough to see, and press PgUp four times to get a reasonable SNAP distance. This transformation is not as complete as the other methods give, but it works. And on a computer network, where you may not be able to access the configuration file, it may be your only choice.

Update

UPDATE changes the format of NOTES, LABELS, and DIMENSIONS to make them conform to the current SET command choice. After you initiate the UPDATE command, select the entities you want to change and press Return.

Settings that Affect Lettering

3 DETAIL
8 UPDATE

The SET commands control the format of DIMENSIONS, NOTES, and LABELS. These commands normally apply to entities not yet created, but UPDATE lets you apply most of them to existing entities. You first use the set commands to specify what you want. Then you initiate the UPDATE command and select the entities you want to change. The list that follows tells which of the DETAIL—SET—TEXT commands Cadkey updates. See LETTERING for detailed descriptions.

DIM HT and **NOT HT** set the heights of letters and numbers.

DIM FNT and **NOT FNT** let you choose the font (BOX, or BOLD, FILLED or UNFILLED), and the slant angle of the letters.

The DETAIL—SET—TEXT commands that Cadkey *does not* update are:

DIM PLC and **NOT PLC**. Update leaves the position of the lower left corner of the dimension, note, or label unchanged.

NOT ANG. Update does not change the angle at which Cadkey writes NOTES (don't confuse this angle with the slant angle of individual letters).

CHR ASP. Update does not change the character aspect ratio (width-to-height ratio) of letters and numbers.

See CHANGE for ways to control the parameters that UPDATE cannot control.

Settings that Affect only Dimensions

The other set commands that you can update affect dimensions but not notes or labels. Figure U-1 shows the variety that UPDATE can produce from a single 2.69" dimension.

The DETAIL—SET—TOLER commands determine how large tolerances are, the format used to show them, and whether they show at all. Tolerances can show as ± values or they can be

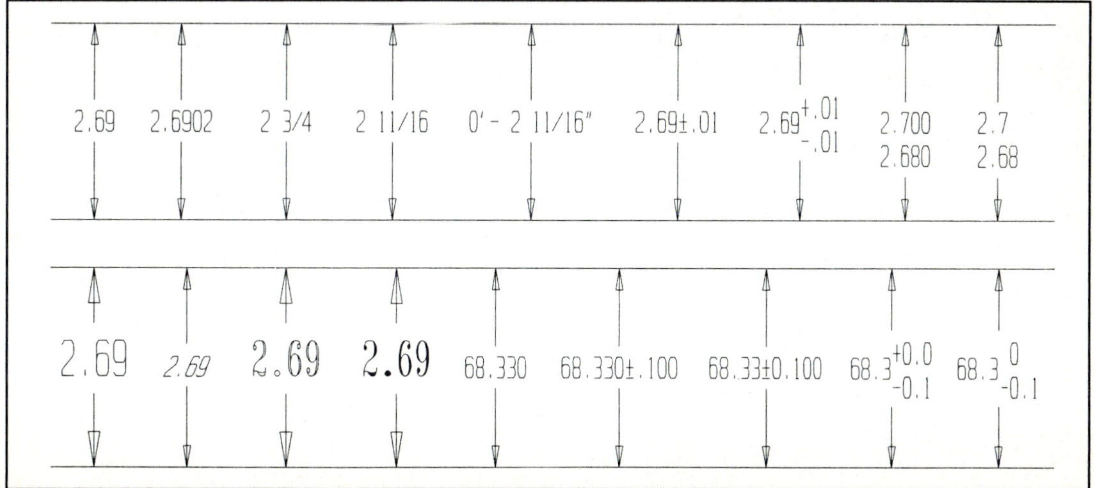

Figure U-1 Dimension formats created by the UPDATE command

implied by upper and lower limit dimensions. Tolerances of equal absolute value can be spelled out (e.g., +.01 and —.01) or doubled up (e.g., ±.01). If one tolerance is zero, its sign may show (e.g., +.01, —.00) or it may be omitted, with the zero tolerance written without a decimal point (e.g., +.01, 0). See TOLERANCES for details.

The DETAIL—SET—DIM REP commands determine whether Cadkey represents dimensions as decimals, as fractions (for example, 6 7/8), or as feet, inches, and fractions of an inch. The DIM REP commands also let you specify precision—for decimal dimensions, the number of decimal places and, for fractions, whether to round to the nearest 1/2, 1/4, etc. CADKEY Light 4.0 gives you the option of writing angular dimensions as degrees, minutes, and seconds. See DIMENSIONING STANDARDS.

The DETAIL—SET—STANDRD—ZEROS commands let you choose whether to show or omit leading and trailing zeros. See DIMENSIONING STANDARDS.

DETAIL—SET—UNITS can, for example, make Cadkey show dimensions in inches even though the drawing is created in millimeters. See UNITS.

UPDATE does not handle the commands that affect dimension-line arrows and extension lines, such as whether dimension-line arrows are IN or OUT. Use CHANGE instead.

Neither UPDATE nor CHANGE affects dimension alignment—whether the text is written horizontally or parallel to the distance being dimensioned (see DIMENSIONING STANDARDS).

Verify

The VERIFY commands list the parameters in the Cadkey DATABASE that define a selected entity. In most cases the list you see is several lines long, presented one line at a time. Press Return to see the next line or F10 to back up and look again at an earlier line. After the last line, Cadkey lets you select another entity to see similar data.

```
7 CONTROL
  1 VERIFY
    1 ATTRIB
    2 COORD
    3 DIST
      1 2 POS
      2 POS+ENT
      3 2 ENTS
    4 ANGLE
  2 ATTRIB
```

Attributes

CONTROL—VERIFY—ATTRIB lists the attributes of the entities you select. The first line starts by listing **Type** and **Form**. Type indicates the type of entity. Form is best thought of as just a number from Cadkey's database. The type code is:

1 POINT	13 DIAMETRIC DIMENSION
2 LINE	14 ANGULAR DIMENSION
3 ARC or CIRCLE	15 NOTE
6 POLYGON	16 LABEL
7 POLYLINE	17 ARROW
11 LINEAR DIMENSION	18 WITNESS LINE
12 RADIAL DIMENSION	19 CROSSHATCHING

On the same line, Cadkey also lists the entity's **LEVEL** and its **defining view**. The defining view for a line is the one Cadkey was in when you created it. The defining view for an arc or circle is one parallel to the plane of the entity.

Pressing Return shows numbers corresponding to **Color**, **Style**, **Width**, and **Pen number**. See ATTRIBUTES for descriptions of these attributes. Style is either LINE TYPE (1 = solid, 2 = dashed, etc.) or font (1 = BOX; 2 = BOLD—see LETTERING). If the entity is a member of a GROUP, pressing Return again shows its **group name**, **group number**, and **subgroup number**. If the entity contains text, the third line shows **text height**, **aspect ratio**, and **arrow number**, which has the value 1 for entity types that normally include arrows.

CONTROL—ATTRIB: The command ATTRIB appears twice in Cadkey's menu structure. The CONTROL–ATTRIB command is mentioned here only to distinguish it from the VERIFY–ATTRIB commands. CONTROL–ATTRIB assigns such attributes as COLOR and LINE TYPE. See ATTRIBUTES for details.

Coordinates

For lines, points, arcs, and circles, **COORD** gives complete geometrical data to six decimal places (entities may be recorded more accurately than this in the DATABASE). For lines, the information includes coordinates in both view and world systems, actual length, and the length as projected into the current view. For arcs and circles, COORD gives the center coordinates, the start point (for a circle, the 3 o'clock position) and the end point. Next it shows, in degrees and radians, the start angle, the end angle, and the sweep angle. The start and end angles apply in the defining view. The ATTRIB command tells which view this is.

For POLYGONS and POLYLINES, you see no coordinate data. Cadkey gives only the number of POLYGON vertices or the number of polyline points (6 for a closed pentagon because Cadkey counts the start point and end points separately). If you want the coordinates of an end of a polyline segment, use CREATE–LINE–ENDPTS–ENDENT in 3D mode to draw a line to it, and verify the coordinates of the line.

Cadkey also gives coordinate data for most of the DETAIL entities: You can check NOTES, DIMENSIONS, LABELS, ARROWS, and WITNESS LINES, but not CROSSHATCHING.

Distance

DIST calculates *projected* distances (distances as they show on the screen) and *actual* distances (distances in three-dimensional space). For POS+ENT and 2 ENTS, Cadkey gives eight lines of data, one line at a time, showing the coordinates and lengths of the shortest connecting lines.

2 POS shows the shortest distances between two positions. Use the POSITION MENU to select these locations. If the locations are at different depths, check the STATUS WINDOW to be sure that CONST is set to 3D when you select the points.

POS+ENT finds the shortest distances between a point and an entity. Cadkey draws a dashed line to show the shortest projected distance, shows how long the line is, and gives you the x and y coordinates of its endpoints. Then Cadkey draws a solid line to show the actual distance, gives that distance, and gives endpoint locations in both view and world COORDINATES. REDRAW (^R) removes the dashed and solid lines.

2 ENTS finds the shortest distances between two entities. The data are the same as for POS+ENT.

The DIST commands take longer to execute than most Cadkey commands. Time and reliability problems can be extreme for polylines and POLYGONS. An 80386 computer needed eight minutes to find the distance between an eight-sided POLYGON and a three-segment polyline string, both of which were lying parallel to the display plane. Moreover, the projected and actual distances, which should have been the same, were not. When you can see which parts of entities are the closest, use the 2 POS or POS+ENT option—it saves time.

Angle

ANGLE measures, in degrees and in radians, the projected angle between two LINE entities. This is not the angle in space, but the projected angle, the angle as you see it in the display plane. This command does not recognize sides of POLYGONS or polylines.

View

The drawings Cadkey creates are three-dimensional. Once a part is properly drawn in three dimensions, you can switch from any view of that part to a front view, a side view, or any other of the eight predefined views. The inside front cover shows the numbers Cadkey assigns to these eight views. These views are:

1	Top	5	Right
2	Front	6	Left
3	Back	7	Isometric
4	Bottom	8	Axonometric

```
6 DISPLAY
  4 VIEW*                 Alt-V
    1 –
    2 ENTITY
    3 NEW
      1 KEY-IN
        1 TOP IN
        2 TOP OUT
        3 RGT IN
        4 RGT OUT
        5 CW
        6 CCW
        7 DONE
      2 3 PTS
    4 SAVE
```

*The STATUS WINDOW also gives access to the VIEW menu.

The first option of the view menu is blank. Pressing F1 does nothing. This option is just a reminder that you can immediately specify a view by entering a number. To switch to the isometric view, press 7 and press Return.

ENTITY switches the viewing plane to a plane in or parallel to the plane of an arc or circle. Simply select the entity. (This command does not create a new view. Every arc or circle has associated with it a viewing plane that coincides with or is parallel to the plane of the entity. If there is no such view when you create an arc or circle, Cadkey automatically creates the new view at the time. The ENTITY command switches you to that already-created view.)

NEW lets you create an additional viewing plane. This new view is assigned the number —1, indicating that it is temporary. Use the SAVE option to make it permanent, or switch to a different view to delete it.

3 PTS creates a plane through three points. The first two points define the X axis in the new view, with the second point indicating the positive X direction. The third point indicates the positive Y direction.

If the points you pick are points on an object, check the STATUS WINDOW to confirm that CONST is set to 3D. Otherwise the new view will be like the current one except that the X and Y axes will in general be shifted and rotated.

KEY-IN creates a new view by rotating the part in space. Rotation angles are in degrees. The new view can be a combination of three types of rotation:

TOP IN and **TOP OUT** rotate the current view around a horizontal axis—the x axis in view coordinates. TOP IN moves the top of the screen toward you.

RIGHT IN and **RIGHT OUT** rotate the view around a vertical axis—the y axis in view coordinates.

CW and **CCW** rotate the view clockwise or counterclockwise around an axis normal to the face of the screen and through the origin.

DONE tells Cadkey to switch to the new view. At this point, you can either SAVE the view or make further changes to refine the results.

SAVE adds the view created by NEW to Cadkey's permanent list of views for the current drawing. If ten views are already listed, the new one automatically becomes number eleven. You can add as many views as you want to this list, with additional view numbers automatically assigned. Unless you SAVE a new view, Cadkey does not keep a record of it it in the DATABASE.

Application

RIGHT IN or OUT 45°, followed by TOP IN 35.2644°, converts a front view to an isometric. But in an exact isometric it isn't unusual for lines at different depths to overlap. To avoid this, you may want to try different values, creating a view that is not quite isometric.

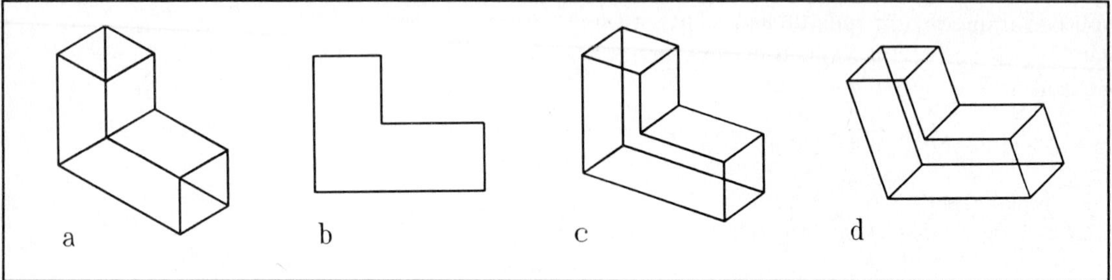

Figure V-1 Steps in creating a new view of a wire-frame drawing

Figure V-1a shows an object that has this problem of overlapping lines in view 7, the isometric view. Figure V-1b shows the same object in view 2, the front view. If, starting in the front view, you specify RGT IN 35° and TOP IN 30°, you get the result in Figure V-1c.

The sequence of operations makes a difference. If you specify TOP IN 30° first and then specify RGT IN 35°, you get the view in Figure V-1d.

Cadkey's Bottom View

Conventional drafting practices call for the bottom view of an object to be adjacent to the front view, as is the view labeled 9 in Figure V-2; but Cadkey's bottom view is like the one labeled 4, drawn in a way that would put it adjacent to the back view. If this orientation bothers you, catch Cadkey at startup when the screen is blank, switch to view 4, press Alt-V, and select NEW—KEY-IN—CW—180—DONE—Alt-V—SAVE. This creates view 9 as a proper bottom view, giving Cadkey an even higher level of respectability than before. Save the result, using *blank* (or a name of your choice) as the file name, and load this file whenever you start a drawing that you expect will require a bottom view.

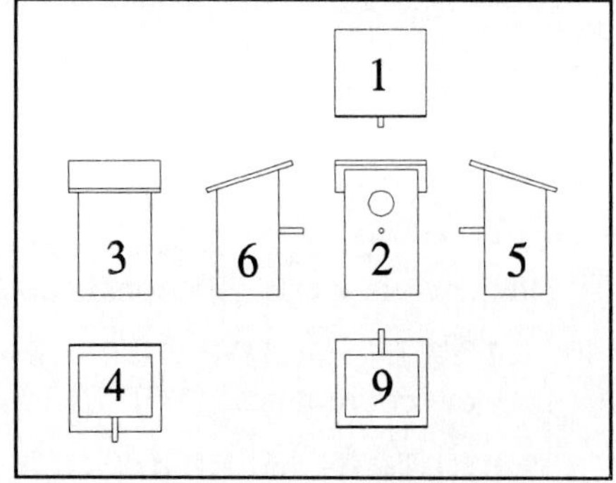

Figure V-2 Alternate position for bottom view

View Coordinates

VIEW coordinates are fixed with respect to the screen, regardless of the view being shown. In view coordinates, XV is measured to the right; YV, vertically; ZV, toward the viewer.

The other coordinate system is WORLD. The world coordinate axes, X, Y, an Z, are fixed with respect to the part. See COORDINATES and the inside front cover for more information.

Viewports

6 DISPLAY
5 VWPORTS
5 AUTO SET

Construction of a three-dimensional drawing is easier and errors are easier to catch when you can watch more than one view at a time. The AUTOSET command lets you choose whether Cadkey's display shows one view or four.

When you select the four-view option, Cadkey asks which is to be the primary viewport. Use the cursor to select one. Your choice makes a difference only if you intend to draw a GRID. Cadkey lets you put the grid either in all four viewports or in just the viewport you designate as primary.

(In prompts that involve the viewports, Cadkey uses CR (carriage return) instead of the usual Return. Most keyboards have either two Enter keys or an Enter key and a Return key. Press either one when CR is called for.)

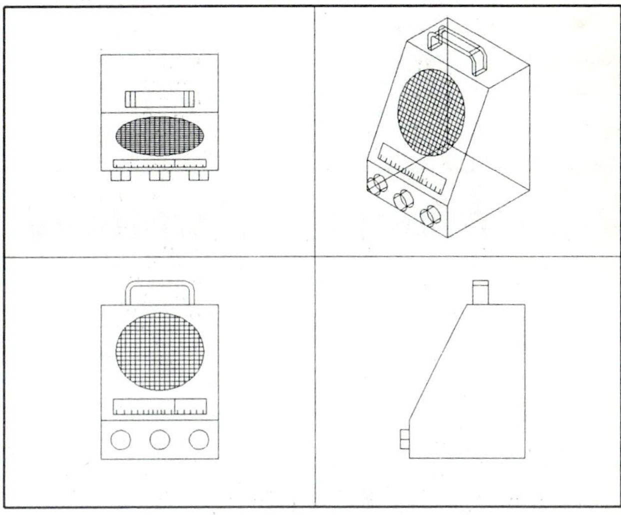

Figure V-1 Four-viewport option

Figure V-1 shows the type of display that the four-viewport choice gives you. Initially, the front view is at the lower left, with the top view above it and the right-side view on its right. The isometric view is on the upper right. But you can change this arrangement and put any view in any quadrant. See VIEW for a list of standard views and for ways to set up new viewing angles, or see the inside front cover for illustrations of the eight standard views.

You can work freely between the views, starting a line in one view and selecting its end point in another. You can draw a circle through points picked in three different views. And you can use two or more viewports to show different parts of the same view.

Some Rules

When you create a PATTERN and select ALL DISP, Cadkey asks you which viewport shows the entities you want to select. This choice does *not* determine the view in which Cadkey creates the pattern. Cadkey uses the view the cursor is in when you indicate the base position for the pattern.

The MOVE/COPY/JOIN commands follow a rule like the rule for PATTERN. No matter how you select the entities involved, the transformation, if it is view sensitive, depends on which view you use when you select your final reference point. And if you are keying in a reference point using VIEW coordinates (see COORDINATES), Cadkey uses whatever view the cursor happens to be in.

Window

6 DISPLAY	
3 ZOOM	
4 WINDOW	Alt-W

WINDOW appears twice in the Cadkey menu system. The ZOOM—WINDOW command shown in this menu asks you to define a rectangular area by specifying the positions of diagonally opposite corners. It then expands the window area until it reaches the edges of the screen. See ZOOM for more detail.

The other WINDOW command is part of the SELECTION MENU. When you create a rectangular window Cadkey selects the entities the window completely encloses. See SELECTING ENTITIES.

Windows in the Cadkey Display

The Cadkey display includes four windows:

The **menu options window** in the upper left corner of the screen shows the portion of the menu system from which you can select the next command. The numbers 1 through 9 in this window correspond to the function keys F1 through F9.

The **status window**, below the menu options window, shows the current settings of various parameters (for example, the scale of the drawing). See STATUS WINDOW for details.

The **cursor tracking window**, in the bottom left corner, normally shows the coordinates of the last point you selected. ^T changes this display to show the cursor position at all times. See CURSOR for details.

The **drawing window** occupies most of the screen. In addition to the drawing, along the top it shows the **history line**, which lists the menu selections you have made to get to where you are in the menu structure. Along the bottom it shows the **prompt line**, which tells you the next step to take.

The drawing window can be subdivided into four parts, showing your three-dimensional drawing from four different viewing angles. See VIEWPORTS for details.

Witness Lines

Witness lines, conventionally called extension lines, are lines that mark the distance over which a dimension applies. The DIMENSION routine supplies these lines automatically, but you can suppress them and then drawn them in as you need them for specific dimensioning layouts.

See ARROWS/WITNESS LINES—CONTROL for ways to eliminate one or both from dimensions. Or see ARROWS/WITNESS LINES—CONSTRUCTION for ways to create them separately.

World Coordinates

WORLD coordinates are fixed in space. As you look at different views of a drawing of a part, world coordinates do not stay the same with respect to the computer screen but instead remain fixed with respect to the part. In this system, X is measured toward the right side of the part; Y, toward the rear, Z, toward the top. The inside front cover shows what world coordinates look like in Cadkey's eight standard views.

The other coordinate system is VIEW, which is fixed with respect to the computer screen. XV is toward the right side of the screen, YV is up, and ZV is toward the viewer. ^V toggles between view and world coordinates.

See COORDINATES for more information.

X-CURSOR

When **X-CURSOR** = (followed by a number) appears at the bottom of my computer screen, it is usually because I accidentally pressed a number key. F10 gets rid of the message. The message appears when it is time to select an entity to move it, delete it, verify its coordinates, etc. Its purpose is to let you select an entity using the keyboard rather than a mouse. Typing 2 produces the message **X-CURSOR = 2.** If you continue typing a number, adding, for example, .2 and pressing Return; and if you then type 3 and press Return, the message becomes

X-CURSOR = 2.2 **Y-CURSOR = 3**

and Cadkey selects the entity that, in view COORDINATES, is nearest XV = 2.2 and YV = 3. This option does not appear when you want to select an entity in order to use ENDENT or some other POSITION MENU command.

X-Form

X-FORM (transform) leads to a series of commands for moving or copying entities. You have several options: You can move selected entities to a different place in the drawing. In a repetitive drawing, you can copy entities any number of times instead of constructing them individually. You can convert a flat figure into a three-dimensional extruded shape. And you can produce mirror images of existing figures. See MOVE/COPY/JOIN for details.

Zeros

Whether to show leading and trailing zeros in decimal dimensions is controlled by the DETAIL—SET—STANDRD—ZEROS commands. DETAIL—UPDATE lets you change the format of existing dimensions. See DIMENSIONING STANDARDS and UPDATE for more detail.

Zoom

The ZOOM commands let you adjust the size and position of the image on the screen. You can make the drawing smaller to make room for additions, or you can expand a small region to make fine detail easier to work with. Because PRINTS and PLOTS show only what is on the screen, the zoom commands also control how much of the drawing appears in hard copies.

Although Cadkey does not list PAN and VIEW as zoom commands, they are closely related to the zoom commands and are discussed here.

```
6 DISPLAY
  2 PAN              Alt-P
  3 ZOOM
    1 HALF           Alt-H
    2 DOUBLE         Alt-D
    3 SCALE*         Alt-S
    4 WINDOW         Alt-W
    5 AUTO           Alt-A
    6 BACK-1         Alt-B
  4 VIEW*            Alt-V
    1 -
    2 ENTITY
    3 NEW
    4 SAVE
```

*The STATUS WINDOW lists these parameters as S and VIEW.

PAN shifts the drawing on the screen. Select the point on the drawing you want to bring to the center of the screen. CADKEY expects you to be dissatisfied with your first choice. After it moves the drawing it asks again which point you want to bring to the center. F10 or Esc exits the operation.

WINDOW asks you to define a rectangular area by selecting diagonally opposite corners. Cadkey then expands that area to fill the computer screen. Use this command when you need to see fine detail more clearly. When you finish with the expanded view and want to restore the previous display, use BACK-1.

SCALE affects the size of your drawing on the computer screen, in printouts, and sometimes in plots; but neither scale nor any other ZOOM command alters the basic dimensional data for the part. When Cadkey wakes up, S is about 1, which, if the CONFIGURATION file is properly set, makes drawings on the screen full-size. S = 0.5 gives half-size drawings. But in printouts, S = 1 produces drawings that are only roughly full size. If the printing area is larger than the monitor display area, the drawing in the printout will be larger than the drawing on the screen. (See also PRINT and PLOT)

After you have entered a new value for scale, Cadkey asks which point on the drawing you want to bring to the center of the screen. Use the cursor to indicate this position, or, if you want to keep the drawing centered as it is, press Return.

HALF cuts the drawing scale in half.

DOUBLE doubles the scale.

AUTOSCALE adjusts the size and position of the drawing, making it as large as possible while still allowing everything to fit comfortably on the screen. It can be a help when you switch to a new VIEW, because it's not unusual for the entire drawing to be hidden somewhere off the screen. Autoscale finds it and brings it back. Once this is done, you may want to use SCALE to restore it to its original size.

BACK-1 restores the display you had before the current one, provided that the latest change was from one of the six ZOOM commands. (BACK-1 does not undo a change from one VIEW to another or a change produced by PAN.) Repeatedly pressing Alt-B toggles you between the two most recent displays.

VIEW lets you look at a three-dimensional object from different directions. You ask for a particular view by keying in its number. If you are looking at the front view and want to see the isometric, press 7 and then press Return. The inside front cover shows the numbering system.

Briefly, the ENTITY option switches you to a view parallel to the plane of the arc or circle you select; NEW lets you rotate an existing view in space to create a new one; and SAVE permanently records the view created by the NEW command. See VIEW for more detail.

Chapter 4

Installation and Configuration

You can install and run CADKEY Light on your computer if it meets these specifications:

IBM PC/XT/AT, PS2, or compatible
640 KB of RAM
Hard disk
DOS 2.1 or higher
Graphics card
Math coprocessor (recommended but not required)

Although CADKEY Light can take over 4 megabytes of hard disk space, you can install it in less space than this and trim it further after installation. See the next section for details.

Installation

The installation procedure is straightforward: Insert CADKEY Light disk #1 into your floppy disk drive. Make that floppy disk drive your default drive–if the disk is in drive A:, type **A:** and press Return (this key may be labeled Enter on your keyboard). Then type **install** and press Return.

Cadkey shows you a list of disk drives. Use arrow keys to highlight the drive on which you wish to install CADKEY (probably C:) and press Return.

If you are installing CADKEY Light 1.5, the default directory for the program is CADKEY. If you are installing CADKEY Light 4.0, the default directory name is CKLIGHT. If the directory name that Cadkey suggests is the one you want to use, press Return to accept it. If not, use Backspace to erase it, enter the name you want, and press Return. The INSTALL program creates the directory you choose and installs Cadkey in that directory. Follow the prompts to insert the other CADKEY Light disks as they are needed.

CADKEY Light 4.0 gives you three options not offered by CADKEY Light 1.5:

1. Where CADKEY Light 1.5 installs about fifty drivers to accommodate whatever graphics card your computer might have, CADKEY Light 4.0 lets you limit the installation to just the driver or drivers you need. The 1.1 megabytes of disk space the installation program mentions applies only if you choose to install all the graphics drivers. You can install the drivers separately, so if you need a different one later you can add it without going through the entire installation ritual. Just run the graphics drivers part of the installation program.
2. CADKEY Light 4.0 lets you direct PART and PATTERN files to a different disk than the one for the main program. (With CADKEY Light 1.5, only the configuration file can do this.)

3. CADKEY Light 4.0 provides extra flexibility in setting up overflow files for the Cadkey DATABASE. You need these overflow files whenever your drawing becomes too complex to fit in conventional memory. Cadkey runs faster if the overflow files are on a RAM disk, but the greater storage capacity on the typical hard disc can accommodate larger PART files. CADKEY Light 4.0 lets you have it both ways, using RAM storage, if your computer provides it, for overflow files and hard or floppy disk space as more space should your drawing overflow the RAM disk.

You may exit the install program at any time during execution by pressing the escape (Esc) key. Cadkey prompts you to verify your intention. Press Y if you really want to terminate install, or N if you want install to continue.

When the installation is complete, the program returns you to the DOS prompt, leaving you in the directory that contains Cadkey.

When CADKEY Light 1.5 is installed, the files add up to over 3.6 megabytes. If hard disk space is at a premium, you can transfer some sample part files from the \PRT subdirectory to a floppy disk and reduce the total to under 2.8 MB; then you can remove the video drivers you don't need and reduce it to under 1.9 MB. To remove these drivers, delete (or move to a floppy disk) every .EXE file but three. Keep CADKEY.EXE, CONFIG.EXE, and the .EXE file for the video driver you selected.

All the files in CADKEY Light 4.0 add up to not quite 4.1 megabytes, taking up about 4.3 megabytes of disk space if the sector size on your hard disk is 2048 bytes. Not loading all the graphics drivers reduces this by almost a megabyte. Cadkey gives you some part files to look at, and you can save over 0.9 megabyte by moving them to another disk. If you don't expect to use CADUTIL.EXE often, you can move it also to save another 0.18 megabyte. These changes leave you with only a little over 2 megabytes needed to run version 4.0 of CADKEY Light.

Configuration

When you run the CONFIG program to configure Cadkey for your computer, you will be asked for information about your system, including:

- the make and model of
  - your graphics card,
  - your monitor,
  - your input device (mouse or digitizer)
  - any plotter or printer,
- the height and width of your computer screen (see the notes that follow on Select Graphics Device if you want to be fussy about these measurements),
- the path to any RAM disk that your system may have, and
- the serial or parallel ports used to connect an input device (such as a mouse) and an output device (a plotter or printer).

After you get into the configuration program, you may find that you also need to know the name of a plotter, printer, mouse, or digitizing tablet with which your devices are compatible. If your devices are well-known brands, you will probably find them listed directly and are not likely to need this additional information.

The configuration program is well documented. For the most part, you need no help beyond the instructions you see on the screen. One problem you might have is finding where to look for specific options. The configuration program covers a broad range of operational details, and many options refuse to fit neatly into the six categories of the main menu. Two places to look for miscellaneous information are Set Graphics Options (under Select Graphics Device) and Set Program Options.

The notes that follow offer a few words of explanation on some options and few tips to get you around an occasional problem. The tips cannot be complete—this would require running the program on all possible systems—but fortunately the program is largely trouble free.

To run the configuration program, switch to the directory in which Cadkey is installed, type **config**, and press Return. Cadkey displays the main menu:

1) Set graphics options
2) Set input device options
3) Set plotter options
4) Set printer options
5) Set program options
6) Set default pathnames for data files
7) Exit Without Saving Changes
8) Exit and Save Changes

To select the part of the configuration program you wish to run, type the appropriate number and press Return. The first time through, you may want to accept most of the default choices that Cadkey shows in parentheses. To do so, just press Return.

If, when you are running any part of the program, you accidentally type the wrong data, erase it with the backspace key and retype it. If you press Return before you notice the error, you cannot correct it immediately. Instead, continue to enter data until CONFIG returns you to the main menu. Reselect the same main menu option, press Return to accept your earlier entries, now shown in parentheses. When you get to the incorrect entry, enter the correct information; then continue to press Return until you get back to the main menu.

Set Graphics Options

The Set Graphics Option offers three choices:

1) Select graphics device
2) Set color options
3) Return to Main Menu

Select Graphics Device

Select your video graphics device from the list that appears. If your graphics device is not on the list, consult the instruction book for that device to see whether it is compatible with one of the listed devices.

If you selected a graphics card that runs in different modes, you will see a list of the modes that Cadkey supports. Enter the number of the desired mode and press Return.

Next you see a list of graphics display monitors. If your monitor is on the list of monitors, enter its number. If your monitor is not on the screen, select one that has the same screen size as yours or enter the screen size of your monitor. The purpose of this step is to set the horizontal and vertical scales of the Cadkey display. The overall height and width of the screen usually give good results; but if, when you use Cadkey, your circles are egg shaped, return to this part of the configuration file to correct the problem. To determine screen dimensions accurately, measure an 80-character line of text for the width and 25 rows of text for the height.

Miscellaneous Options

Option 1, Select Graphics Device, also includes seven miscellaneous items:

cursor size
graphics marker size
the maximum number of grid points
the smoothness of the display for circles and arcs
the minimum segment length in sketch lines
cursor appearance when it is in the menu section
configuration for computers using two monitors

Unless you have used Cadkey enough to have developed some preferences, your best bet is to press Return to accept each default value and skip the rest of this subsection.

The minimum **cursor dimension** is 0.01 inch. The maximum dimension, which is twice the width of the computer screen, gives a cursor the full width and height of the viewport.

Graphics markers are the temporary symbols Cadkey uses to mark the start points of lines, etc. Make them any size between 0.0001 inch and 10 inches.

Set the number of **grid points**—the number of rows and columns in the display grid—to any number up to 200. Cadkey does not draw grids finer than what you specify. Because fine grids take longer to draw, there is an advantage to limiting the number of grid points.

Low values of the **smoothness factor** show curves on the screen as regular polygons and arcs as straight-line segments. With a factor of 1, the display is quite coarse: Typical segment lengths are an inch or more. As a circle gets smaller, it shows as a diamond, then as a triangle, and finally as a horizontal line. Plots and printouts are unaffected—circles look like circles.

A **sketch line** (see POLYLINE) is a line you draw freehand, using the mouse to drag the cursor along the path you want the line to take. The result, which can look like a smooth curve, is actually a string of straight-line segments. To keep the number of segments from becoming uncontrollably large, Cadkey sets a minimum segment length. You may assign any value over 0.00005 inch.

The **menu cursor type** is the form the cursor assumes when you bring it into the windows along the left edge of the screen. Choose between using inverse video to highlight the option the cursor is on and pointing to the option with an arrow.

The default **monitor configuration** is for one monitor. If you have two monitors (monochrome for text display and color for graphics), one must be primary and therefore active when the system boots. Enter the appropriate number and press Return.

Set Color Options

Set Color Options controls the colors of the Cadkey display. If you are configuring Cadkey for the first time, you probably want to skip this long routine and accept the defaults; however, Cadkey may force you to do otherwise. If, for example, you have a CGA monochrome monitor, you see this message when you try to exit the configuration program:

The color settings are invalid for the selected graphics device.
Do you wish to change them now?

Fortunately, the solution is simple. Run through this section of the program and press Return to accept every default. This changes nothing, but it keeps Cadkey happy.

The Set Color Options routine lets you set background colors, colors for text or graphics, and styles and colors for border lines. You set these choices separately for nine screen areas and then for the cursor, rubber banding, and graphics markers.

1) Menu options window
2) System mode indicator (the upper left corner of the screen)
3) Break window (the window that shows BACK-UP and ESCAPE)
4) Status window
5) History line
6) Prompt line
7) Cursor tracking window
8) Pop up menus
9) Graphics viewport
10) Cursor and marker
    Cursor
    Rubber banding
    Markers (the marks that show start points of lines, etc., and those that show which entities you have selected)
11) Return to Set Graphics Options menu

Choose from the following colors:

0-Black	4-Yellow	8-Blue	12-Lt Red
1-Green	5-Cyan	9-Lt Blue	13-Lt Magenta
2-Red	6-Magenta	10-Lt Green	14-White
3-Amber	7-Grey	11-Lt Cyan	15-High White

Option 11 returns you to the Set Graphics Options menu. From there, you can continue to work with graphics options or return to the main menu.

Set Input Device Options

Select your input device (mouse or digitizing tablet) from the displayed list. If your input device is not listed, check the instruction book to see whether it is compatible with one of the listed devices. If you have to use trial and error to select a mouse driver, Microsoft Mouse and Mouse Systems Mouse are good possibilities. A quick way to check whether you picked the right option (and also whether you picked the right serial port) is to see whether the device works smoothly in the routine that follows for assigning the cursor puck buttons.

If you have neither a mouse nor a digitizing tablet, select the None option. This choice lets you use the keyboard arrow keys to move the cursor.

Specify the serial port (com1 or com2) used by your input device.

When you identify a tablet as your input device, you may accept the default work area dimensions for that device, or you may elect to change those dimensions. You should change the dimensions of the active area—the area that can return coordinate data—only if the default values are incorrect or if you are using an unsupported tablet. If you need to change these dimensions, use the documentation that came with your tablet to determine the correct values.

Professional versions of Cadkey can use a function selection area to initiate macros. Because CADKEY Light lacks macro capability, the function selection area does not affect CADKEY Light operation.

Answer Y to the invitation to assign the cursor puck buttons. As noted earlier, this choice lets you confirm that you have selected the right mouse or digitizing tablet and the right serial port. It also lets you make better use of the mouse. There are certain functions you use often—Back-up (F10), Esc, Ctrl-R (redraw), and Enter (alias Return or CR)—and it is convenient to assign some of these functions to mouse buttons. If you have a three-button mouse, you might try Cursor (the primary mouse function) on button 1, Enter on 2, and either F10 or Esc on 3.

Set Plotter Options

If you do not have a plotter, select NONE (or just skip item 3 in the main menu). Otherwise, select your plotter (or one compatible with yours) from the displayed list.

Specify the **paper size** your plotter uses.

CADKEY Light 4.0 has you check the **clip limits** for the plotter you selected. Plotters cannot plot to the edges of the paper, and these limits set the margins the plotter uses.

Check the **x and y offsets**. Normally you accept the default values, but if these values would give plots that are off center you can change them. Positive values move the plot up and to the right. See your plotter manual for guidance. Because the PLOT routine also lets you set offset values, you can experiment while running Cadkey to find what values work best.

Enter the **plotter pen width** in millimeters. This tells Cadkey the offset to use from one pen stroke to the next when filling areas.

See your plotter's documentation for the recommended **pen velocity** in centimeters/second

Enter a **curve tolerance factor** between 0.0 and 5.0 (CADKEY Light 1.5) or greater than 1.0 (CADKEY Light 4.0) to determine the smoothness of arcs and circles.

Choose a **pen sorting** method to determine the sequence in which pens are used. No sort plots entities in the order Cadkey encounters them as it reads the DATABASE. Low to high order draws first all entities that use pen #1. In order found draws first all entities that use whatever pen is assigned to the entity Cadkey encounters first.

You can change the **assignment of plot pens** to vary the way color numbers (see ATTRIBUTES) control plotter pens. Normally, color #5 calls for plotter pen #5, but you can make it call for pen #3. Cadkey enters, one at a time, the sixteen color numbers, and you enter the corresponding plotter pen number. Consequently, you can, if you wish, assign the same pen to more than one color number. Note that to use this system you must use color numbers, not Cadkey's pen numbers, to select the plotter's pens (see PLOT).

Tell Cadkey whether to send plot data to a **parallel port, a serial port, or a file**. Enter -1 for COM1, -2 for COM2, +1 for LPT1, +2 for LPT2, or enter the file name. (Note the instructions the configuration program gives you if you are on a network.)

For serial port plotters, enter the **baud rate**.

Set Printer Options

If you do not have a printer, select NONE (or just skip item 3 in the main menu). Otherwise, select your printer (or one compatible with yours) from the displayed list.

Printing resolution (low, medium, or high) is a compromise between speed and quality. (The quality of the image on the computer screen does not limit printout quality.)

If you reassign **printer paper limits**, leave a margin between the printing area and the edge of the paper. On a dot-matrix printer, failure to do so can give double-length printouts (22" long on 8-1/2" x 11" fanfold paper), with 1/8" lines of data alternating with 1/8" gaps.

Tell Cadkey which **parallel or serial port** connects to your printer. Enter —1 for COM1, —2 for COM2, +1 for LPT1, or +2 for LPT2. (Note the special instructions the configuration program gives you if you are on a network.)

Set Program Options

Specify the DOS pathnames for database **overflow and scratch files**. See item 3 under INSTALLATION for comments.

Allocate some system **memory for on-line printing** and other CADKEY functions.

Select the **units** (inches, millimeters, feet, centimeters, yards or meters) for construction.

Specify the number of **register variable** names Cadkey can allow. This number is much less important in CADKEY Light than in the professional versions of Cadkey, where the variable names are used for CALCULATOR functions and for CADL (CADKEY Advanced Design Language) files. The default is 85 for CADKEY Light 1.5. For CADKEY Light 4.0, the default value of 200 is also the minimum value.

Font size is not the size of the font, but the kilobytes of memory allotted to font files. A small value leaves more free memory for running Cadkey and can help it respond more rapidly to your commands. With too small a value, the font file is truncated and letters and numbers become garbled. If you encounter this problem as you use Cadkey, rerun the configuration file and assign more memory for fonts.

Chaining tolerance is the maximum distance between endpoints of entities in a chain. If two endpoints lie closer to one another than this, Cadkey recognizes them as coinciding.

The selection marker or **highlighting style** lets you see which entities Cadkey selected, telling you whether the ones selected were the ones you wanted to select. A flashing marker does not flash repeatedly, but shows for a fraction of a second at the time Cadkey makes the selection. Drawn markers, because they stay on indefinitely, make it easier to see what you have selected, but it takes a REDRAW operation to get rid of them. In simple drawings, where redraw time is short, you will probably prefer the highlighted entities. See Select Graphics Device—Select Color Options—Cursor and Marker for setting the marker color.

It is a good idea to save files periodically, and **Auto-save** does this for you automatically. Autosave is active only when Cadkey is at the main menu—a habit that can be annoying. You can stare at a drawing for ten minutes wondering what to do next, and the minute you decide and start pressing keys, autosave tells you to wait while it saves the drawing. If you are saving to a hard disk with a fast response time, the save time is short and the inconvenience is minimal. If you usually save large files to a floppy disk, you will probably choose to disable autosave and resolve to save files manually. If you enable autosave, you specify the time interval between saves and the directory and file name to use.

Set Default Pathname for Data Files

Tell Cadkey where you want to store PART, PATTERN, PLOT, and NOTE files. In CADKEY Light 1.5, the defaults are the subdirectories PRT, PTN, PLT, and NOT in the directory that houses the main program. In CADKEY Light 4.0, you may have changed the defaults for part and pattern files during the installation program.

Exit Without Saving Changes

If you select this option, Cadkey prompts you to reaffirm that choice. Enter Y to do so and the configuration program will terminate, leaving the earlier CONFIG.DAT file unchanged. If you enter N, Cadkey will return you to the main menu.

Exit and Save Changes

This option terminates the configuration program and updates the CONFIG.DAT file to incorporate all the data you have entered.

The Configuration Data File

Cadkey stores your configuration data in the file CONFIG.DAT. Although it was not designed for readability, it is an ordinary text file and is documented well enough to let you see the choices you have made. A printed copy of this file is helpful if (1) you reconfigure Cadkey but want to return to the earlier configuration or (2) you switch to another version of Cadkey and want to see how you configured it before.

Because it is a text file, you can edit it with any word processor that reads and writes ASCII files. And the word processor lets you set one parameter that the configuration program skips. The line "grvpaxes 0 0 ;display axes on entry: display viewport, construction viewport" controls whether Cadkey's AXES show initially. The default numbers are 0 0 for CADKEY Light 1.5 and 1 1 for CADKEY Light 4.0. Setting the first number to 0 shows the axes at startup; setting it to 1 suppresses them.

Index

Bold face in a series of entries indicates the place or places where you are most likely to fine the information you need. Entries in upper-case letters are command names or status window abbreviations rather than purely descriptive titles.

With CADKEY® Light™ on your own computer, you can avoid that long trip to the computer lab and the frustration of finding all the computers in use by other students. If your school uses CADKEY 3.5, order CADKEY Light 1.5 and you will find that the difference in versions is not a problem. Either program reads files generated by the other. If your school has upgraded to CADKEY 4.0, order CADKEY Light 4.0 for compatibility with that program. Features such as SPLINE that are available only in professional versions of CADKEY are easily added to the files you prepare in CADKEY Light.

Whether your school uses CADKEY Light 1.5, CADKEY Light 4.0, CADKEY 3.5, or CADKEY 4.0, your own CADKEY Light program lets you work on assignments at home. And it's yours to keep and continue to use after you've finished the course.

This order blank entitles you to purchase one set of CADKEY Light program disks for $59.95 plus $5.00 shipping and handling. This special offer is available only to students.

Equipment you need:

IBM PC/XT/AT, PS2, or compatible
or COMPAQ 286 or 386-based machine
640 kb of RAM
Hard disk drive
DOS 2.1 or higher
Graphics card
Mouse

What you need to send:

This order blank (a photocopy can't be accepted)
A photocopy of your current student I.D
A money order or cashier's check for $64.95 in US funds
Telephone numbers we can use if we have questions or there are delivery problems

Where to send it:

Cadkey, Inc.
Educational Programs
4 Griffin Road North
Windsor, CT 06095-1511

Ship to ______________________________________ (No P. O. box, please)

____

____

Phone: (______)______________________________

School: ______________________________________

Instructor's name: ____________________________

Instructor's phone: (______)______________________

Disk size (check one): ☐ 3 1/2" (720k) ☐ 5 1/4" (360k)

CADKEY Light version (check one): ☐ 1.5 ☐ 4.0